This is the first full-length study of the vernacular motet in thirteenth-century France. The motet was the most prestigious type of music of that period, filling a gap between the music of the so-called Notre-Dame School and the Ars Nova of the early fourteenth century. This book takes the music and the poetry of the motet as its starting point and attempts to come to grips with the ways in which musicians and poets treated pre-existing material, creating new artefacts. The book reviews the processes of texting and retexting, and the procedures for imparting structure to the works; it considers the ways we conceive genre in the thirteenth-century motet, and supplements these with principles derived from twentieth-century genre theory. The motet is viewed as the interaction of literary and musical modes whose relationships give meaning to individual compositions.

CAMBRIDGE STUDIES IN MEDIEVAL AND RENAISSANCE MUSIC

French motets in the thirteenth century

CAMBRIDGE STUDIES IN MEDIEVAL AND RENAISSANCE MUSIC

GENERAL EDITORS

Iain Fenlon, Thomas Forrest Kelly, John Stevens

This series continues the aims of the Cambridge Studies in Music but now focuses on the medieval and Renaissance periods. As with the earlier series, the central concern is to publish books which make an original contribution to the study of music in its widest sense. Thus the relationship of music both to a broad historical and social context and to the other arts is seen as an important feature.

PUBLISHED TITLES

The organ in western culture, 750–1250
PETER WILLIAMS

Gothic song: Victorine sequences and Augustinian reform in twelfth-century Paris
MARGOT FASSLER

French motets in the thirteenth century: music, poetry and genre
MARK EVERIST

French motets in the thirteenth century

music, poetry and genre

MARK EVERIST

CAMBRIDGE
UNIVERSITY PRESS

Published by the Press Syndicate of the University of Cambridge
The Pitt Building, Trumpington Street, Cambridge CB2 1RP
40 West 20th Street, New York, NY 10011–4211, USA
10 Stamford Road, Oakleigh, Melbourne 3166, Australia

First published 1994

Printed in Great Britain at the University Press, Cambridge

A catalogue record for this book is available from the British Library

Library of Congress cataloguing in publication data

Everist, Mark.
French motets in the thirteenth century: music, poetry and genre / Mark Everist.
   p. cm. – (Cambridge studies in medieval and Renaissance music)
Includes bibliographical references and indexes.
ISBN 0 521 39539 9 (hardback)
1. Motet – France – 550–1400.   I. Title.
II. Title: French motets in the 13th century.   III. Series.
ML2927.E94   1994
782.2'6'094409022 – dc20   93–28322 CIP MN

ISBN 0 521 39539 9 hardback

For Jeanice

Vostre douz viaire cler
Fair por cuers enamorer
M'a saisi sanz moi grever
D'uns jolis maus a sentir.
Dame, grant desir
Ai de faire vo plesir

Contents

Preface

This book is about music and poetry in the motets composed in France during the thirteenth century. Collected together in voluminous manuscripts that are often beautifully written and decorated, motets constitute an extensive and imposing repertory that dominates the musical landscape of the period. Arising out of the liturgical polyphony of Paris around 1200, the corpus of motets is the first in which vernacular poetry encounters polyphonic music.

The repertory of motets presents an attractive subject for scholarly enquiry. The standard bibliography of the motet lists over 1200 motet voices in both French and Latin from the hundred years up to 1300. Translating that figure into numbers of motets poses problems because a single work can make use of anything between one and three voices. However one arrives at a number of surviving motets, thirteenth-century music is dominated by these pieces. Editorial problems, such matters as notation, transcription and editing of these works, have, by and large, been overcome, and editions of this music are available on the shelves of most research libraries. It should therefore be possible – perhaps even easy – to give a satisfactory account of the thirteenth-century motet based on the original manuscript sources.

The manuscripts that preserve this music are scattered all over Europe, most noticeably in Florence, Wolfenbüttel, Montpellier and Bamberg. Each preserves large numbers of pieces (the Bamberg manuscript has 100; the Montpellier Codex has over 300) but they betray very little about the origins – geographical or cultural – of their contents. Even if it has been possible to demonstrate where and when these books were copied – and this has been shown with some success – we still know relatively little about the types of people who wrote the music and poetry of the motets, the people who performed and heard them, and the values that were attributed to the works. The late thirteenth-century writer on music, Johannes de Grocheio, was usually forthcoming about such historical and aesthetic matters. Even he, however, only went as far as proposing that the motet was more suited to the *literati* than the *laici vulgares*. Grocheio contrasted the 'literate' motet with the 'lay' dance-song. Such a distinction is clear from even the most cursory comparison of the two types of music. The motet is sophisticated, complex, and full of musical and poetic allusion whereas the dance-song has a function that demands clarity and simplicity. In terms of helping with answering questions of cultural context, Grocheio says more than most, but even that is not very much.

We know little of the cultural background to the motet because those who wrote its music and poetry are today anonymous; to judge from the rarity of attribution in the surviving manuscripts, relatively few composers were known by name in the thirteenth century. Under these circumstances, the motet can emerge as opaque and impenetrable. Such a view is a striking contrast to the brilliance of these polyphonic miniatures that were prized so highly in their time.

Writing the history of thirteenth-century music is hampered by the absence of the ranks of administrative documents that one associates with the historiography of fifteenth- or sixteenth-century music. Recourse to alternative sources – sermons, treatises on the Seven Deadly Sins, manuals for confessors, theological encyclopedias and vernacular romances – has resulted in extraordinarily revealing accounts of the *mentalités* of individuals who wrote about music, and of the place of certain aspects of music in thirteenth-century society. This approach, with rare but striking exceptions, fails to illuminate the music that, for over a century, has been considered the focus of thirteenth-century endeavour: organum, clausula, motet and conductus. The result is a danger of being forced into viewing the thirteenth-century motet in a vacuum, and of considering this large number of extraordinary pieces entirely out of context. This is certainly one of the less attractive fates that has befallen the motet. It has been subjected to various sorts of statistical investigations, some of which have been useful (if sometimes unwieldy) and others that have been of less value.

The originality of the 300 works in the Montpellier Codex, for example, is something that must surely strike any critic of the thirteenth-century motet. After 700 years of near-silence, individual works should now be encouraged to speak. This book is an attempt to listen, and to understand what they say. Criticism of single works is central, and methods of criticism that arise out of a consideration of specific works, rather than out of amorphous groups of works, are preferred. This is not a history either of the musical culture of the period or of the genre that gives the book its title. As the foregoing comments suggest, the first seems hopelessly ambitious; the second – the intrinsic history, or chronicle, of a single genre – seems inappropriate today.

The idea that an individual motet from the thirteenth century is worthy of investigation raises the problem of genre and of typology. Genre, together with music and poetry, governs the scope of this enquiry. Various attempts to categorise the thirteenth-century motet have been made, some medieval and some modern, and often for very different purposes. A review of twentieth-century attempts to classify the thirteenth-century motet underlies the discussion of the *motet enté*, rondeau-motet and refrain cento in Chapters 4–6. The conclusions reached in these chapters are, first, that the taxonomies that have been handed down to us are flawed, and second, that an understanding of genre, in any case, implies something more than simply a taxonomy. This gives a methodological context to the discussion of devotional forms in Chapter 7, in which a single thread (the idea of devotional poetry within the context of secular music) is drawn through a small portion of the repertory. Important here is the fact that a taxonomy has only a slight role to play, and that the subject matter of Chapter 7 is not genre but *mode*. This opens up the possibility of a systematic review of the concept of genre in the thirteenth-century motet, and this task is undertaken in Chapter 8. A sympathetic view of contemporary genre theory is blended with medieval distinctions between borrowed and composed material. The result is a persuasive interpretation of the motet that will prompt further investigation.

I have prefaced the chapters devoted to a discussion of genre with three chapters grouped together under the title 'Origins'. The first of these outlines the technical background on which subsequent chapters build, and also summarises some important material that is discussed in detail elsewhere, especially discussions of the original manuscript sources of the music. Chapters 2 and 3 explain the relationship between words and notes in the motet, and I have taken the opportunity, in Chapter 2, to discuss the crucial role of the Latin motet, even though it technically falls outside the scope of this book.

One of the characteristics of the motet that emerges is the importance of allusion and reference, both in text and music, to other works. Such allusions and references have dictated the methods with which I have approached this repertory. In general, methods that have revealed the ways in which words and notes interact have been preferred to those that demonstrate that a work conforms to some sort of normative pattern. So there is scant treatment of melodic mode, minimal concern with questions of closed and open forms, and little description of the surface of music or poetry. On the other hand, space is made for an account of poetic and musical patterns as they are found in specific works: line-length, rhyme, register and articulative gesture in poetry; constructions of phrase, proportion and the continuous reuse of material in music. The most telling element in the relationship between words and music, and between different compositions, the refrain, appears at the centre of much of the discussion in Chapters 4–8. It is introduced and explained in Chapter 3.

The identification of organa, clausulae and motets can be complicated. I have followed conventional practice in identifying all works derived from liturgical chant with Ludwig's M[ass] or O[ffice] numbers. Motet tenors are similarly identified, and upper parts are given the numbers found in Gennrich's *Bibliographie der ältesten lateinischen und französischen Motetten*. Where there is no room for confusing one work with another, however, I have used less formal means of identification. I have also tried to keep manuscript shelfmarks out of the prose, and referred to primary source material by a variety of more or less formal means.

Although this book contains no new editions, the examples are freshly edited according to principles that give *perfectiones* a higher priority than modern bars. The latter are reserved for the ends of phrases in individual voice-parts. This results in editions where bar-lines do not coincide, and that reflect the phrase-structures of the music under discussion. I found the editions and translations of texts in the editions by Tischler and Anderson a useful point of reference, if only to disagree with them.

I have incurred many debts during the process of assimilation and learning that passes for research. I directed two graduate seminars, one in the Department of

Music at King's College London in 1987, and one at the Ecole Normale Supérieure (Groupe de Formation Doctorale) in Paris in 1991; both were of enormous value in lending precision to parts of my thinking that were at that stage less well focused than they might have been. Parts of Chapters 5 and 6 were reworked from articles in *Music and Letters* and the *Journal of the Royal Musical Association*; I am grateful to Oxford University Press and the Secretary of the Royal Musical Association for permission to reproduce this material. Thanks are due to Penny Souster of Cambridge University Press and to Ann Lewis who copy-edited the text. Finally, I would like to thank those who read parts of this book in typescript: Craig Wright, Sylvia Huot, and especially Thomas Forrest Kelly.

Part One

Origins

1

Introduction

Composition

During the 1280s, a monk from the Abbey of Bury St Edmunds wrote a treatise on music in which he cast a critical eye over the musical events of the previous hundred years.[1] Anonymous IV, as he came to be called, wrote mostly about technical matters: dissonance treatment, rhythm and notation.[2] Since he had spent some part of his career in Paris, he was also able to chronicle the history of music in that city. He was especially forthcoming about music at the Cathedral of Notre Dame de Paris. At the time he was writing, he felt able to review all the genres that we know from the late twelfth and thirteenth centuries: organum, conductus and motet. Although the composition of organum and conductus had almost completely stopped by the 1280s, Anonymous IV reserved the greatest praise for two composers whom we associate with the Notre-Dame school. Leoninus and Perotinus were active in the twenty-five years either side of 1200, and Anonymous IV described them respectively as *optimus organista* and *optimus discantor*: the best composers of organum and of discantus.[3]

From his other comments about the activities of Leoninus and Perotinus, it is clear that Anonymous IV was identifying two different compositional styles: organum and discantus. In doing so, he pointed to two of the major achievements of the Notre-Dame school. Although the individual organum composition was a setting of a liturgical item – a gradual, alleluya or responsory – the generic term 'organum' subsumed two stylistic categories. One is confusingly also called organum, and the other discantus.[4]

[1] The treatise is edited in Fritz Reckow, ed., *Der Musiktraktat des Anonymus 4*, 2 vols., Beihefte zum Archiv für Musikwissenschaft 4–5 (Wiesbaden: Franz Steiner Verlag, 1967), and translated in Jeremy Yudkin, ed., *The Music Treatise of Anonymous IV: A New Translation*, Musicological Studies and Documents 41 (Neuhausen-Stuttgart: American Institute of Musicology, 1985) which replaces Luther Dittmer, trans., *Anonymous IV* (New York: Institute of Mediaeval Music, 1959).

[2] He received his name when his treatise was the fourth anonymous treatise to be edited in the first volume of Charles Edmond Henri de Coussemaker, ed., *Scriptorum de musica medii aevi nova series a Gerbertina altera*, 4 vols. (Milan: Bolletino bibliografico musicale; Paris: A. Durand, 1864–76; R Hildesheim: Georg Olms, 1963) 1: 327–65.

[3] Reckow, *Musiktraktat*, 1: 46.

[4] This confusion was known to the author of the treatise that served as the source for Anonymous IV's text. In the thirteenth chapter of his *De mensurabili musica*, Johannes de Garlandia introduces his description of

n.4 continued on p.4

Organum and discantus played important roles in Parisian music between 1170 and 1220. Leoninus and his followers built on a long-established musical tradition of writing organum in which an elaborate upper voice (duplum) was combined contra-puntally with the notes of a plainsong. The chant was arranged in very long note values and called the tenor. Whereas earlier traditions had explored both note-against-note techniques and more elaborate polyphonic treatments of a plainsong, Leoninus wrote music in which the tenor was deployed in such long values as almost to lose its melodic identity. Above this, the duplum spun virtuoso threads of melody that created elaborate patterns and sequences. These exuberant dupla characterised the style of early Parisian organum.

Composers also evolved a contrasting style of composition named discantus in which both voices moved in strictly controlled rhythms. The sections in discantus style were called clausulae. During the course of composing clausulae, they also experimented with ways of conceptualising and notating rhythmic patterns that ultimately resulted in the formulation of the rhythmic modes. Many clausula settings were made of the same section of plainsong, and one clausula could have been swapped with another. By the time the earliest manuscript of organum and discantus was copied, around 1250, large numbers of clausulae were copied in a discrete part of the book and separate from the organum that had spawned them. In writing compositions for many of the important feasts in the liturgical year, Leoninus created what Anonymous IV called the *Magnus liber de gradali et antifonario*. This cycle of organum settings both for the Mass and the Office formed the basis of subsequent developments in liturgical polyphony. Perotinus is acknowledged, again by Anonymous IV, both as a composer who revised the *Magnus liber* and as a composer of clausulae.

Revising the organum sections of the *Magnus liber* and writing new clausulae were two responses to Leoninus' achievement; writing texts to the discantus sections of organum was a third.[5] This process resulted in what would, later in the century, be called a motet. At its most basic, a motet consists of a piece of discantus to which words have been added; however, early practitioners of the genre would still have considered it a piece of discantus. Later theoretical accounts call a piece of texted discantus a motetus, and this term is also used for the voice-part that carries the text.[6] For theorists of the second half of the thirteenth century, a two-part motet

organum as follows: 'Organum dicitur multipliciter: generaliter et specialiter. De organo generaliter dictum est superius; nunc autem decendum est de ipso in speciali' (Organum has several meanings, [both] generic and specific. Organum in the generic sense was discussed above [Chapter 1]; now, however, it must be discussed in its specific sense; Erich Reimer, ed., *Johannes de Garlandia: De mensurabili musica: kritische Edition mit Kommentar und Interpretation der Notationslehre*, 2 vols., Beihefte zum Archiv für Musikwissenschaft 10–11 (Wiesbaden: Franz Steiner Verlag, 1972) 1: 88; translation from Stanley H. Birnbaum, trans., *Johannes de Garlandia: Concerning Measured Music (De mensurabili musica)*, Colorado College Music Press Translations 9 (Colorado Springs: Colorado College Music Press, 1978) 42–3). Garlandia terms organum in its specific sense *organum per se* (*ibid.*, 43). See also Edward H. Roesner, 'Johannes de Garlandia on *Organum in speciali*', *Early Music History* 2 (1982) 129–60.

5   Wilhelm Meyer, 'Der Ursprung des Motett's: vorläufige Bemerkungen', *Nachrichten von der königliche Gesellschaft der Wissenschaften zu Göttingen: Philologisch-historische Klasse, 1898*, 4 vols. [paginated consecutively] (Göttingen: Luder Horstmann, 1898) 2: 113–45; *R* in *Gesammelte Abhandlungen zur mittellateinischen Rhythmik*, 3 vols. (Berlin: Weidmannsche Buchhandlung, 1905–36; *R* Hildesheim: Georg Olms Verlag, 1970) 2: 303–41.

6   Klaus Hofmann, 'Zur Entstehungs- und Frühgeschichte des Terminus Motette', *Acta musicologica* 42 (1970) 138–50.

consisted therefore of a motetus and a tenor. From its earliest days, the motet was also characterised by the addition of voices: a third part was called a triplum, a fourth, quadruplum.

Two forces, the addition of texts to pre-existing melismatic polyphony and the addition of new voice-parts to two-part counterpoint, marked the growth of the motet. By the middle of the thirteenth century, these techniques had become an indispensable part of compositional practice. They also resulted in a bewildering combination of voice-parts and texts. Over a tenor taken from plainsong, for example, were composed both the words and notes of a new motetus in Latin or French, or two new voice-parts texted in either language. It was even possible to have constructed a motet using one text in French and one in Latin. Composers also returned to a two-part clausula and simply added a Latin or French text. The texting of a three-part clausula opened up even more opportunities of combining poems and music.

Thirteenth-century musical culture made free with pre-existing materials, and many motets share music and text with other pieces. Originality had a very different meaning in the thirteenth century than in the late twentieth. Traditionally, a motet's value has been determined by the complexity of its context, and scholars have taken great trouble to group the surviving works into families of clausulae and motets that share the same music, and then to explain how one individual relates to its fellows. This is a complex task, owing to the extent of the surviving music and poetry, and has been the work of more than one productive lifetime. Any critic of the motet must be thankful that this work is not only complete, but that it has been done with so much flair and accuracy.[7]

The question of how these works interact one with another has received less attention. It has received preliminary answers based on conceptual models that do insufficient justice to the complexity of the genre. For example, it has almost always been assumed that there exists a single compositional route from clausula to two-part Latin motet,

---

[7] Fundamental to all enquiry is Friedrich Ludwig, *Repertorium organorum recentioris et motetorum vetustissimi stili*, 2 vols. (1/1 – Halle: Verlag von Max Niemaeyer, 1910; *R* [ed. Luther A. Dittmer, Musicological Studies 7] Brooklyn, N.Y.: Institute of Mediaeval Music; Hildesheim: Georg Olms Verlag, 1964); (1/2 – [345–456 ed. Friedrich Gennrich including *R* of 'Die Quellen der Motetten ältesten Stils', *Archiv für Musikwissenschaft* 5 (1923) 185–222 and 273–315, Summa musicae medii aevi 7] Langen bei Frankfürt: n.p., 1961; *R* [345–456], [457–783, ed. Luther A. Dittmer, Musicological Studies 26] [Binningen]: Institute of Mediaeval Music, 1978); (2 – [1–71 ed. Friedrich Gennrich, Summa musicae medii aevi 8 – 65–71 in page próof only] Langen bei Frankfürt: n.p., 1962; *R* [1–64, 65–71 corrected], [72–155 ed. Luther A. Dittmer (Musicological Studies 17)] Brooklyn, N.Y.: Institute of Mediaeval Music, n.d.; Hildesheim: Georg Olms Verlag, 1972). An important addition for the motet repertory is Friedrich Gennrich, *Bibliographie der ältesten französischen und lateinischen Motetten*, Summa musicae medii aevi 2 (1957). For the conductus, see Eduard Gröninger, *Repertoire-Untersuchungen zum mehrstimmigen Notre-Dame Conductus*, Kölner Beiträge zur Musikforschung 2 (Regensburg: Gustav Bosse Verlag, 1939), revised as Robert Falck, *The Notre Dame Conductus: A Study of the Repertory*, Musicological Studies 33 (Henryville, Ottawa and Binningen: Institute of Mediaeval Music, 1981); see also Gordon A. Anderson, 'Notre-Dame and Related Conductus: A Catalogue Raisonné', *Miscellanea musicologica* 6 (1972) 153–229; 7 (1975) 1–81. Trouvère song is indexed in Gaston Raynaud, *Bibliographie des chansonniers français des xiiie et xive siècles comprenant la description de tous les manuscrits, la table des chansons classées par ordre alphabétique de rimes, et la liste des trouvères*, 2 vols. (Paris: F. Vieweg Libraire Editeur, 1884), revised as Hans Spanke, *Raynauds Bibliographie des altfranzösischen Liedes*, Musicologica 1 (Leiden: E. J. Brill, 1955), and again by Robert White Linker, *A Bibliography of Old French Lyrics*, Romance Monographs 31 (University, Miss.: Romance Monographs, 1979). A recent attempt to combine and revise Ludwig's and Gennrich's work is Hendrik van der Werf, *Integrated Directory of Organa, Clausulae and Motets of the Thirteenth Century* (Rochester, N.Y.: Author, 1989).

to French two-part motet, and so on.[8] Further reflection suggests that there is no reason why this model should apply to every work. More importantly, it omits the possibility of several motets in a single family deriving directly from the clausula in a collateral fashion, rather than in the single filial pattern suggested by this example.

Interpretation of the motet is complicated by an absence of a secure chronology for the music of the thirteenth century, and by the almost complete anonymity of the composers.[9] Although there is general agreement as to the dates of the surviving manuscript sources for the clausula and the motet, unfortunately this does not help with the earliest stages in the motet's history. Because these are largely retrospective collections, much of the material for the early Latin motet is preserved in the same sources as the clausulae on they which they were based. This means that great caution has to be exercised in the use of the manuscript chronology when attempting to come to terms with a single family of clausulae and motets.

Composers of the thirteenth-century motet are never identified in the surviving manuscripts, and theorists rarely speak of composers. Anonymous IV's account of the works of Leoninus or Perotinus is an exception. Indeed, there is a certain irony in that most theorists who speak about the motet are identified by name – Johannes de Garlandia, Franco of Cologne and Lambertus, for example – whereas the names of those responsible for the works they discuss remain unknown. This anonymity needs to be understood in the light of the continuous reworking of material that made up much of the activity of the thirteenth-century composer. In a given motet, any number of composers could have left their mark on the work. Some modern commentators are reluctant to confront this collaborative activity, and avoid the use of the word 'composer' entirely.[10] This might be helpful if it drew attention to the fact that those responsible for the motet handled poetry as well as music. However, to replace the word 'composer' with 'creator', for example, simply because the art of the motet involves the reuse of material, implies a nineteenth- and twentieth-century view of originality that disadvantages the thirteenth-century composer.

8   In particular, this is a characteristic of the work of Gordon A. Anderson. See, for example, 'Notre Dame Bilingual Motets: A Study in the History of Music, 1215–1245', *Miscellanea musicologica* 3 (1968) 50–144; *The Latin Compositions in Fascicules VII and VIII of the Notre Dame Manuscript Wolfenbüttel Helmstadt 1099 (1206)*, 2 vols., Musicological Studies 24 (Brooklyn, N.Y.: Institute of Mediaeval Music, 1971–6); 'Notre Dame Latin Double Motets ca.1215–1250', *Musica disciplina* 25 (1971) 35–92.

9   However, Richard de Semilli, Richard de Fournival and Philip the Chancellor are poets known to have written the texts of motets and conductus. They may even have composed music, but evidence for this is difficult to find, and more difficult to evaluate. The number of works with which named artists can be associated is tiny when compared with the enormous repertory of surviving unattributed motets. For Richard de Semilli, see Georg Steffens, 'Der kritische Text der Gedichte von Richart de Semilli', *Festgabe für Wendelin Foerster* (Halle: Niemeyer, 1902) 331–2, and Christopher Page, *The Owl and the Nightingale: Musical Life and Ideas in France 1100–1300* (London: Dent, 1989) 241 note 50. The motet texts composed by Richard de Fournival are edited in Paul Zarifopol, *Der kritische Text der Lieder Richarts de Fournival* (Halle: Niemeyer, 1904); see also Robert Falck, 'Richart de Fournival', *The New Grove Dictionary of Music and Musicians*, 20 vols., ed. Stanley Sadie (London: Macmillan, 1980) 15: 843. The most recent studies of the complex issues surrounding the attribution of poetry to Philip the Chancellor are Peter Dronke, 'The Lyrical Compositions of Philip the Chancellor', *Studi medievali*, Third Series 28 (1987) 563–92, and Thomas B. Payne, 'Poetry, Politics, and Polyphony: Philip the Chancellor's Contribution to the Music of the Notre Dame School', 2 vols. (Ph.D. diss., University of Chicago, 1991) 2: 327–98.

10   Dolores Pesce ('The Significance of Text in Thirteenth-Century Latin Motets', *Acta musicologica* 58 (1986) 93) favours the use of the term 'creator'. Norman Smith ('The Earliest Motets: Music and Words', *Journal of the Royal Musical Association* 114 (1989) 151) offers the expression 'motet-maker'.

In the thirteenth century, a composer could manipulate words and notes with equal ease, and his skill lay as much in the combination of pre-existent materials with new ones as in the original composition of poetry or music. *Compositor* certainly meant a literary author as early as the thirteenth century. *Compositio* implied synthesis in logic, and *compositum* a compound of matter or form.[11] These usages, together with the etymology of the word 'composer' (*componere*, meaning 'to place together'), are an encouragement to use the word to refer both to an individual working with words and notes, and to someone manipulating pre-existent and newly constructed materials.

With this wider definition of composition in mind, it is possible to explore the shifting ambitions of composers during the course of the thirteenth century. They constantly changed the balance between innovation and renovation. The 'renewing' of pre-existent materials becomes just as varied, and just as imaginative, as the creation of new works. When we compare the earliest motets with mid-century works, we may see that the former tend to borrow and elaborate an entire musical structure, but that, although the latter are termed 'newly composed', they are still based on pre-existing tenors. Despite this difference in the use of pre-existent materials, both early and mid-century works are characterised by a balance between the creation of the new and the carefully crafted reuse of the old.

Despite the large body of commentary on the music of the motet, its French poetry has only recently received similar levels of attention.[12] There are two impulses behind this recent interest in the poetic content of the motet. One has been a concern to reinstate the poetry alongside verse that has long been considered its superior, and to show that motet poetry has qualities equal to trouvère songs or other lyrics.[13] The other is a relish for the intertextual richness of two poems declaimed simultaneously, as is found in the three-part motet.[14] Latin texts, however, do not seem to have aroused the same interest as French ones.[15] Discussion of

[11] *Revised Medieval Latin Word-List from British and Irish Sources*, ed. R. E. Latham (London: Oxford University Press, 1965; *R* 1983) 101.

[12] Early attempts were Gaston Raynaud, ed., *Recueil de motets français des xiie et xiiie siècles publiés d'après les manuscrits, avec introduction, notes, variantes, et glossaires*, 2 vols., Bibliothèque française du moyen âge (Paris: F. Vieweg, 1881–3; *R* Hildesheim and New York: Georg Olms Verlag, 1972), and Yvonne Rokseth, *Polyphonies du treizième siècle*, 4 vols. (Paris: Editions de l'Oiseau Lyre, 1935–9).

[13] This has certainly been one of the impulses behind Beverly Jean Evans, 'The Unity of Text and Music in the Late Thirteenth-Century French Motet: A Study of Selected Works from the Montpellier Manuscript' (Ph.D. diss., University of Pennsylvania, 1983), and Evans, 'The Textual Function of a Refrain Cento in a Thirteenth Century French Motet', *Music and Letters* 71 (1990) 187–97. Evans opposes the view of the motet espoused in sources as diverse as Raynaud, *Recueil de motets*, and Pierre Bec, *La lyrique française au moyen âge (xiie–xiiie siècles): contribution à une typologie des genres poétiques médiévaux, études et textes*, 2 vols., Publications du Centre d'Etudes Supérieures de Civilisation Médiévale de l'Université de Poitiers 6–7 (Paris: Editions A. and J. Picard, 1977–8).

[14] Sylvia Huot approaches this question directly in 'Polyphonic Poetry: The Old French Motet and Its Literary Context', *French Forum* 14 (1989) 261–78, and slightly more obliquely in Huot, 'Transformations of Lyric Voice in the Songs, Motets and Plays of Adam de la Halle', *Romanic Review* 78 (1987) 148–64. Huot's more recent work has been to explore the relationship between vernacular texts in motets and the literary origins of tenor incipits.

[15] Guido Maria Dreves, ed., *Lieder und Motetten des Mittelalters*, 2 vols., Analecta hymnica medii aevi 20–1 (Leipzig: O. R. Reisland, 1895) edited a large proportion of the Latin motet repertory, but commented little. See, however, Joel Relihan's introduction to the edition and translation of the Latin texts in Hans Tischler, ed., *The Montpellier Codex*, 4 vols. [vol. 4 ed. and trans. Susan Stakel and Joel C. Relihan], Recent Researches in the Music of the Middle Ages and Early Renaissance 2–8 (Madison, Wis.: A. R. Editions, 1978–85) 4: xx–xxi, and Pesce, 'The Significance of Text'.

French motet poetry, however, rarely encompasses its relationship with the music, and the converse is often true. The parallel existence of musicological and literary modes of commentary on the motet is a possible cause and an undesirable result.[16] This book attempts to steer these parallel existences towards some sort of juncture.

An interpretation of the motet cannot be established without a concept of number. From the simplest proportions of mensural notation to the most complicated numerical ground plan, number underpins much of the innovative, and a certain amount of the borrowed, in the motet.[17] The ideas of numerical planning, symmetry and proportion play an important role both in the reworking and original composition of the motet. A borrowing (a plainsong tenor, for example) may be deployed in a way that stresses structural features of the work; reworking (a texting of a melismatic clausula or a retexting of a motet voice) may either ignore, or select for emphasis, numerical or symmetrical elements in the original material. The relationships between clausula and motet show a continual exchange of numerical and proportional concerns with textual and poetic priorities.

Sources: typology and origins

The interpretation of the thirteenth-century motet has been facilitated by the rapid advances in identifying the date and provenance of the surviving manuscript sources.[18] We may distinguish three important types of musical source in the thirteenth century: chansonnier, *liber motetorum* and service book. All play a role in the preservation of polyphonic music. Although chansonniers are primarily the sources for trouvère song, motets are however found in two of these: the so-called Roi and Noailles chansonniers.[19] The motets are preserved in separate quires in the manuscript. One further chansonnier, Paris, Bibliothèque Nationale, fonds français 845, contains motets that will form an important part of the evidence in Chapter 4. The *liber*

---

[16] Gennrich long ago cautioned against such a division. See his *Musikwissenschaft und romanische Philologie* (Halle: Niemeyer, 1918); 'Die Musik als Hilfswissenschaft der romanischen Philologie', *Zeitschrift für romanische Philologie* 39 (1919) 330–61.

[17] Ernest Sanders laid out many of the ways in which number controls the functioning of both clausula and motet ('The Medieval Motet', *Gattungen der Musik in Einzeldarstellungen: Gedenkschrift Leo Schrade*, ed. Wulf Arlt *et al.* (Berne: Francke Verlag, 1973) 525–8), and John Stevens has given us a more general introduction to the ways in which number may be expressed in, and determine the structure of, medieval music and verse (John Stevens, *Words and Music in the Middle Ages: Song, Narrative, Dance and Drama, 1050–1350*, Cambridge Studies in Music (Cambridge: Cambridge University Press, 1986) 45–7).

[18] The only resistance to reworking the history of thirteenth-century music is found where complex chronologies have already been built on (sometimes contentious) observations of musical style. See, for a rare example, Hans Tischler, ed., *The Earliest Motets (to circa 1270): A Complete Comparative Edition*, 3 vols. (New Haven and London: Yale University Press, 1982) 3: 33, where he writes: 'Since the dating of the manuscripts is only approximate and the music collected in them often reflects periods earlier than those of their compilation or writing, a chronological order cannot be established and would not be fruitful'.

[19] Paris, Bibliothèque Nationale, fonds français 844 and 12615. The first of these is edited in facsimile in Jean and Louise Beck, eds, *Le manuscrit du Roi, fonds français no 844 de la Bibliothèque Nationale: reproduction phototypique publié avec une introduction*, 2 vols., Corpus cantilenarum medii aevi 1; les chansonniers des troubadours et des trouvères 2 (London: Humphrey Milford; Oxford University Press; Philadelphia: University of Pennsylvania Press, 1938).

motetorum, as its name makes explicit, is dedicated to motets. In the thirteenth century, this entails a consistent format. A *liber motetorum* is almost always prefaced by a polyphonic setting of the versicle *Deus in adiutorium*. Important examples are the Bamberg manuscript, the Turin motet book and the eighth fascicle of the Montpellier Codex.[20] Even the rather later motets in the Brussels rotulus are prefaced by *Deus in adiutorium*.[21] Service books encompass missals, breviaries with and without notation, antiphonals, graduals, psalters, sequentiaries, and so on. In general, they are organised according to the subdivisions of the liturgical year and the difference between Mass and Office. The so-called 'Notre-Dame' manuscripts now housed in Florence and Wolfenbüttel (W_1 and W_2) are service books in layout.[22] Liturgical organum is grouped according to a division between Mass and Office, and then according to the sequence of the liturgical year beginning with Advent. The distinction between organa for two, three and four parts, and *Benedicamus Domino* corresponds to the subdivisions found in other service books into *temporale*, *sanctorale*, proper and common. For much of its early career, the Florence manuscript was known as the Antiphonary of Piero de' Medici.[23]

The liturgical ordering of service books and of the derivative 'Notre-Dame' manuscripts contrasts with the organisation of the other two types of book. The chansonnier tends to group most of its contents according to author in descending order of aristocratic rank; anonymous works, where there are any, are placed in alphabetical order.[24] In the *liber motetorum*, where all the works are anonymous, alphabetical ordering, usually by the incipit of the motetus, is the norm. However, in the early Latin collections of motets found in such composite anthologies as the Florence manuscript, liturgical order is still found. In the near-contemporary manuscript W_2, otherwise very similar to Florence in arrangement, the French motets are grouped alphabetically.

Genre and *mise-en-page* are related. Organum and conducti are invariably copied in score, the parts one above another. Polytextual motets with almost textless tenors were copied in parts to save space. In the earliest examples, the tenor was simply copied at the end of the motetus part. In the earliest layers of the Montpellier

[20] Bamberg, Staatsbibliothek, Lit. 115; Turin, Biblioteca Reale, vari 42; Montpellier, Bibliothèque Interuniversitaire, Section Médecine H 196. Facsimiles and editions of both Bamberg and Montpellier are Pierre Aubry, ed., *Cent motets du xiiie siècle*, 3 vols. (Paris: A. Rouart, Lerolle; Paul Geuthner, 1908; *R* New York: Broude Brothers, 1964); Rokseth, *Polyphonies du treizième siècle*. An (idiosyncratic) edition and facsimile of Turin is in Antoine Auda, ed., *Les 'motets wallons' du manuscrit de Turin: vari 42*, 2 vols. (Brussels: chez l'auteur, [1953]).

[21] Brussels, Bibliothèque Royale Albert 1er, 19606. Edited in facsimile, *Rotulus (1 conductus & 9 motets), early 14th c.* ([Brussels]: Alamire, 1990).

[22] Florence, Biblioteca Medicea-Laurenziana, Pluteus 29. 1. Facsimile in Luther Dittmer, ed., *Facsimile Reproduction of the Manuscript Firenze, Biblioteca Medicea-Laurenziana Pluteo 29,1*, 2 vols., Publications of Mediaeval Musical Manuscripts 10–11 (Brooklyn, N.Y.: Institute of Mediaeval Music, [1966]–7); Wolfenbüttel, Herzog-August-Bibliothek 628 (W_1): James H. Baxter, *An Old St Andrews Music Book (Cod. Helmst. 628) Published in Facsimile with an Introduction*, St Andrews University Publications 30 (Oxford: Humphrey Milford; Oxford University Press; Paris: Librairie Ancienne Honoré Champion, 1931); Wolfenbüttel, Herzog-August-Bibliothek 1099 (W_2): Luther Dittmer, ed., *Facsimile Reproduction of the Manuscript Wolfenbüttel 1099 (1206)*, Publications of Mediaeval Musical Manuscripts 2 (Brooklyn, N.Y.: Institute of Mediaeval Music, 1960).

[23] Mark Everist, *Polyphonic Music in Thirteenth-Century France: Aspects of Sources and Distribution* (New York and London: Garland, 1989) 58.

[24] This is easily seen in the manuscript inventories in Raynaud, *Bibliographie des chansonniers français*.

Codex, this is replaced by a procedure whereby the triplum and motetus of three-part pieces are copied side-by-side in columns; the tenor is then copied across the bottom of the page underneath the two upper parts. This was more economical, and allowed scribes to synchronise page turns.[25]

With typology of manuscript sources in mind, we may point to some exceptions that help to focus such general rules. The collection of fragments of motets in Munich quite clearly organises its contents according to the liturgical order of the motets' plainsong tenors.[26] But these are French motets, and a similar repertory to that alphabetically arranged in W_2. A chansonnier in the Bibliothèque Nationale – fonds français 846, the Chansonnier Cangé – imitates contemporary motet books, not only in its notation and format, but also in its alphabetical arrangement of contents.[27] Fascicles 2 to 6, the *corpus ancien*, of the Montpellier Codex are each devoted to a particular genre much in the same way as those of Florence or W_2. They are then framed by fascicles 1 and 7. *Deus in adiutorium* thus appears at the beginning of this section of the manuscript in the manner of a *liber motetorum*. The eighth fascicle is already a self-contained *liber motetorum*, again prefaced by *Deus in adiutorium*.

The typology of thirteenth-century music books offers a basis on which to examine the interrelation of chronology, manuscript provenance and repertory. In previous surveys of the motet, the lack of consideration of the co-existence of these three elements has led to some anomalies. Chief among these has been the undue weight that has been attached to certain subgenres of the motet on the basis of a statistical, as opposed to a critical, view of distribution.

The 'bilingual motet' is an excellent example of a subgenre that has been given more than its fair share of attention.[28] This consists of one Latin- and one French-texted voice-part above a plainsong tenor. Almost every account of the thirteenth-century motet, of whatever scope, gives space to this subgenre. It is treated as if it had the same generic status as the three-part French motet or the Latin motet. But in fact the distribution of the bilingual motet is tiny, numerically speaking, and consists of parts of two manuscripts only. Both sources are Parisian, and confirm the strongly localised interest in this particular type. It is almost exclusively preserved in the third fascicle of the Montpellier Codex and the so-called 'La Clayette' manuscript.[29]

[25] Whether this suggests that such books as Bamberg or the later fascicles of Montpellier were conceived with performance in mind is an open question. For a view that supports the idea that these books were associated with performance, see Patricia L. P. Norwood, 'Performance Manuscripts from the Thirteenth-Century?' *College Music Symposium* 26 (1986) 92–6. An opposing view, based on the uses to which non-musical books of similar quality were put, has yet to be advanced.

[26] Bayerische Staatsbibliothek, c. g. m. 42. See Luther Dittmer, ed., *Eine zentrale Quelle der Notre-Dame Musik: Faksimile, Wiederherstellung, Catalogue raisonné, Besprechung, und Transcriptionen*, Publications of Mediaeval Musical Manuscripts 3 (Brooklyn, N.Y.: Institute of Mediaeval Music, 1959).

[27] Edited in facsimile, in Jean Beck, ed., *Reproduction phototypique du chansonnier Cangé: Paris, Bibliothèque Nationale, Ms. Français No 846*, 2 vols., Corpus cantilenarum medii aevi 1; les chansonniers des troubadours et des trouvères 1 (Paris: Librairie Ancienne Honoré Champion; Philadelphia: University of Pennsylvania Press, 1927).

[28] Anderson, 'Notre Dame Bilingual Motets', 52–3.

[29] Paris, Bibliothèque Nationale, fonds français 13521. See Luther Dittmer, ed., *Paris 13521 and 11411: Facsimile, Introduction, Index and Transcriptions from the Manuscripts Paris, Bibl. Nat. Nouv. Acq. Fr.13521 (La Clayette) and Lat.11411*, Publications of Mediaeval Musical Manuscripts 4 (Brooklyn, N.Y.: Institute of Mediaeval Music, 1959); Friedrich Gennrich, ed., *Ein altfranzösischer Motettenkodex, Paris B.N. 13521*, Summa musicae medii aevi 6 (Darmstadt: n.p., 1958).

Although these are both Parisian books, the relationship between source and repertory in the La Clayette manuscript is problematic. Its repertory overlaps substantially with Montpellier, but the paleographical and art-historical evidence indicates that it was probably copied at the very end of the century, whereas those parts of Montpellier that contain French-texted motets were probably copied in the 1270s.[30] Furthermore, many of the bilingual pieces in this manuscript are in four parts. So, to judge from surviving sources, motets surviving in bilingual versions were initially collected in one source only (the third fascicle of Montpellier). If we judge the preservation of this particular type by the number of manuscript locations where it made an impact rather than by the total number of specimens, a very different, even marginal, picture of the bilingual motet begins to emerge. Much has not survived, but there is no particular reason to assume that a larger proportion of bilingual motets has been lost than of the three-part motet with Latin texts or of the two-part French motet. The absence of bilingual motets in mid-century sources outside the Montpellier Codex is very telling.

The chronology of the thirteenth-century motet begins to pick up a certain focus as more and more manuscripts are grouped according to paleography, manuscript decoration and format. Since the definitive dating of the Florence manuscript,[31] most of the major sources of thirteenth-century music have been subjected to scrutiny with the result that it is possible, first, to make some generalisations about the chronology of the manuscript sources, and second, to begin to use this information to formulate a chronology of the thirteenth-century motet.

Three immediate problems arise however. The first of these is that one of the largest sources of the music, the Montpellier Codex, has been the most reluctant to yield to the sort of enquiry outlined in the previous paragraph. Its history is complex, and there still remain problems concerning the date of the later layers in the manuscript and their relationship to the *corpus ancien*.[32] The second problem is that two of the other key manuscripts, Florence and W_2, are both anthologies, and seem to fall into the same chronological gap: 1245–55 for Florence[33] and 1244–60 for W_2.[34] The bases for these dates are cross-relations with single manuscripts which themselves may be either at the earliest or latest point in the development of the particular paleographical element that is being used to locate the manuscript.[35] There are clear repertorial and notational reasons for dating W_2 later than Florence: W_2 includes French motets whereas Florence only preserves Latin ones, and W_2 uses a slightly more progressive notational style. The grouping of artists of the miniatures and

---

[30] Everist, *Polyphonic Music*, 153.

[31] Rebecca Baltzer, 'Thirteenth-Century Illuminated Miniatures and the Date of the Florence Manuscript', *Journal of the American Musicological Society* 25 (1972) 1–18.

[32] See most recently, Everist, *Polyphonic Music*, 110–34, and Mary Wolinski, 'The Montpellier Codex: Its Compilation, Notation and Implications for the Chronology of the Thirteenth-Century Motet' (Ph.D. diss., Brandeis University, 1988).

[33] Baltzer, 'Thirteenth-Century Illuminated Miniatures', 18.

[34] Everist, *Polyphonic Music*, 109.

[35] In the case of W_2, the evidence is based on comparisons with Oxford, Wadham College, MS 1, and Branner's 'Dominican Bible Group' (see Robert Branner, *Manuscript Painting in Paris During the Reign of St Louis: A Study of Styles*, California Studies in the History of Art 18 (Berkeley, Los Angeles and London: University of California Press, 1977) 207–8).

historiated initials in W_2 certainly makes one incline towards the late 1250s or early 1260s, but the minor initial decoration does just the opposite, and suggests the 1240s. We need to beware circular arguments concerning repertory, notation and decoration. The third problem concerns the dating and status of the manuscript W_1, now preserved in the Herzog-August-Bibliothek in Wolfenbüttel. Although it clearly borrows its layout from the Parisian predecessors of Florence and W_2, it is the earliest of the surviving Notre-Dame manuscripts but almost certainly originates far from Paris and its cathedral, in the Augustinian Cathedral of St Andrews.[36] Since it contains no motets, it is of only tangential interest to this study, but its preservation of the earliest copy of the *Magnus liber organi* of Leoninus – as Ludwig observed nearly a century ago – makes it one of the most important documents of medieval polyphony. This manuscript's centrality to our thinking about the music of the 'Notre-Dame School' contrasts oddly with its provincial origin.

Despite these basic problems, it is indeed possible to present a chronology of the thirteenth-century motet, but it needs to be treated with great caution. Nevertheless, it allows us to isolate the arrival of the French motet in a written form in the manuscript W_2, probably before 1260, and to contrast this layer of activity with that represented by the earliest parts of the Montpellier Codex, copied in the 1270s. This ability to compare and contrast two types separated by a known period of time gives a degree of chronological purchase on motets with French texts composed and copied between *c.* 1250 and *c.* 1270. This repertory is therefore the focus of the discussion in Chapter 8.

A concentration on music between 1250 and 1270 also provides a point of comparison with the chronological implications of contemporary theory. There is a large cluster of post-Garlandian theorists – Lambertus, the St Emmeram Anonymous, Franco of Cologne and Anonymous IV – all writing apparently within the period 1275–85.[37] The problems associated with the often explicit relationships between these theorists are great, but are nothing compared with the challenges of trying to align the chronology of musical repertories with a sometimes doubtful chronology of theory.[38] The basis of the associations between the dates of theoretical and musical sources is mostly that of notation. Assumptions behind much of the thinking on this question have been built on a strictly linear view of the development of notation that, as has already been pointed out elsewhere, is not the only or the most obvious way of interpreting the surviving evidence.[39]

---

[36] These are the conclusions reached in Mark Everist, 'From Paris to St. Andrews: The Origins of W_1', *Journal of the American Musicological Society* 43 (1990) 1–42 which supersede those in Edward H. Roesner, 'The Origins of W_1', *Journal of the American Musicological Society* 29 (1976) 337–80, and Julian Brown, Sonia Patterson and David Hiley, 'Further Observations on W_1', *Journal of the Plainsong and Mediaeval Music Society* 4 (1981) 53–80.

[37] Various chronological relationships between this group of theorists have been proposed. For a representative sample, see Mark Everist, *French 13th-Century Polyphony in the British Library: A Facsimile Edition of the Manuscripts Additional 30091 and Egerton 2615 (folios 79–94v)* (London: Plainsong and Mediaeval Music Society, 1988) 7–9, and the sources cited there.

[38] One attempt, to explain the theoretical background to Bamberg, is Patricia L. P. Norwood, 'A Study of the Provenance and French Motets in Bamberg Staatsbibliothek Lit.115' (Ph.D. diss., University of Texas at Austin, 1979) 88–90.

[39] Everist, *French 13th-Century Polyphony in the British Library*, 9.

Critical practice

The study of distribution and concordance-base has pushed discussion of the thirteenth-century motet towards the mechanistic examination of motet families and away from matters of compositional intention. Although the grouping of motets according to shared tenors and clausulae is essential, it has also had the effect of driving the autonomous work of art into the background. At its worst, this has had the result of generating commentaries that take no more account of the artistic nature of the motet than would a description of the history of manufacture of barrels, candles or textiles.[40] The focus on changing versions of the work, status of concordances and structure of 'repertories' has consistently represented the work of art as little more than the sum of its concordances. The individual work may therefore be reinstated at the centre of the field of enquiry. Studies in the past that have attempted to explain the motet without reference to its immediate context or function have rightly been harshly judged.[41] A view of the motet that respects the integrity of a single work while taking account of its possibly complex history is clearly a desirable goal. Such an objective implies a search for the working practices of medieval composers, the materials with which they worked, and the assumptions that they must have made in fashioning and refashioning their cultural artefacts.

If a reassessment of compositional practice and intention is one response to the way we currently perceive the thirteenth-century motet, a re-evaluation of genre is another. A theory of genre is more than the creation of a crude taxonomy, and a more sophisticated approach to genre is essential to understanding the motet. But even in those approaches to genre that have been simply taxonomic, judgement and selection of criteria have been less than adequate. One reason for this is the fact that questions of genre have never been addressed directly. Criteria determining taxonomic choices of genre and subgenre are never made clear. They are absent in such bibliographies as Friedrich Gennrich's work that swept the scholarly field in the late 1950s and are still the only tools available for the examination of the motet.[42] This is one body of literature in which one might expect to read some serious view of the issue of genre. Hardly surprisingly, such discussion is lacking in most general histories of music. Understanding the criteria for Gennrich's generic choices, complementing and proposing alternatives to them, is important to grasping the meaning of the motet.

Gennrich's view of genre was severely hampered by over-ambitious system building. Chapters 4 to 6 of this book discuss the music he attempted to classify, and

---

[40] The most direct target of this challenge is Hans Tischler's *The Style and Evolution of the Earliest Motets (to Circa 1270)*, 4 vols., Musicological Studies 40 (Henryville, Ottawa and Binningen: Institute of Mediaeval Music, 1985).

[41] Noteworthy in this respect is Finn Mathiassen, *The Style of the Early Motet (c.1200–1250): An Investigation of the Old Corpus of the Montpellier Manuscript*, trans. Johanne M. Stochholm, Studier og publikationer fra Musikvidenskabeligt Institut Aarhus Universitet 1 (Copenhagen: Dan Fog Musikforlag, 1966), which attempted to treat its subject without reference to previous musical and textual traditions. Reviews were universally unfavourable.

[42] Gennrich, *Bibliographie der ältesten französischen und lateinischen Motetten*.

conclude by refining or rejecting not only his specific view of the *motet enté*, the rondeau-motet and the refrain cento, but also his strictly normative approaches to questions of genre. Two examples taken from his *Bibliographie der ältesten französischen und lateinischen Motetten* will make the point. Gennrich's discussion of the music in the manuscript Paris, Bibliothèque Nationale, fonds français 845 makes consistent use of the formulation '2st[immige], T[enor] fehlt' (2 parts, tenor is lacking) to describe nothing more or less than a monody.[43] He fails to distinguish between these pieces and, say, a two-part motet in the Roi or Noailles chansonniers whose tenor had not been copied on to the stave lines provided. In all his discussions of the motets preserved in the manuscript Oxford, Bodleian Library, Douce 308, the motets are described as '2st[immige] o[hne] N[oten], T[enor] fehlt' (2 parts, without notation, tenor is lacking).[44] In fact, the manuscript simply preserves the text. Gennrich's norm in both these examples is a two-part motet (motetus and tenor) from which other presentations deviate. While the example from the Douce manuscript is simply obfuscatory, the one from français 845 shows just how badly works suffer on Gennrich's Procrustean Bed. Monophonic works or texts are treated by Gennrich as inadequately preserved or degenerate polyphony.

A more useful view of genre as an interpretative element in the motet is offered here in the spirit of an alternative to Gennrich's over-rigorous systems, not as a substitute for them. One of the conclusions that develops out of this study is that a simple taxonomy of a 'genre' of the motet with a collection of more or less related 'subgenres' is simply not tenable. The only exceptions are the distinctions of kind offered by medieval theory or manuscript organisation between conductus, organum and motet, or between number of parts and language of upper-voice texts. The reassessment of genre in Chapters 4–7 of this book suggests that the concept of 'subgenre' becomes less and less applicable to the French motet, and that the concept of generic 'mode' is of more value to an interpretation of both text and music. This idea is given a theoretical backbone in the last chapter of the book, which forms the basis for a revised interpretation of the genre.

A search for compositional ambition and an attempt to evolve an appropriate theory of genre are thus the two driving forces behind this book. There is no doubt that its title reflects a generic choice even before the covers are opened. For English music of the thirteenth century, with its much closer generic links between conductus, motet and polyphony based on a liturgical cantus firmus, a title that specified country and genre would be impossible. But the view of French music adopted here at least shares generic assumptions with those who compiled thirteenth-century music books and those who theorised about the subject. But if the title seems limiting, its treatment is not restricted to such narrow paths, as the discussion of the origins of the motet in the following chapter will show.

---

[43] *Ibid.*, 97–8.
[44] *Ibid.*, 98–102.

2

The origins and early history of the motet

Introduction

Modern views of the motet see its history as an evolution from the clausula. The clausulae that were preserved in the 'Notre-Dame' sources had apparently been composed to enrich the *Magnus liber organi*, and then served as 'sources' for the motet. The generations who reworked the *Magnus liber organi* of Leoninus replaced the original clausulae with a large number of substitutes. The writing of substitute clausulae apparently generated even more possible sources. There are however problems with this view that concern the nature of the clausula itself. Several clausulae survive for the same passage in organa that can only be performed in the liturgy once a year. It might therefore be questioned whether substitution within the liturgy was their real purpose. There is at least the possibility that some of the 'substitute' clausulae were in fact musical models to facilitate the performance of newly composed motets. Although the notation of motets in the earliest sources is problematic, the notation of the larger part of the clausula repertory is unequivocal. This is because the notes joined in ligatures that identify the modal rhythms of the clausula have to be separated when the motet text is added. The resulting motet notation lacks the combinations of ligatures that make it possible to read the rhythms.[1] This plausible explanation for the multiplicity of clausulae may be difficult to prove, but it must be considered in any description of the conventional view of the progress of the motet. We need, then, to maintain a bifocal view of the clausula that acknowledges the possibility that it could be either a straightforward source, or a notational model, for the motet.

Simply to compare a motet with its 'source' clausula is to ignore many important relationships. These include the connections between the clausula, its host organum, the parent plainsong of the organum itself and the liturgical context of the plainsong. Some or all of these have far-reaching implications for the ways in which the motet develops. Any discussion of musical and textual procedures in the motet will make frequent reference to these backgrounds to musical composition and recomposition.

---

[1] Sanders, 'Medieval Motet', 505–7.

In the earliest years of the thirteenth century, the retexting of clausulae was only one of a variety of procedures that resulted in the creation of the motet.[2] A wide range of compositions arose out of differing attitudes to the combination of poetry and music. This is not, however, to overturn or even to challenge the veracity of the traditional view of the genesis of the motet, but is an attempt to supplement it. The view that motets were created out of the retexting of clausulae is supported by the large numbers of motets and clausulae that share the same music. Although this 'genetic' relationship had, by the middle of the century, proved to be the way forward for composers, we should not be blind to the wide range of experimentation that characterised the emergence of the motet.

The conventional view: motet and clausula

Poetry

Despite the fact that the 'traditional' relationship between motet and clausula has been acknowledged for over a century, few attempts have been made to come to terms with the compositional dynamics of writing new texts to old music. An example will point to some of the ways these relationships may be considered. The clausula embedded in the Pentecost organum, *Alleluya. Paraclitus spiritus sanctus* (M26), served as the source for a number of motets. The fact that it survives embedded in a host organum makes it fairly certain that the clausula is a genuine pre-existent source for the motet, and not simply a newly composed model to aid its composition or performance. The first thirty-three perfections of the clausula are given as Example 2.1. In many respects, this is a good example of the ways in which a clausula functions, and of the material that would challenge the composer of the motet. Rhythmically, the organisation of the upper voice (the duplum) depends on the first rhythmic mode with a substantial degree of *extensio modi*. In transcription, this results in a mixture of two rhythmic patterns. One is based on dotted crotchets and the other on an alternation of crotchets and quavers. The use of two types of rhythm determines the changes in the declamation of the text of any motet subsequently based on this clausula. The tenor moves in the dotted crotchets of the fifth rhythmic mode. The contrapuntal style of the piece is unexceptional. Phrases generally begin and end on what Johannes de Garlandia called perfect concords (unison and octave), imperfect concords (major and minor thirds) and intermediate concords (fifth and fourth).[3]

The overall structure of the clausula is determined by the patterning of the tenor. There are two statements of the tenor, or *cursus*, and each is complete. This has the

---

[2] The challenge to the conventional view of the priority of clausula over motet presented in Wolf Frobenius, 'Zum genetischen Verhältnis zwischen Notre-Dame-Klauseln und ihren Motetten', *Archiv für Musikwissenschaft* 44 (1987) 1–39 is ill directed. Frobenius gives substantially insufficient weight to the question of the clausula's liturgical context, and (critically) is unaware of any of the problems surrounding the definition of refrains and the role they play in polyphony. These will be discussed in Chapters 3 and 4.

[3] Reimer, *Johannes de Garlandia*, 1: 67–9.

Example 2.1 Clausula *Docebit* (M26), perfections 1–33; *I-Fl* Plut. 29. 1, fol. 118v

effect of dividing the piece into two sections. The first *cursus* begins the piece; the second begins at perfection 61. The rhythmic organisation of each is different. Groups of three *longae* and a *longa* rest structure the first *cursus*. Patterns of three *longae*, *longa* rest, *longa duplex*, *longa* and a *longa* rest control the second. Example 2.2 gives the plainsong on which the clausula is based and the two rhythmic patterns that organise it. There are differences in duration between the two *cursus*. In the first, six notes in the tenor occupy eight perfections; in the second, only five notes occupy the same musical space. The duration of the piece is thus determined as follows: the first *cursus* lasts 60 (5 × 12) perfections, the second 72 (6 × 12). The two therefore stand in a 5 : 6 relationship. Within each *cursus*, furthermore, the first ten pitches are repeated as pitches 16 to 25. They correspond to perfections 1–13 and

Example 2.2 Plainsong melisma *Docebit* and two clausula tenor patterns derived from it

21–33 in the first *cursus* shown in Example 2.1. The composer reflects this repetition in the duplum. In the section before the repetition of the tenor pitches, the music proceeds according to simple Mode I patterns. At the point where the tenor repeats (perfection 21) the music moves into patterns using *extensio modi*. Phrases that consisted of crotchets and quavers are replaced by those made up of dotted crotchets. This, too, is visible in Example 2.1. In the second *cursus* however, the repetition of the tenor pitches seems to be ignored. It occurs in the middle of the first limb of the repetition of a duplum phrase in which musical preoccupations lie elsewhere.

There are examples of phrase repetition in the duplum above the tenor in each *cursus*. However, these do not coincide with the internal repetition of the tenor. The duplum repetitions therefore take place over different tenor notes. Both pairs of repetitions are given as Example 2.3.1 and Example 2.3.2. The repetition in the first *cursus* (Example 2.3.1) is marked out by the following rests or *suspirationes* in both parts. By contrast, the repetitions in the second *cursus* merge into the following phrases. The loosest form of melodic repetition occurs at the beginning of each of the two tenor *cursus*: the beginning of the clausula and at perfection 61. It is illustrated in Example 2.4. The duplum pitch *a* in the fourth perfection is absent in the repetition at perfection 64. Its absence may be prompted by aural considerations. The *a* is already present in the tenor in perfection 3, and the duplum pitch is therefore almost a duplication. It is again present in the tenor in perfection 63; here, the duplum doubling is eliminated. There is also a sense in which perfections 4–8 recur in perfections 64–9. The duplum phrase is shifted back a perfection to take account of the new distribution of the tenor pitches. These correspondences are made explicit in Example 2.4. The effect is nevertheless to alert the ear to the repetition of the tenor melody, even though the structure of the duplum phrase has been changed.

Against the unchanging patterns of the tenor *ordines*, the duplum creates a series of phrases of varying lengths. The interplay between the phrase-lengths of the two voice-parts is one of the most important points of interest in the piece. In general, the duplum phrases are constructed so as to overlap with those of the tenor. The few points of coincidence, where the duplum and tenor do in fact pause together, are therefore of significance. In Example 2.3.1, we saw how simultaneous rests in

Example 2.3.1 Clausula *Docebit* (M26), perfections 37–44 and 45–52

Example 2.3.2 Clausula *Docebit* (M26), perfections 79–86 and 91–8

Example 2.4 Clausula *Docebit* (M26), perfections 1–10 and 61–70

both voices articulate the phrase repetitions in the first *cursus* of the piece. Particularly striking are the simultaneous phrase-endings in perfections 28 and 32. These are visible at the end of Example 2.1. The four-perfection phrase that separates the two cadences is curious. This is in fact the exact centre of the first *cursus* of the piece, and is marked by a central four-perfection phrase in which the duplum is divided into two two-perfection phrases. Although the duplum employs other two-perfection phrases in the clausula (perfections 71 and 125, for example) this is the only occasion where two such phrases are juxtaposed.

Questions of number and symmetry should play an important role in structuring a work without a text. The only literary component to the clausula is the residue of the plainsong melisma *Docebit*, and this seems to have little effect on the work. As the clausula is turned into a motet by the addition of words, these numerical and symmetrical patterns may be retained, exaggerated or contradicted.

The general principles for the creation of a text to a pre-existent clausula consist of adding a poetic text to the duplum. In writing poetry to fit the music of the clausula, the composer adheres very strictly to the rhythmic patterns of the upper voice of the clausula, and adds one poetic syllable to each note. Even where the surreptitious addition or subtraction of a note might have made the work more easy, the composer in general faithfully preserved the pattern of his original material.[4]

Example 2.5 shows the first thirty-three perfections of the motet (344) *Doceas hac die – Docebit* (M26) that results from the addition of a poetic text to the clausula:

---

4   Smith, 'The Earliest Motets', 151.

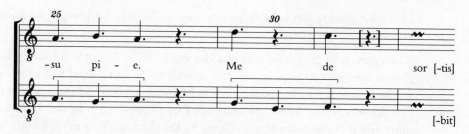

Example 2.5 Motet (344) *Doceas hac die – Docebit* (M26), perfections 1–33; *I-Fl* Plut. 29. 1, fol. 400r–v

Doceas hac die
Viam patrie,
Fons gratie,
Spes venie,
Terminus vie,
Ihesu pie.
Me de sortis vane
Solvas et humane
Carnis carcere.
Rege,
Quem sub lege
Iubes degere,
Sine luce
Tua duce
Nichil prospere
Possum agere.
Vite
Des
Fructum de te vite;
Elicere,
Fecunde
Gratiam funde,
Cuius habunde
Effluant unde,
Unde
Sint anime
Fide munde,
Spe iocunde.
Da gratie rore
Sancti spiritus amore
Proficere,
Me
Qui docebit.

Teach us today the way of the Father, You who are the fount of grace, the hope of pardon and the end of the way, Holy Jesus. Loose me from the emptiness of my fate and from the prison of human flesh. Direct me whom You enjoin to endure under Your law, for without Your light as a guide, I am not able to prosper, nor can I achieve anything. Grant me the fruit of life from You, the vine; come forth, shed abundantly Your grace, whose overflowing waves billow forth whence minds are cleansed by faith and made happy in hope. Grant that I shall grow, by the dew of grace and by the love of the Holy Spirit, which will teach me.[5]

A comparison of the motet with the clausula given in Example 2.1 shows how, in general, one note in the clausula corresponds to one syllable of text in the poem, and how there is only minimal alteration of ornamentation and alignment of notes.[6] Line-lengths in the poem are controlled by phrase-length in the clausula. The composition of the poem is not affected by the alternations of rhythmic mode. The music to which the lines 'Terminus vie / Ihesu pie' etc. are set has no effect on the length of the lines of poetry. It will be remembered that, in the clausula, this change of rhythmic mode in the duplum mirrored the repetition of pitches of the tenor. The addition of a motetus poem that fails to respond to this feature of the clausula has the effect of smoothing over this structural gesture. The dynamics of the new motet poem override those of the old clausula.

The treatment of rhyme in the poem is less dependent on the structure of the clausula. In fact, it seems as if the composer here is setting out to construct a set of rhyme patterns that interweave with, but do not correspond to, the phrases of the duplum, now motetus, and the syntax of the poem itself. The poem is governed by a single rhyme: -e. But there are groups of double rhymes throughout the poem. The first six lines all rhyme -ie and lines 21–5 all rhyme -unde for example. In principle, these double rhymes are grouped so that when one double rhyme ends and is replaced by another, it does not recur. The result is a sequence of double rhymes: -ie, -ane, -ege, -uce, -ite, -unde and -ore. This sequence is contrasted with the recurrence of lines that rhyme -ere at various points in the poem (lines 9, 12, 15, 16, 20 and 31). However one choses to handle the detail of the analysis of the rhyme, it is clear that blocks of double rhyme articulate sections of the poem. The change of rhyme sometimes corresponds to musical phrase and/or to the sense of the poem. Often it does not. In combination with these two other methods of organising words and notes, it creates three layers of structural activity: rhyme, phrase and poetic content.

The melodic repetitions in the clausula change as the poetic text is composed to fit the pre-existing music. In the first *cursus* of the piece, the two limbs of the duplum repetition (Example 2.3.1) are separated, in the motet, by the end of a sense-group in the poem – 'Me de sortis vane solvas et humane carnis carcere' – and the beginning of another – 'Rege, quem sub lege iubes degere'. But this self-contained textual phrase begins before the first limb. The text associated with the second limb continues after the end of the melodic repetition. In fact, apart from the obvious constraints on the composition of the poem dictated by the distribution of notes, there

---

5 In the edition of the text, the poetry is given a new line wherever there is a new musical phrase. This occurs even when the phrase consists of a couple of perfections only, and the line is one syllable long. However, where there is more than one line of poetry to a musical phrase, each line of the poetry is lineated separately.

6 Some differences between motet and clausula may arise from textual disturbance. Despite the fact that clausula and motet were composed at different times, they were both copied more or less simultaneously into the Florence manuscript. There are problems presented by trying to understand a history of this music when different historical layers are preserved in a single source copied at a single point in time. In the case in question, it is far from clear exactly how much time separated the composition of the clausula from the texting of the motet.

Example 2.6 Comparison of clausula *Docebit* (M26) and motet (344) *Doceas hac die – Docebit* (M26), perfections 79–102

is little attempt to respond to these sorts of melodic subtleties. The original melodic repetition in the second *cursus* of the piece is camouflaged even more effectively by rewriting part of the motetus. Example 2.6 superimposes the passage in the motet on that in the clausula.

The two-perfection phrase (93–4) clearly posed problems. In the normal course of events it would have required a two-syllable line. One might have expected the line 'Gratiam funde' to have been extended by a single syllable. But the poem at this point has just initiated a sustained passage based on the double rhyme *-unde*. Choices of vocabulary are narrow here, and the word 'unde' was to be saved for the end of the phrase. It seems that the choice here was either to modify the rhyme-scheme or to change the melodic superstructure. The composer seems to have valued the continuity of rhyme in the poem more highly than the integrity of the melodic repetition in the clausula. Although the original melodic parallelisms of the clausula are lost by this process, the motet replaces the simple A–A^1 repetition of the clausula with an A–B–A^1 structure. This is marked in Example 2.6.

To summarise, we may agree that in general the process of texting respects the musical surface of the melismatic original, but ignores certain purely musical repetitions and numerical structures. The patterns of line-length in the poem very clearly reflect the lengths of phrases in the clausula. Rhymes, however, behave differently, and set up their own patterns over and above those created by the clausula. Where there are collisions between musical elements in the clausula and poetic elements in the newly composed text, the strictly musical concerns of the clausula yield to the musico-poetic dynamic of the motet.

The same processes are used in the creation of three-part motets from three-part clausulae. We may begin with questions of retexting, by comparing a three-part clausula and a so-called conductus-motet. The latter requires a little introduction. It received its name from Ludwig, who pointed to the fact that the two upper voices were homorhythmic and carried the same text. Sometimes, the upper two voices alone were copied, in score, in the manuscripts. The resulting piece looked like a conductus. The conductus-motet was therefore marked out from the 'classic' three-part motet, in which the two upper parts carried different texts and were rhythmically differentiated.[7]

The upper voices in a conductus-motet are rhythmically homogeneous. In a three-part clausula there may be great rhythmic variety between the upper voices. Creating the motet from the clausula may therefore lead to technical problems. Surmounting these difficulties is the larger part of the composer's achievement. Example 2.7 displays the first forty perfections of a three-part clausula *Latus* (M14) with the motet derived from it [(229) *Radix venie*] – (229) *Radix venie* – *Latus* (M14).

---

[7] An alternative to this terminological conundrum has recently been proposed by Darwin Scott: the 'monotextual' motet (Darwin F. Scott, 'The Three- and Four-Voice Monotextual Motets of the Notre-Dame School' (Ph.D. diss., University of California at Los Angeles, 1988)). Although the term has much to recommend it, the sheer weight of the literature that uses the term 'conductus-motet' forces its use in the present context.

Example 2.7 Comparison of three-part clausula *Latus* (M14), perfections 1–40, with motet derived from it [(229) *Radix venie*] – (229) *Radix venie* – *Latus* (M14); *I-Fl* Plut. 29. 1 fols. 24r–v and 385r–v

The composer texts both upper voices of the clausula with the same poem. Any musical complexities in the clausula that stand in the way of this task are likely to be subject to adjustment. We can see here a more extreme example of the subordination of musical sophistication to poetic exigency that we saw in embryo in the previous example.

There is a variety of different rhythmic patterns, each with different numbers of notes, in the triplum and duplum of the clausula. Perfections 1–3 and 17–20 are two clear examples of this. In the clausula, the Mode I triplum presents four and eight notes respectively. The duplum, which mixes Mode I with *extensio modi*, has two and four notes for the same passages. It is clearly impossible to underlay the same text to this music as it stands. The composer responds by dividing each of the dotted crotchets of the passage in *extensio modi* into simple Mode I patterns. This results in alternations of crotchets and quavers on the same pitch.

Some specific cadence formulae in the clausula are rejected by the composer of the motet. At five points in the clausula (perfections 23–4, 31–2, 39–40, 57–8 and 65–6) the upper voices cadence with the tenor and then repeat the same notes in the space vacated by the subsequent tenor rest.[8] In the motet, these cadences are changed wholesale by the excision of the repeated upper-voice pitches. All three voice-parts cadence simultaneously. The first three of these are visible in Example 2.7.

In some cases, the duplum of the clausula has one note fewer than the triplum or vice versa. Here, the solution is to add an extra note to the voice-part that is lacking,

[8]   In only one of these instances, perfections 31–2, does the pitch of the host clausula change.

usually the same pitch as the previous one (perfections 27–8). Later in the piece, the voice-parts are balanced by a process of subtraction. Perfections 33–40 pose slightly more of a problem. The duplum consists of two symmetrical phrases of four perfections each. Each is made up of six notes. The triplum, however, describes a single phrase of eight perfections constituted from fourteen notes, two more than the total of the two duplum phrases. What the composer has done is to adjust the rhythm of the triplum so that two syllables can be placed on each of two dotted crotchet pulses created out of the same four pitches.

The first couple of phrases of the clausula were a particularly vexing problem for the composer of the motet. The two upper voices of the clausula set up an opposition between six- and eight-bar perfections that is not sustained throughout the piece. If the upper voices had remained in such a relationship for the duration of the piece, the clausula would not probably have recommended itself as a likely model to the composer of the motet. The solution to the problem is striking. It involves moving the pitches of perfections 7–8 back two perfections so as to create a cadence in perfection 7. The pitches remain the same and make adequate contrapuntal sense with the duplum and tenor. The music proceeds as before from perfection 9 onwards. From that point, the triplum and duplum phrases of the clausula more closely resemble each other in terms of duration. Creating one text to share between the two voice-parts then becomes easier.

The three-part organum from which the clausula *Latus* (M14) is abstracted also hosts another three-part clausula, *Nostrum* (M14). This, in turn, served as a model for a further conductus-motet (216) *Nostrum est impletum – Nostrum* (M14). Example 2.8 gives the opening of both the clausula and motet versions. The transformation of this clausula into a motet is marked by the fact that the first eight perfections of the clausula are left in their melismatic state, and the process of retexting begins at the ninth perfection. A reason for this procedure might well be the fact that the original plainsong gave four notes to the syllable *Nos-* and the rest of the melisma to *-trum*, although the style of the music for the two syllables is however undifferentiated. The resulting motet exhibits some hybrid characteristics. In its mixture of texted (*cum littera*) and untexted (*sine littera*) passages, it resembles certain conducti that mingle discant-style *caudae* with stanzas in a homorhythmic idiom *cum littera*.[9] Such uncertainty as to genre illustrates the great diversity of experimentation that accompanied the creation of the motet.

These examples outline the more important ways in which the composers of motets set about adding texts to their melismatic originals. The musical foreground was, by and large, respected wherever possible. When the simple relationship between word and note became strained, however, the composers had no hesitation in modifying the clausulae, either for reasons of necessity, or for those of artistic choice. Under circumstances in which, as we shall see, new music was being written to add to the clausula, this is hardly surprising.

---

[9]   *Caudae* are melismatic sections at the beginning and end of the stanzas of complex polyphonic conductus.

Example 2.8 Comparison of three-part clausula, *Nostrum* (M14) and conductus-motet (216) *Nostrum est impletum – Nostrum* (M14), perfections 1-10; *I-Fl* Plut. 29. 1 fols. 24r and 384r–v

Music

There is general agreement that the composition of the clausula precedes that of the motet. There is no such agreement as to the priority of one type of motet over another. No consensus exists, for example, as to whether a two-part motet in Latin must have preceded a three-part bilingual motet, or as to whether a motet whose text alludes to its liturgical context must be older than one whose poetry is independent of its liturgical background. Such disagreement is of course appropriate. By all accounts, there was a spectacular explosion of experimental musical procedures in the early thirteenth century. This element of experimentation was substantially more important than is commonly accepted.

The creation of the conductus-motet from a two-part clausula involves writing new music as well as poetry. The creation of a text for the duplum of the clausula is part only of the compositional enterprise. The composer also adds a new triplum that uses the same text as the motetus. Often, however, what appears in one manuscript as a conductus-motet is preserved elsewhere with only two voices: the motetus and tenor. This raises the question of the relationship between clausula, conductus-motet and two-part motet. To borrow two terms from textual criticism, the relationship must here be filial, and not collateral. The two motets share the same text, and both are derived from the clausula. The problem is how to arbitrate between two possible compositional processes. One involves writing the three-part piece (conductus-motet) directly from the clausula, in other words adding text and the third voice-part at the same time. The two-part motet is then a 'reduction' of a three-part original. The composer could also text the pre-existent clausula, and then he, or someone else, could later add the triplum that shares the same text. The question can be condensed to asking whether the text and new music were composed at the same or at different times, and in what order.

The motet [(635) *Ad veniam perveniam*] – (635) *Ad veniam perveniam* – *Tanquam* (O2) well illustrates some typical procedures and problems associated with the addition of text and voices to a two-part clausula. Unlike the previous examples, its state of preservation is complex. The two-part clausula is copied in the Florence manuscript and W_1. In both manuscripts, it is found among a group of pieces that are not embedded in organa. Differences between the two sources are minimal and mostly concern the distribution of notes and ligatures. The three-part conductus-motet is found in three sources, but in three different states: complete in Florence, missing its tenor in W_2, and its two upper parts only in the Madrid manuscript. The last two versions are subtly different. The version in W_2 has space left for the tenor, and the piece is copied among other conductus-motets; the omission of the tenor is simply an oversight. However, the version in Madrid is copied among two-part conductus never intended to be supplied with tenors. In addition to these concordances, there is a two-part motet that corresponds to the lower two parts of the conductus-motet in W_2. It has been suggested that the two-part motet must be a reduction from a three-part model, and therefore that the conductus-motet must be derived directly from the clausula.[10] None of the surviving evidence permits such an assertion. The fact that the clausula and conductus-motet both appear in Florence, while the two-part piece appears in the near-contemporary (but in fact slightly later) W_2, tells us nothing about the relative chronology of the different versions of this music. For our present purposes however, both possibilities – that the two-part motet was the first derivative from the clausula and that the conductus-motet was the first to derive from the clausula – need to be entertained in the following discussion. However, the relationship between the two-part motet and clausula suggests that the process of texting preceded the addition of the triplum. Example 2.9 gives the first twenty perfections of *Ad veniam perveniam* and the corresponding portion of the clausula from which it is derived. The clausula that forms the basis of this group of pieces is an extraordinary composition. Most of its phrases are constructed out of a simple alternation between duplum and tenor. This is the normal procedure in the first of the piece's two *cursus*. In the second, in which the tenor leads off, most phrases are constructed according to a pattern that consists of alternation of tenor and duplum. They then continue with music in which both voice-parts are presented together briefly, and then cadence. The two *cursus* of the tenor divide the piece in two more or less equal parts. The cadences, however, divide the structure of the piece into sections as follows (durations are in perfections):

38P + 12P + (2 × 8P) + 12P + 8P.

---

10   Anderson, *Latin Compositions . . . Wolfenbüttel*, 1: 42.

Example 2.9 Comparison of clausula *Tanquam* (O2), perfections 1–20 with [(635) *Ad veniam perveniam*] – (635) *Ad veniam perveniam* – *Tanquam* (O2); *I-Fl* Plut. 29. 1, fols. 147v and 381r

The opposition between one large phrase, unbroken by any cadence, and the neat asymmetry of the rest of the piece is a direct result of the exchange of voices in the first section and the coupling of voice-exchange with short phrases in the second. The very strict alternation of voices in perfections 1–25 is underpinned by two sequences. Strictly speaking, the first of these involves the tenor (perfections 3–10) and the duplum (perfections 5–12). But the contrapuntal sequence that lies behind it is constructed out of a chain of three descending parallel-fifth progressions. They are placed at the beginnings of perfections 3, 7 and 11. These relationships are mapped out in Example 2.10.

Example 2.10 Clausula *Tanquam* (O2), perfections 3–12

This sequence is followed by another. Its structure parallels the first but in a more complicated way. Example 2.11 shows these relationships.

Example 2.11 Clausula *Tanquam* (O2), perfections 13–27

Again, there are melodic sequences in the duplum: perfections 13–16, 17–20, 21–4 and (modified) 25–7. These are mirrored in the tenor: perfections 15–18, 19–22 and 23–6. The single change in pitch (arrowed) is the original melodic profile of the chant that the composer chose not to modify. The composer of the clausula creates a contrapuntal structure spanning perfections 13–27 that is more exhaustively sequential. The beamed notes at the top of the upper stave and at the bottom of the lower one indicate the overall progression in parallel fifths that governs this section. The second layer of beamed notes indicates a subordinate progression of parallel fourths. The ways in which these two sets of parallel motions interact sequentially are outlined in unstemmed noteheads at the bottom of the graph. Both types of sequence – the melodic and the contrapuntal – will be seen to be of significance in the process both of adding text and of composing a third voice.

The poem added to this clausula is as follows:

> Ad veniam
> Perveniam,
> Si veniam
> Cum oleo
> Quod debeo
> Et caveo
> Sedulis
> Oculis
> Ne dormiam
> Sompnique desidiam
> Si procul admoveam
> Ut vigil aperiam;
> Nam
> Sic itur ad gloriam,
> Quam
> Consequar per gratiam;
> Si veniam
> Obviam
> Ornatu non careo
> Nuptiis regiis idoneo.

I shall come to pardon if I come with oil which I owe, and if I beware, with unremitting eyes, not to sleep, and if I remove far from me the desire of sleep, so that watchful, I shall remain. For thus is the road that leads to glory, which, through grace, I am to follow. If I come, I do not lack adornment seemly for the royal marriage.

Although it does not trope any words of the tenor text, the poem makes a clear reference in its recurrent use of -*am* rhymes, and also in the symbolism adopted by the first and final lines of the poem: 'Ad veniam perveniam, si veniam cum oleo' and 'Si veniam obviam ornatu non careo nuptiis regiis idoneo'. These lines refer to the parable of the wise and foolish virgins and therefore share the imagery of the beginning of the verse: 'Tanquam sponsus Dominus procedens de thalamo suo et exivit'. In both the responsory verse (explicitly) and the motet text (implicitly) Christ is symbolised as the bridegroom.

The short phrases of the duplum result in short lines of poetry. The opening six musical phrases, for example, all of four perfections duration in Mode III, give rise to lines of four syllables each. The sense of the poem consistently overlaps the division of these phrases. In fact, the first major articulation of the sense of the poem comes over half way through, after the line 'Ut vigil aperiam'. In the discussion of *Doceas hac die*, we saw how a single rhyme dominates the poem, and how individual pairs of rhymes alternate with a single overriding line. Here, in *Ad veniam perveniam*, we can see -*am* rhymes alternating with one other rhyme: -*eo*. These two rhymes dominate most of the poem. It is difficult to envisage this simply as a by-product of composing a new text to a pre-existent clausula. Such a procedure might enable the composer to maintain a grasp of the rhyme of the tenor text without exhausting -*am* rhymes. In this case, there is such a wealth of words ending -*am* that it hardly seems a problem.

The first change of rhyme in the poem reflects the sequential structure of the source clausula. The first three rhymes are -*am*. The second three lines use the first new rhyme. The change quite clearly matches the change in the first two sequences illustrated in Examples 2.10 and 2.11: -*am* for perfections 3–12 and -*eo* for 13–27.

The motet poem on its own seems very modest. When the constraints of rhyme, musical phrase and rhythm are taken into account, however, it is a very impressive undertaking indeed, and contrasts with the compromises that the composer is required to make in the creation of the triplum.

Although the poetic text reflects some aspects of the structure of the clausula, the added triplum adopts a rather different position. In the first of the two sequences graphed in Example 2.10 the melodic sequence is abandoned, but the contrapuntal sequence is duplicated in the descending *e*, *d* and *c* in perfections 3, 7 and 11. This may be compared with the upper part of the contrapuntal summary in unstemmed noteheads at the bottom of Example 2.10. However, in the second sequence, the composer of the new triplum makes no attempt whatsoever to make his contribution correspond melodically with the clausula. Example 2.12 is a contrapuntal summary of perfections 13–27 of the three-part version of the piece. The contrapuntal sequence is enhanced by octave duplications to the G8–5 and the F8–5 sonorities. The rest of the voice-part duplicates pitches already present in the contrapuntal structure.

Example 2.12 Contrapuntal structure of [(635) *Ad veniam perveniam*] – (635) *Ad veniam perveniam* – *Tanquam* (O2), perfections 13–27

The new triplum adds significant new sonorities to the contrapuntal vocabulary of the clausula. The intervals between duplum and tenor found at the beginning of perfections are unisons, fourths, fifths, octaves and a single third. Sometimes, the new triplum simply creates sonorities existing elsewhere in the piece: for example, adding an upper or lower fifth to a unison. Adding a third to a unison creates an interval that is only present once in the original clausula. The original third in the clausula is left untouched by simply repeating the duplum pitch. We have already seen the duplication of an upper octave to create an 8–5 sonority in the second sequence at the beginning of the piece. Octaves are also enriched by the addition of a fifth to create the same configuration.

The most far-reaching contrapuntal change brought about by the addition of the triplum is the creation of 5–3 sonorities, by adding a third to a pre-existent fifth. There are three such 5–3s in the piece, and two of them are placed just before and just after (two perfections in each case) the exact centre of the piece. This is the point at which the second tenor *cursus* begins. In this way, the triplum brings out a structural feature of the clausula that was avoided in the phrase-structure of the duplum of the original clausula. In contrast to the duplication of pre-existent pitches to create 8–5 sonorities, which enhance texturally with the duplication of pitches, these 5–3s add a striking new harmonic dimension to the piece. They are used with powerful structural effect.

Creating a conductus-motet out of a pre-existent three-part clausula caused problems when the clausula chosen was not built up out of triplum and duplum phrases of the same length. Deciding which three-part clausula to turn into a motet was thus of paramount importance, even though some further modification would occasionally be required. In a three-part motet with separate triplum and motetus voices, each with its own text, there is no necessity for simultaneous cadences. The entire repertory of three-part clausulae is readily available for this type of treatment.

Problems do arise, however, in a piece that exemplifies the move from three-part clausula to double motet (a three-part motet with separate texts for the two upper voices, in Ludwig's parlance): (221) *Salve salus hominum* – (222) *O radians stella* – *Nostrum* (M14). There are both French and Latin branches to the family of which this motet is a member. Since the French tradition will be discussed in the next chapter, we may here limit our enquiry to the Latin double motet.[11]

The importance of *Salve salus hominum* lies in the ways in which the two upper-voice texts are constructed. Whether there is an intermediary between it and its source clausula (in the form of one or more of the French motets), or whether it depends directly on the source clausula, is of less than immediate significance. Even to speak of a source clausula is, in this case, to make several assumptions that should not go unchallenged. First, there is no single source clausula; there are two. The hypothetical three-part piece is made up out of two two-part ones based on an identical tenor pattern. It could be suggested that a lost three-part clausula was broken up into two by combining each of the upper voices separately with the tenor.[12] However, since we no longer have the original three-part piece, it is difficult to judge. Employing two two-part clausulae to create a three-part one implies a degree of opportunism, not to say luck. So does finding a three-part clausula that will respond to being dismembered into two successful pieces of two-part counterpoint. Second, and more important, we have no evidence that this clausula was ever used in any liturgical context. It is preserved uniquely among clausula collections in the Florence manuscript, and is not found embedded in organum. It may therefore have been a notational model, rather than a source, for the motet.

---

[11] Anderson believed that the French versions, both in three and in four parts, prefigure the Latin ones: 'The texts in this version [three-part motet with two upper-voice texts in Latin] present many indications of being contrafacta, for they are Marian and the T[enor] chant is from the Mass and no attempt has been made to trope the text . . . . The 4 pt French version in [La] Cl[ayette] and Mo[ntpellier] is representative of the earliest pieces known in this form, yet it betrays none of the crude experimentation evident in some of these early 4 pt works, and the added 4th part shows considerable skill. The first motet in the motet fascicles [*sic*] of Mo in its Cl version must be very close to W₂ 3 [the third motet fascicle of W₂ = fascicle 9 of the manuscript] in time, the Qua[druplum] perhaps being added by the same composer who wrote the basic 3 pt source clausula, even if all the parts were not written at the same time (*ibid.*, 1: 329–30).' Anderson's comments are seriously flawed by the assumption that the absence of tropic reference to the tenor in the upper voices implies that a work is a contrafactum, and a narrow 'filial' view of the reworking of the motet family.

[12] *Ibid.*, 1: 329.

Example 2.13 gives the first twelve perfections of (221) *Salve salus hominum* – (222) *O radians stella* – *Nostrum* (M14) superimposed on a reconstruction of the three-part clausula whose music it shares.

Example 2.13 Reconstruction of the three-part clausula *Nostrum* (M14), perfections 1–12, and derivative motet (221) *Salve salus hominum* – (222) *O radians stella* – *Nostrum* (M14); *I-Fl* Plut. 29. 1, fol. 157v and *D–W* 1099, fol. 186r–v.

The music consists of two upper voices in Mode III with a Mode V tenor. Mode III produces lines of four, seven, ten or thirteen syllables when the text is added. With one exception, all the poetic lines are of this length. The two texts are as follows:

(Triplum)
Salve salus hominum,
Spes misericordie,
Spes venie,
Purgatrix criminum,
Cecis lumen luminum,
Mater
Prudencie,
Signum vie,
Terminus patrie,
Spes venie,
Nectar, flos glorie,
Iusticie
Sol pie,
Clemencie,
Sobrie
Ros, Virgo mundicie.

Hail, safety of men, hope of pity, hope of pardon, cleanser of sins, light of light to the blind, Mother of prudence, sign-post of the way, boundary of Heaven, hope of pardon, nectar, flower of glory, sun of holy justice, dew of temperate pardon, Virgin of cleanliness.

(Motetus)
O radians stella pre ceteris,
Summi Dei mater et filia,
Eximia proles degeneris,
Tu generis mundi leticia,
Tu de via tribulos conteris,
Spes miseris hominis,
Nescia Maria,
De lateris
Luto nos libera,
Regenerans genus in posteris regia;

O shining star, outshining all others, Mother and Daughter of the highest God, peerless offspring of a degenerate race, You are the joy of the people of the world. You turn away the perils of the way, O hope of wretched man. Mary, not knowing, free us from the mire surrounding us, regenerating the human race in Your kingdom for all ages.

The exception is in the triplum (perfections 27–30) where the clausula breaks a pattern of Mode III *ordines* with *extensio modi* for the only time in the piece. This moment is selected for very careful treatment in the motet. It is the only time a new rhyme is introduced beyond the two presented at the beginning of the triplum poem. The choice of word is entirely appropriate as well: 'Mater' summarises in a single substantive the entire preoccupation of both upper-voice texts. The passage is given as Example 2.14.

Example 2.14 (221) *Salve salus hominum* – (222) *O radians stella – Nostrum* (M14), perfections 27–30

What is striking about these two Marian texts is how little they share with each other in terms of imagery. The lack of correlation with the tenor is not uncommon. As will be seen when we turn to the French double motet, the distances that can separate motetus and triplum texts can be very great or very small. Here it seems as if every effort is being made to separate the two texts. There is no overlap of rhyme:

the pairs of rhyme used in each poem are mutually exclusive. Invocations are couched in different terms: 'Salve' in the triplum, 'O' in the motetus. Images are different – 'iusticie sol pie' and 'radians stella' – and change independently throughout. The only point of comparison is the use of the word 'spes' in the two poems, and the presence of the same formulation twice in the triplum – 'spes venie' might suggest that the use of the same word in the two texts might not have been the result of specific lexical choice, but the absence of a sufficiently rich poetic imagination.

There are two procedures used to create a motet out of a clausula: the writing of poetry to pre-existent music, and the construction of additional voice-parts to enhance two-part clausulae. In the (re)composition of music, procedures already found in the clausula are further exploited. The constraints of the phrase-patterns of the host clausula create a style of poetry that exploits curious irregular line-length. This is not only an important and consistent feature of early motets but continues to have a significance into the rest of the century. The untexted clausula retains its influence on the poetic style of Latin and French motet texts long after its music ceases to provide the source for newly composed works.

The alternative view: format and texting

The basis for the construction of an alternative view of the growth of texted discantus is the variety of repertories and individual works. Only four specimens of the three-part motet with Latin texts survive in the two so-called 'Notre-Dame' manuscripts that contain motets of any description: Florence and W_2. This is a pointer to chronology since we can be reasonably sure of the dates of copying of these two manuscripts: *c.* 1250 and *c.* 1260. Furthermore, the first formal presentation of a 'repertory' of Latin double motets does not occur until the fourth fascicle of the Montpellier Codex. This was copied at least a decade after W_2 and Florence, perhaps up to twenty-five years later, and it is far from representative. This fascicle of Montpellier has been the subject of much speculation concerning the 'peripheral' nature of its contents. Whether or not we are convinced by arguments for 'Rhenish' provenance or not, the collection is characterised by a heterogeneity that marks it out from other collections in Montpellier, as well as from other sources.[13] In sum then, the Latin double motet has only sporadic representation before 1270. The four isolated examples that were copied before the middle of the century therefore warrant a degree of attention. They are roughly contemporary with the three-part motet with two upper-voice texts in French. By this time, however, the French double motet was accorded a place of some status in the motet fascicles of W_2. This is the date of the copying of these Latin double motets. Given the numerical

[13]   The 'peripherality' of the fourth fascicle of the Montpellier Codex was proposed by Ernest Sanders ('Peripheral Polyphony of the Thirteenth Century', *Journal of the American Musicological Society* 17 (1964) 261–87). Responses are Dolores Pesce, 'A Revised View of the Thirteenth-Century Latin Double Motet', *Journal of the American Musicological Society* 40 (1987) 405–42, and Everist, *Polyphonic Music*, 275–90.

strength of the two-part Latin motet in both Florence and W$_2$, and the classic status of the French double motet by 1250, the paucity of Latin double motets before the fourth fascicle of Montpellier is most curious.

The four Latin double motets copied before 1270 therefore merit our attention. They are:

> (221) *Salve salus hominum* – (222) *O radians stella* – *Nostrum* (M14)
> (647) *Stirps Jesse* – (648) *Virgo cultus* – *Flos filius eius* (O16)
> (255) *Mors que stimulo* – (254) *Mors morsu* – *Mors* (M18)
> (316) *Ypocrite pseudopontifices* – (315) *Velut stella* – *Et gaudebit* (M24)

Salve salus is a work with a curious clausula background which may well be preceded or paralleled by French-texted works. *Stirps Jesse* is perhaps a unique example of the way in which a three-part Latin 'double' motet could be fashioned out of a three-part clausula. The French component of both motet families and the Latin component of the *Stirps Jesse* complex are to be discussed in the next chapter. *Mors que stimulo* is an even rarer case. It is a Latin double motet, found in Florence and W$_2$, fashioned from a four-part clausula. There is even a version of this piece in Montpellier where all three upper voice-parts of the clausula are texted.

The fourth of these pieces, (316) *Ypocrite pseudopontifices* – (315) *Velut stella* – *Et gaudebit* (M24), is one of the very best-known thirteenth-century motets. The complex of motets of which it forms part includes two-part motets in Latin and French, a French double as well as the Latin double motet, and a bilingual double motet. They are all based on a two-part clausula in Florence. For our present purposes, its most interesting appearance is among the manuscript fragments now preserved in Châlons-sur-Marne.[14] A view of the motets in this fragmentary collection begins to take us towards an alternative to the conventional view of the growth of the motet.

This version of *Ypocrite pseudopontifices*: (317) *O quam sancta* – [*Et gaudebit* (M24)], preserved in Châlons-sur-Marne 3. J. 250, is based, as is the rest of the complex, on the two-part clausula in Florence. However, it not only employs a unique triplum, but deploys its borrowed material in a radically different way to what we have so far witnessed. The music is not notated in parts, as is the norm for motets, but in score. The single text is written under the tenor which is however in ligatures. Score notation and the presentation of the text under the tenor are characteristics of the conductus repertory. Writing the tenor in ligatures points up the ambivalent position of this piece and the two similar works in the manuscript. Three compositions follow exactly the same pattern of presentation in this source. In addition to *Ypocrite pseudopontifices*, there are (451) *In veritate comperi* – [*Veritatem* (M37)] and (448) *O Maria maris stella* – [*Verita* (M37)]. Both these latter works exist in straightforward conductus-motet versions in other sources. In these concordances, the tenor is notated at the

---

14 Archives Départmentales de la Marne et de la Région de Champagne-Ardenne, 3. J. 250. See Jacques Hourlier and Jacques Chailley, 'Cantionale Cathalaunense', *Mémoires de la Société d'Agriculture, Commerce, Sciences, et Arts du Département de la Marne* 71 [2e série 30] (1956) 141–59; Jacques Chailley, 'Fragments d'un nouveau manuscrit d'Ars Antiqua à Châlons sur Marne', *In memoriam Jacques Handschin*, ed. Higinio Anglès *et al.* (Strasbourg: P. H. Heitz, 1962) 140–50.

end, and is furnished with an incipit. It is presumably to be sung either to syllables from this incipit or vocalised. The poetic text appears under the motetus, and is only carried by the upper two parts. All this is normal for a conductus-motet. The intention and audible result of the procedure found in Châlons-sur-Marne may have been to create something that sounded like a conductus. The three parts would have moved homorhythmically and would have declaimed the same text. Some intervention would have been required to split up the notes of the tenor. However, there are other ways in which the Châlons pieces are not like conductus. The texts are not strophic, but more importantly, their clausula origins mean that the texts are characterised by the unequal line-lengths and irregular rhyme-patterns typical of the motet. The resulting poems are very different to the strophic lyrics with regular rhyme and line-length that are found in the repertory of conductus or *cantio*.

The generic status of the motets in the Châlons fragments lies somewhere between a conductus and a motet proper. Such generic ambiguity characterises the entire contents of the manuscript. This collection of fragments is difficult to interpret because a tiny proportion only of what was once originally a large manuscript remains. Nevertheless, what survives of the collection is characterised by an extraordinary eclecticism. The three motets in Châlons-sur-Marne were interspersed among a group of conducti by a scribe who apparently drew no distinction between a conductus and a motet rewritten to sound like a conductus. Furthermore, in the leaves that do remain, there are not only motets in score and conducti, but also monophonic sequences and individual motet voices copied as monodies. Some of the latter have similar origins to some of the three motets notated in score. For example, the motetus only of (216) *Nostrum est impletum – Nostrum* (M14) is preserved on fols. 5r–v of Châlons-sur-Marne, but it is also found as a conductus-motet in the Florence manuscript. The motetus voices of two other motets are preserved in the Châlons fragments, (451) *In veritate comperi – [Veritatem* (M37)] and (448) *O Maria maris stella – [Verita* (M37)], while the entire conductus-motet is found in Florence.

The three motets preserved in the Châlons-sur-Marne fragments bear comparison with a group of compositions in the central part of the manuscript London, British Library, Egerton 2615. This manuscript contains an abbreviated selection of the repertory preserved in Florence.[15] In addition to conducti and organa, there are three other pieces, two of which are similar to the three motets in the Châlons-sur-Marne fragments: [(532) *Agmina milicie*] (532) *Agmina milicie – Agmina* (M65) and (69) *Serena virginum – Manere* (M5). The origins of the former are doubtful. It is related to a clausula preserved in the so-called St Victor manuscript that may be either a source for the motet or a version of the motet without text. Those of the latter are complex: it is derived from a series of four successive clausulae which served as the model for a four-part conductus-motet. The version in the Egerton manuscript consists of the lowest three parts.

As in the Châlons-sur-Marne fragments, the two motets are here notated in score with the text under the tenor. It is left in ligatures and must be altered if the text is

---

[15]   Everist, *Polyphonic Music*, 42–57.

to be sung. The third piece that stands apart from the organa and conducti in the Egerton manuscript is very different. (359) *Veni doctor previe – Veni sancte spiritus* (M27) consists of a three-part setting of the entire solo portion of the verse of the *Alleluya. Veni sancte spiritus.* The tenor is disposed in organal long notes which carry the text of the verse while the upper parts move in a homorhythmic pattern and carry the same text, underlaid to the motetus, as in the conductus-motet. The three preserved versions of the piece demonstrate how difficult it was to accommodate such a work in manuscripts clearly designed to acknowledge the generic differences between conductus, organum and motet. In the Egerton manuscript, it separates a collection of organa from a group of conducti; in Florence, it occurs in the first motet fascicle and is thus viewed as a type of conductus-motet. Exactly what generic status the piece has in its third source, the Beauvais Circumcision Feast, is unclear; it appears in the first polyphonic supplement and is cued into the Office liturgy. This version of the piece in the London manuscript has no text to the tenor, and is thus separated from the other two versions of the piece.

In general terms, motets are derived from chant and use poetry that avoids strophic repetition. Conducti, composed without reference to chant, are characterised by their use of strophic texts. Strophic poetry is therefore rare in chant-derived polyphony of the thirteenth century. (228) *Latex silice – Latus* (M14) is one of the few apparently chant-based polyphonic works from the first half of the thirteenth century whose text is strophic. Other examples are the two-part version of the conductus-motet (231) *Homo quam sit pura – Latus* (M14) preserved in the manuscript Rome, Santa Sabina XIV L3; contrafacta of this piece are also strophic. A contrafactum of the motet (307) *Scandit solium – Ta* (M23), *Celi semita,* is also strophic. A French contrafactum of the same piece, unfortunately incomplete but whose text ends 'que tout ce nos viegne', is a further example.

Another strophic motet, at least on first inspection, is (59) *Qui servare puberem – Ne* (M3), as preserved in W_1. This is one of the six motets preserved in W_1 without tenors as conductus; *Latex silice* and *Serena virginum* are two of the others. The subsequent stanzas to the text of *Qui servare puberem* were added locally and do not form part of the original conception of the piece. Whether or not the poetry of *Qui servare puberem* was conceived strophically, the strophic composition of texts to chant-derived polyphony clearly played an important role in the works discussed here. But to speak of 'chant-derived' or 'chant-based' music may be an illusion in such a composition as *Latex silice.* It may have originated as a three-part conductus to which a cantus firmus was added. Given the limited harmonic range of the music, this is not as difficult as it sounds. Both *Latex silice* and *Serena virginum* are contained within conductus collections in Florence, and even *Serena virginum,* which is clearly based on a group of clausulae, was changed into a conductus by the omission of the tenor. The inclusion of the tenor at the end of this transmission of the piece in Florence may simply be 'misleading'.[16]

It is clear that the pieces found in the Châlons fragments and in the Egerton manuscript share stylistic characteristics of both motet and conductus. These pieces

---

[16] Sanders, 'Medieval Motet', 515–16.

are clearly important in the growth of the motet. Another juncture, between motet and organum, is also important. We have already seen how (359) *Veni doctor previe – Veni sancte spiritus* (M27) borrows much of its musical style from organum. A further way in which the motet may interact with organum is in the texting of one or more of the dupla, tripla and quadrupla in an organum. The result of this is different to texting a clausula to create a motet because the source is a passage of organum whereas the clausula is a passage in discantus. The basic premiss, though, of fitting a text to pre-existing rhythmic voice-part is similar. There survive quite a number of these so-called 'troped organa'. One of the interesting features of their preservation is that a substantial number of the texts may have been composed by Philip the Chancellor. This, coupled with the fact that two of the most significant host organa were composed by Perotinus (*Viderunt omnes* (M1) and *Sederunt principes* (M3)), has prompted speculation as to collaboration between the two. Following this line of argument, Perotinus may have contributed to the early growth of the motet.[17]

Experimentation was a characteristic of thirteenth-century musical practices, and nowhere is it more evident than at the very outset of the creation of the motet. Although the conventional view of the growth of the motet was a reflection of the state of affairs that dominated by around 1250, surviving compositions, deceptively cloaked in the mantle of neat generic subdivision in Florence, show a wide range of practices in play in the early years of the century. The 'genetic' view of the motet emerged from a rich variety of experimental procedures that has left us with a large number of pieces that defy neat compartmentalisation. The fragmentary remains of this experimentation cannot be allowed to be pushed aside in future discussions of the origins of the motet.

[17] See Thomas B. Payne, '*Associa tecum in patria*: A Newly Identified Organum Trope by Philip the Chancellor', *Journal of the American Musicological Society* 39 (1986) 233–54; and Payne, 'Poetry, Politics, and Polyphony'.

3

The French motet

The French language and the motet

Motets in French, or adaptations from clausulae and pre-existent Latin motets, involve many of the same procedures found in the Latin tradition. Irregularity of musical phrase and poetic line-length are hallmarks of the French as well as the Latin motet. Although in principle the composer could vary the number of syllables in a poetic line written to pre-existent music by repeating pitches, this hardly ever happened. In cases where French motets are modelled on Latin-texted originals, the composer of the French motet respected his model as much as the creator of the Latin motet adhered to the structure of his clausula prototype.[1] Even when composers began writing motets that did not depend on polyphonic models but struck out from a plainsong, poetic lines of irregular length remained the norm. Rhyme was a different matter. Here a number of opportunities presented themselves. Duplicating the Latin rhyme-scheme or ignoring it completely were the simplest and most extreme. More interesting is the possibility of contradicting the rhyme-scheme in motets that reflected some original patterning in the clausula model.

We may begin our exploration of the derivation of a French motet from the tradition of the clausula and Latin motet with a family of motets based on one of the most popular tenors: *Flos filius eius* (O16). Many combinations of text and music arose out of the *Flos filius* plainsong. It is almost impossible to construct a simple chronology for this group of compositions. The three-part clausula is found in a single source only, and not embedded in an organum setting.[2] The clausula might therefore not be a source for the motet, but simply a notational sketch. The French motet that forms part of the family, (650) *Quant revient et fuelle* – (651) *L'autrier joer* – *Flos filius eius* (O16), makes use of a refrain in its motetus. This fact might well suggest that the motet with French texts might depend directly on the clausula. Both the French piece, and the Latin – (647) *Stirps Jesse* – (648) *Virga cultus* – *Flos filius eius* (O16) – could therefore descend independently from the same clausula. These uncertainties suggest that the music should be discussed in a way that avoids making

---

[1] Georg Reichert, 'Wechselbeziehungen zwischen musikalischer und textlicher Struktur in der Motette des 13. Jahrhunderts', *In Memoriam Jacques Handschin*, ed. Higinio Anglès *et al.* (Strasbourg: P. H. Heitz, 1962) 151–69.
[2] Florence, fol. 11r.

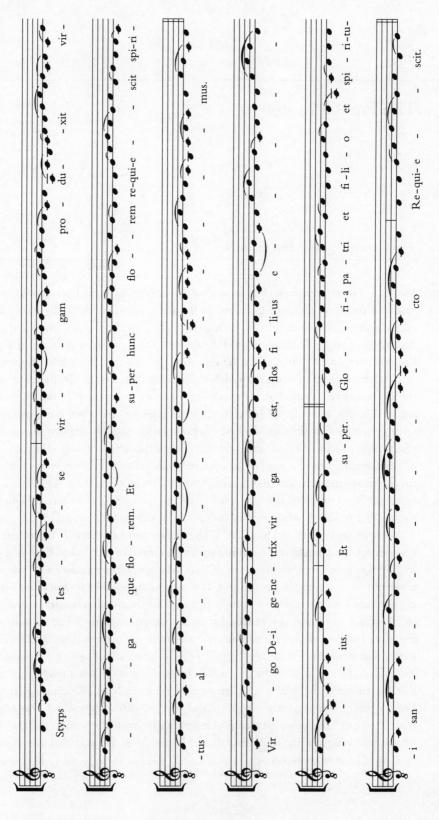

Example 3.1 Plainsong responsory *Stirps Jesse* (O16)

simple assumptions about the history of the motet family, and that examines the nature of the relationship between clausula, French motet and Latin motet as independent, but related, entities.

We may begin with the plainsong responsory on which the complex of motets is based: *Stirps Jesse virgam produxit*. Example 3.1 is an edition. This responsory is prescribed in thirteenth-century Parisian liturgies as the sixth at Matins for the feast of the Annunciation of the Blessed Virgin (25 March) and as the Vespers responsory for the Assumption of the Blessed Virgin (15 August).[3] Organum settings survive in both two and three parts, and there are clausulae on *Flos filius eius*, *Stirps*, *Jesse*, *Virgo* and *Genetrix virga est*. Of the eleven clausulae on *Flos filius eius*, four have a reflection in the motet repertory.[4]

Example 3.2 consists of an edition of the beginning of the three-part clausula *Flos filius eius* (O16) and its derivative Latin motet (647) *Stirps Jesse* – (648) *Virga cultus* – *Flos filius eius* (O16). We will return to the structure of the poetry later. The first thing to observe about the clausula is the phrase-structure of the triplum and duplum. It would have been difficult, if not impossible, to have constructed a conductus-motet with homorhythmic upper parts out of them. The two voices were constructed so as to avoid any simultaneous cadence before the end of the movement. The phrases of the duplum are constructed as follows:

6P + 6P + 6P + 2P + 4P + 2P + 2P + 8P.

The regular repetitions of six-perfection phrase-lengths at the beginning of the piece oppose the irregular structure in the second part. This opposition is numerically structural. The three phrases of six perfections constitute exactly half the duration of the duplum; the remaining five phrases make up the second half. The triplum, on the other hand, has the following structure:

8P + 1P + 4P + 2P + 4P + 3P + 3P + 4P + 7P.

Apart from a few obvious symmetries (4–2–4; 4–3–3–4 (followed by 7, the sum of the two previous numbers)), the phrase-structure of the triplum is less than clear. But perhaps the most important structural consideration is that the phrase-structures of the duplum and triplum are patterned so that they do not cadence together until the end of the clausula. The wide range of differing phrase-lengths in the two voices, especially in the triplum, is a consistent feature of this particular piece.

The tenor structure of this clausula is complex. There are two complete *cursus*. They use the same rhythmic pattern: *longa, brevis, longa, brevis, longa, brevis* rest. But the first *cursus* begins with a *longa ultra mensuram*, a dotted crotchet in transcription, followed by another *longa*, before the beginning of the pattern. Furthermore, the second *cursus* starts by omitting the first pitch of the plainsong melisma (see Example 3.3). This second *cursus* begins immediately with the rhythmic pattern of the first *cursus*, but reverses two of its pitches. The last four perfections of the piece are made up out of the last five notes of the tenor *cursus* but in a different (cadential) pattern that makes

---

[3]   Paris, Bibliothèque Nationale, fonds latin 15181 fol. 368v and *ibid.*, 15182 fol. 304 bisr.

[4]   Ludwig, *Repertorium*, 2: 95–7.

Example 3.2 Three-part clausula *Flos filius eius* (O16) and derivative Latin motet (647) *Stirps Jesse* – (648) *Virga cultus* – *Flos filius eius* (O16), perfections 1–15; *I-Fl* Plut. 29. 1 fols. 11r–v and 409v–10r

Example 3.3 Tenor patterns in clausula *Flos filius eius* (O16)

use of further *longae ultra mensuram*. Of the thirty-six perfections that make up the piece, the repetitions of the tenor *cursus* divide the clausula into three sections of 17, 15 and 4 perfections respectively. Constructing a second *cursus* that mimicked the first, either exactly or in terms of duration, would have been the simplest procedure. The actual pattern seems to be an attempt to unbalance the tenor and to complement the exact binary division of the duplum. The tenor cadences twice only with the duplum and twice with the triplum (perfections 8 and 29). In a piece where the tenor phrases are three perfections long, this is a striking example of a sustained and successful attempt at creating three overlapping voice-parts.

In the Latin motet based on the clausula, there are changes to the rhythm of the duplum. These are entirely in line with the procedures for deriving Latin motets from clausulae seen in the previous chapter. There are exceptions to the principle that the model should be followed slavishly. Where the clausula made use of *fractio modi*, the motet might modify the rhythm of the clausula. This is especially common where *semibreves* are introduced into the motet and where some ornamental group-ings are shifted forward by a *brevis*.[5] The modification of instances of *fractio modi* are clear in this clausula; they usually concern the replacement of *longa-brevis-longa* patterns with three *breves*, a standard procedure in Mode I *fractio modi*. When this pattern is taken over in the motet, it often results in a *longa* followed by two or three *semibreves*. Examples are in perfections 7 (triplum), 11 (motetus), and so on.

Mode I results in clausula phrases consisting of odd numbers of notes; this produces like numbers of syllables in the lines of poetry in the motet. There is even a one-note phrase towards the beginning of the triplum whose single syllable is the first of a longer segment of text. Although the first half of the motetus occupies itself with thirty-three syllables (three equal phrases consisting of eleven syllables each), the second comprises twenty-seven syllables (three lines of three syllables, one of seven and one of eleven). The two temporally equal halves have numbers of syllables that stand in an irrational 11 : 9 proportion. Although the duplum of the clausula is

5   Smith, 'The Earliest Motets', 151–60.

clearly mathematically patterned, the fitting of words does not match the pattern. In the triplum, the one symmetry in the structure of the clausula is partially contradicted in the text setting. The triplum poem, *Stirps Jesse*, is given below with line-lengths, rhymes and phrase-lengths in perfections indicated.

7a	Stirps Jesse progreditur,	4
7b	Virga prodit celitus	4
	Ex	1
7a	Virga flos producitur.	4
3b	Spiritus	2
7c	Septiformis gratie	4
5d	Florem perficit	3
5c	Fructu glorie.	3
7d	Flos electos reficit	4
11e	Cuius odor mentium remedium.	7

The stem of Jesse flourishes and produces a small twig from Heaven, and a flower blooms from this twig. The Spirit of seven-fold grace makes perfect the flower through the fruit of glory. The flower whose fragrance is a remedy of minds restores the elect.

We can see the symmetrical phrases of four, three, three and four perfections in lines 6 to 9. These give rise to lines with seven, five, five and seven syllables respectively. But rather than mirroring the ABBA structure of the line-lengths that are derived from the phrase-lengths of the clausula, the rhyme-scheme is ABAB. This is clearly more to do with the overall rhyme-scheme of the poem than with the phrase-structure of the clausula. The third line, the single syllable 'Ex', falls outside a scheme that relies, as does that of lines 6 to 9, on pairs of rhymes: ABAB. Again, it seems that consistency in the poem is prized more highly than reflecting the musico-mathematical relationships in the original clausula.

Both texts depend heavily for images, in addition to biblical references, on the words of their tenor melisma and on those of the host plainsong. Most obvious is the use of the symbol of a flower, *flos*, both in its substantive and verbal forms, derived directly from the text of the tenor melisma: *Flos filius eius*. The symbol of a flower is found both in the triplum and the motetus, three times in the former, and twice, once as a verb, in the latter. As we have seen, this is a common characteristic of poetry in early Latin motets.

Less common is the technique of resorting to the original plainsong for images. Clearly references to *virga* (twig) in both triplum and motetus refer back to the responsory, as of course do those to *flos*, which occurs there three times, twice in the responsory itself, and once in the verse from which the tenor melisma is taken. The first four lines of the triplum poem in fact only lightly amplify the first phrase of the responsory.

> Stirps Jesse virgam produxit virgaque florem

becomes in the motet poem:

> Stirps Jesse progreditur,
> Virga prodit celitus
> Ex
> Virga flos producitur.

Example 3.4 Four-part motet (652) *Plus bele que flor* – (650) *Quant revient et fuelle* – (651) *L'autrier joer* – *Flos filius eius* (O16), perfections 1–16; *F-MO* H 196, fols. 26v–8r

Apart from the use of the verb *progredior* and the adverb *celitus*, this part of the text simply elaborates the plainsong. *Celitus* is the adverbial cognate of the adjective *celestis* which is found in the motetus. The two words, as can be seen from a glance at perfections 7 and 8 of Example 3.2, are presented in their respective voice-parts at exactly the same time. One powerful image that is shared between the two motet texts, *fructus glorie*, seems to have no model either in the plainsong or in the *capitulum* or *lectio* that precedes the chant at Assumption Vespers or Annunciation Matins.[6]

The first sixteen perfections of the four-part version in French, (652) *Plus bele que flor* − (650) *Quant revient et fuelle* − (651) *L'autrier joer* − *Flos filius eius* (O16), are given as Example 3.4. The three lower parts may then be compared with the Latin version of the piece already discussed. Musically, differences are slight, and the phrase-lengths of both Latin and French poetic line-lengths are the same as the length of phrases in the clausula. Their rhymes, and other structural features, are different. We may begin with a comparison of the two motetus poems: the Latin (648) *Virga cultus* and the French (651) *L'autrier joer*. The two texts are given side by side below. The French motetus ends with a refrain, here italicised.

Virga cultus nescia dum floruit	L'autrier joer m'en alai par un destor.
Quam celestis gratie ros imbuit	En un vergier m'en entrai por quellir flor.
Ree virge diluit contagia.	Dame plesant i trovai, cointe d'ator.
Glorie	Cuer ot gai.
Fructum flos exhibuit.	Si chantoit en grant esmai:
Trabeam carneam	'Amors ai. Qu'en ferai?
Verbum induit.	*C'est la fin, la fin.*
Sol levi nube latuit.	*Qe qe nus die j'amerai'.*

A small stem, not knowing the cultivator while it flourished, which the dew imbued with heavenly grace, washed all the filth from sinful man. The flower brought forth the fruit of glory; the Word put on a stately robe of flesh, and now the Sun lies behind a transparent cloud.	The other day I was going along a path; into an orchard I entered to gather flowers; there I found a sweet lady, dainty of appearance. She had a gay heart, and she was singing in great distress: 'I have love; what shall I do about it? It's the end, the end, whatever anyone says, I must love.'

Immediately, we can see a completely different structure in the two texts. Line-lengths, as previous comments have suggested, have to be identical; but rhyme-schemes differ widely. The French poem uses three rhymes only whereas the Latin uses five. Furthermore, one of the rhymes in the French poem, *-in* in the pen-ultimate line, is related to the direct speech of the last four lines. More striking are

---

6   By contrast, Rebecca Baltzer has shown how one of the other *Flos filius* motets, (665) *Flos ascendit de radice* − *Flos filius eius* (O16) depends on material from the fifth lesson at Matins, on the Nativity of the Virgin (see Rebecca Baltzer, 'Aspects of Trope in the Earliest Motets for the Assumption of the Virgin', *Festschrift for Ernest Sanders*, ed. Brian Seirup and Peter M. Lefferts (New York: Trustees of Columbia University, 1991) 17).

the internal rhymes in the first three lines of the two poems. The French one rhymes consistently whereas the Latin does not. But on the other hand, the cross-references between the rhymes of the Latin poems are much more subtle, and show an end-rhyme in line 1 becoming an intermediate rhyme in line 3. Exactly the reverse process is also found, and an internal rhyme in line 2 becomes an end-rhyme in line 4.

To compare the rhyme-scheme of two triplum poems is to witness something similar. The poems begin in a similar sort of way but then continue differently. Points of interest, that might suggest the priority of one text over the other, are the similar responses to the symmetrical patterning of the phrase-lengths of the clausula towards the end of the poem discussed earlier. The Latin poem, it will be remembered, takes the ABBA phrase-structure of the model and contradicts it with a rhyme-scheme CDCD. The French poem does exactly the same. This could be the result of direct modelling of the Latin on the French, or mere coincidence. The choice of identical rhymes is also striking, although the French exclamation is hardly uncommon.

The poetry of the two upper-voice poems in the three-part French work well exemplifies two of the most common types used in motet texts. The motetus is a *pastourelle*-type text, the triplum is a courtly *requette* that borrows substantially from the *pastourelle* register. The four-part work shares two of its three upper-voice texts with those of the three-part one. Its quadruplum adds a devotional poem to the work. The music of the quadruplum occasionally doubles pre-existent pitches, or fills out the sonority of the vertical aggregations of pitches. The function of the quadruplum can be better explained by reference to a second French motet. This, too, shares its musical superstructure with Latin motets.

We have already seen how (221) *Salve salus hominum* – (222) *O radians stella* – *Nostrum* (M14) functions in relation to its clausula model. The version of the motet with French texts, (218) *Qui d'amors velt bien joïr* – (219) *Qui longuement porroit joïr* – *Nostrum* (M14), raises questions about the priority of the one over the other. Example 3.5 is an edition of the first twelve perfections of the piece that also includes the quadruplum.[7] There is a close musical identity with the Latin version of the piece given as Example 2.13, although there are consistent variations between the clausula and the Latin and French motet traditions; these may offer some assistance with questions of priority. At three points in the triplum of the clausula, there are melodic figurations that are consistently shared with the French motet versions, and that are always modified in the Latin ones. These are given as Example 3.6. Such variants clearly separate the clausula and French motet from the Latin motet. The Latin version changes the configurations of the clausula/French motet to a dotted crotchet followed by a dotted crotchet rest. The French motet follows the clausula. It seems clear that the French version did not descend from the Latin one, for this would have entailed three changes between the clausula and the Latin motet; all would have had to have been consistently reinstated in the French-texted piece.

---

[7] The version of the piece made up of the lower three parts is also found in W_2 and Turin, Biblioteca Reale, MS vari 42.

Example 3.5 (220) *Qui la vaudroit* – (218) *Qui d'amors velt bien joïr* – (219) *Qui longuement porroit joïr* – *Nostrum* (M14), perfections 1–12; *F-MO* H ¹⁹6, fols. 23v–5r

Although we can be certain that one set of priorities may be eliminated, there remain two possibilities. Either the Latin version of the motet descends from the French (and in turn from the clausula) or both motet versions descend directly from the clausula.[8] In the latter case, it has to be assumed that the French motet adheres closely to the clausula model and that the Latin one introduces a level of editorial consistency. A comparison of the Latin and French texts adds nothing to this particular discussion.

The construction of the quadruplum in Example 3.5 reinforces the picture of the quadruplum as essentially a textural, rather than a contrapuntal, addition.[9] The additions of pitch created by the quadruplum most often duplicate those already present in the polyphonic complex. There is only one technique of adding new pitches, and that is to take a pre-existing fifth and to add the upper octave to create

---

8   Anderson allowed only the first of these two possibilities in his commentary to this work (*Latin Compositions*, 1: 329–33).
9   See the discussion of *Plus bele que flor* (above, pp. 49–51).

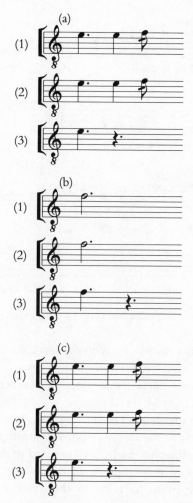

Example 3.6 Comparison of three points in triplum of (a) clausula *Nostrum* (M14), (b) (218) *Qui d'amors* and (c) (221) *Salve salus hominum*

an 8–5 chord. This happens only to chords on *g* and *a*. A third is never added to a pre-existent fifth. In a piece with a large number of 8–5s but only two 5–3s, this is striking. These latter two sonorities are both on *a*, and are two chords to which the upper octave was not added by the quadruplum. It seems as if the 8–5–3 chord was unwelcome, and that the composer preferred 8–5 or 5–3 sonorities.

The tone of the quadruplum poem is courtly and its register *aristocratisant*. The rhythms of the voice-part generally mirror those of the Mode III *ordines* of the triplum and duplum. However, in two instances, the poet-composer allows himself the luxury of making use of a declamation that depends on the rhythm of *fractio modi*. In the two places given as Examples 3.7.1 and 3.7.2, the first *longa perfecta* is broken into a *brevis* and a *longa imperfecta*. *Fractio modi* is however found in both the triplum and motetus of this motet, and had been present in the clausula. Setting the text to rhythms of *fractio modi* speeds up the declamation of the poetry. The

Example 3.7 Declamation in quadruplum (219) *Qui longuement*, perfections 19–22, 65–8, 23–40

declamation follows this rhythm. By way of contrast, the declamation in Example 3.7.3 is slowed down by the introduction of *longa* rests. This results in extraordinary single-note phrases with single-syllable lines. In all other textings of the clausula, the declamation follows basic Mode III patterns.

This flexibility in speeding up or slowing down the declamation of the poem is an important property of the newly composed quadruplum. In the composition of new text and music, the poet might have reverted to the isosyllabicism – or at least the regular patterns of line-length – of other lyric genres, since none of the constraints resulting from the reuse of the music now applies to such newly composed poetry. But irregular line-length and duration of phrase are as much characteristics of newly composed voice-parts as they are of those parts of motets based on clausulae. We have seen how typical these are of clausula composition, and how they result in irregular phrases and concomitantly unequal lines of text in motets based on clausulae. Here, the composer has appropriated exactly the same sort of style in a compositional context where his only constraint is fitting his composition to pre-existent counterpoint.

The refrain

An important change took place in the composition of motets when, instead of writing French contrafacta or adding voice-parts to pre-existing motets derived from clausulae, composers began writing new motet upper voices over old plainsongs. Both Latin and French texts adorned these new upper voices. Although these motets still depended on a borrowed tenor, we may today term them 'newly composed' to distinguish them from works in which all the voices are borrowed. Newly composed French motets might appear to offer an even larger range of possibilities to the analyst of compositional process than do the Latin works derived from clausulae, because, in addition to being built on pre-existent tenors, many French motets make use of what have come to be called refrains.

The refrain is present in almost all vernacular musico-literary genres of the thirteenth century. In its simplest form, it consists of two self-contained lines of poetry with their own music. It is found in the motet and in the monophonic chanson repertory. The same refrain can occur at the end of each stanza (chanson à refrain), or different refrains may be found at the end of each stanza (chanson avec des refrains). An essential point of departure in the rondeau, the refrain crops up in a variety of other less easily defined contexts that range from courtly romance to proverb.

There are few problems with the identification of refrains in all genres except the motet. In the chanson avec des refrains, the refrain disrupts the regular metre and rhyme of the rest of the strophe. In two manuscripts, the chansonniers Roi and Noailles, music is provided for the refrains in every stanza. In the chanson à refrain, the repetition of the refrain itself points to its presence. The rondeau consists of either six or eight lines, and includes an internal repeat of all or part of the refrain; its identification is unproblematic. Even in the romance, the refrain disrupts the rhyme and metre of the narrative. It is either provided with music, or the surviving manuscripts make it clear that music was intended for inclusion even although it was never copied.[10]

It is often taken as axiomatic in writing about the motet that refrains are always quoted or borrowed.[11] In subsequent discussion of the motet, we will see that this is far from always being the case. Furthermore, and to digress only briefly, we might also be sceptical of the idea that a refrain is always a quotation, citation or borrowing, not only in the motet, but also in the other lyric genres just mentioned. In working with these materials, it is dangerous to assume that the refrain sprang out of nowhere and was then cited in a rondeau or chanson à refrain, for example. Some evidence from the motet seems to suggest that the occurrence of the refrain in the motet may sometimes be its original manifestation. Other lyric genres may well behave similarly.[12]

A pressing question that arises when one examines the use of refrains in motets is whether or not both words and music travel from one composition or genre to another. In general, refrains circulate with either both words and music or with the text alone. There is no evidence of the melody of the refrain circulating independently

---

[10] Typically, empty stave-lines or space for them betray the fact that music was destined to accompany these refrains.

[11] Two quotations from a standard textbook on medieval music are typical: 'It must already be clear that the practice of quoting refrains spread beyond the limits of trouvère song' (Richard H. Hoppin, *Medieval Music*, Norton Introduction to Music History (New York: W. W. Norton; Toronto: R. J. Mcloed, 1978), 295); 'One of the most distinctive practices in thirteenth-century French motets [is] the quotation of texts and melodies *that presumably originated as refrains of monophonic songs* [emphasis added]' (*ibid.*, 338).

[12] This is a view expressed by Samuel Rosenberg: 'There is . . . a certain diffuseness in the endeavor to identify cited refrains in existential terms: where were the refrains quoted from? or were they, or some of them, really composed for a particular context rather than cited from elsewhere?' (Review of Eglal Doss-Quinby, *Les Refrains chez les trouvères du xiie siècle au début du xive*, American University Studies 2: 17 (New York, Berne and Frankfurt am Main: Peter Lang, 1984), in *Speculum* 62 (1987) 411).

of its poetry. Problems evidently arise when both text and music of a refrain appear in one work, but the text alone appears in a work that is not normally provided with music: any stanza except the first of a chanson avec des refrains, in a source other than the Noailles or Roi chansonniers, for example. In such cases, we have to accept the fact that the surviving written documents do not preserve enough information to make secure judgements, and we therefore need to proceed with appropriate caution.

Scholars of medieval French poetry have recognised that the use of the refrain in the motet poses problems that are not shared by other genres.[13] Exhaustive bibliographical control over the refrain has tended to conceal many of these problems of identification and function. Friedrich Gennrich drew up various lists of refrains between 1921 and 1964.[14] His work on identifying correlations between refrains in a variety of sources was immensely valuable, and was an unmistakable point of departure for van den Boogaard's revision. Much of Gennrich's work in the field of the chanson à refrain and the chanson avec des refrains was exemplary and an essential foundation for later work. He was however a little over-adventurous in his quest for refrains in motets. Passages of direct speech are often called a refrain, even when this is the sole occurrence of the lines of poetry in the literature. The ramifications of this sort of over-optimistic procedure are only apparent when the repertory of refrains is considered as a whole. Van den Boogaard lists 1933 refrains in his inventory. Of these, about one-third have some reflection in the motet repertory; the remaining two-thirds circulate in the chanson and *contextes non chantés*. But less than half of the motet refrains occur in rondeau, chanson or romance. The remainder are unique in their motet contexts, and, to borrow Doss-Quinby's terminology, they have to be understood as *intratextual* entities; we have to look at the way in which they work within an individual composition to decide if they are, or are not, refrains.[15]

The position of the refrain in the chanson à refrain, rondeau or *roman* makes the identification of an intratextual refrain a simple matter. In the motet, on the other

---

13   Two studies of the refrain which appeared in the early eighties subjected the genre to a systematic literary scrutiny which it had not received since the largely bibliographical work of Nico van den Boogaard published in 1969 (Doss-Quinby, *Les Refrains chez les trouvères*; Susan M. Johnson, 'The Role of the Refrain in Old French Lyric Poetry' (Ph.D. diss., Indiana University, 1983)). Both are strikingly successful in their attempts to adduce a poetic for the refrain in monophonic song and in what Eglal Doss-Quinby calls 'les contextes non chantés'. Strikingly unsuccessful are their attempts to come to terms with the refrain in the motet. Doss-Quinby admits that 'C'est dans les motets que la définition et le rôle du refrain sont le plus difficile à préciser' (Doss-Quinby, *Les Refrains chez les trouvères*, 61). In his otherwise very flattering review of the published version of Doss-Quinby's dissertation Rosenberg comments that 'the refrains figuring in motets . . ., partly because of their irregularity of placement, pose the question of detection' (Rosenberg, Review of Doss-Quinby, *Les Refrains chez les trouvères*, 411).

14   *Rondeaux, Virelais und Balladen aus dem Ende des xii., dem xiii., und dem ersten Drittel des xiv. Jahrhunderts mit den überlieferten Melodien*, 3 vols [1] Gesellschaft für romanische Literatur 43 (Dresden: Gesellschaft für romanische Literatur, 1921); [2] Gesellschaft für romanische Literatur 47 (Gottingen: Gesellschaft für romanische Literatur, 1927); [3 (titled *Das altfranzösische Rondeau und Virelai im 12. und 13. Jahrhundert*)] Summa musicae medii aevi 10 (Langen bei Frankfurt: n.p., 1963); Gennrich, 'Refrain-Tropen in der Musik des Mittelalters', *Studi medievali* 16 (1943–50) 242–54; Gennrich, 'Refrain-Studien: sind die Refrains Fragmente von populären oder populär gewordenen Liedern oder vollständige Volkslieder', *Zeitschrift für romanische Philologie* 71 (1955) 365–90; Gennrich, *Bibliographisches Verzeichnis der französischen Refrains*, Summa musicae medii aevi 14 (Langen bei Frankfurt: n.p., 1964).

15   Doss-Quinby, *Les Refrains chez les trouvères*, 57–8.

hand, not only is there no predictable position for the refrain, but the types of distinction that one is able to make between line-length, rhyme, register and content in other genres, are that much more difficult because of the style of the motet itself. In this respect, then, the motet is markedly different from all other genres under consideration here. This means that identifying refrains in motets is more difficult than in other genres, but also reinforces the importance of refrains as a characteristic of the French motet.

There is one piece of evidence that may be adduced in support of Gennrich, although this does little to counter the general scepticism with which many of his identifications are greeted. It does however improve on the rather blunt critique of Gennrich that completely fails to take into account the possibility of occurrences of refrains in works that have subsequently disappeared.[16] The piece of evidence is statistical, and crude in the extreme. 651 refrains are found in motets, and, of these, 282 are found only once. 43 per cent are therefore unique. Discussion of refrains in this book will suggest that there is a certain doubt about some of the remaining 57 per cent. If we conduct the same experiment with a genre where we can be certain of the status of unique refrains, the chanson avec des refrains for example, we would have an interesting comparison to make with the motet. There are a total of 470 refrains used in the *corpus* of the chanson avec des refrains. Of these, 200 are unique, and represent a proportion of 43 per cent of the total: exactly the same proportion as in the motet. There seem to be two ways of interpreting this information: either to acknowledge that Gennrich was correct and that all his refrains were correctly identified. We may alternatively accept that the motet and chanson avec des refrains have different origins and functions, and that this statistical information is of limited value. These options point to the importance of the criteria that we use in identifying a refrain that occurs in a single motet only.

We approach the use of refrains in the thirteenth-century French motet with two questions in mind. First, are we dealing with a genuine refrain that either occurs in several compositions or for which we have good reason to posit lost contexts, or are we attempting to handle a refrain that may have come into being through Gennrich's over-zealous bibliographical manipulation of this material? Second, does any refrain represent a borrowing or quotation, or might any given occurrence be the refrain's origin? We can only answer the second question by scrutiny of individual pieces, and even then, results may be equivocal. We may respond to the first question simply by restricting our enquiry to motets that use refrains found in more than one composition.

Example 3.8 consists of an edition of a three-part composition taken from the fifth fascicle of the Montpellier Codex: (11) *Je m'en vois* – (12) *Tiex a mout le cuer hardi* – *Omnes* (M1). The two upper-voice texts follow the example and are annotated with rhyme-schemes and line-lengths.[17]

---

[16] A good example of the use of such blunt techniques is Robyn Smith, 'Gennrich's "Bibliographisches Verzeichnis der französischen Refrains": Paper Tiger or Fat Cat?' *Parergon* 8 (1990) 73–101.

[17] Normal practice is here followed in counting syllables in a line of French medieval poetry: feminine rhymes are discounted and indicated with '.

Example 3.8 (11) *Je m'en vois* – (12) *Tiex a mout le cuer hardi* – Omnes (M1); *F-MO H 196*, fols. 118v–21r

(11) *Je m'en vois*

1.	3a	Je m'en vois,
2.	4'b	Ma douce amie;
3.	7a	Si vous les, ce poise moi,
4.	6'b	Qu'onques mes en ma vie
5.	7'b	Ne fis si grief departie.
6.	7c	Bien sai c'om m'a encusé,
7.	5c	C'om m'a desevré
8.	5'b	De vo compaignie;
9.	7c	Ne sunt aillours mi pensé.
10.	9'd	*J'aim la bele, la blonde, la sage,*
11.	7c	*Si li ai mon cuer doné;*
12.	7c	Bien le tieng a assené.
13.	3c	A son gre
14.	7c	Fere en puet sa volenté,
15.	7c	Ne li fera fors bonté,
16.	7c	Car pleine est d'umilité.

(12) *Tiex a mout le cuer hardi*

1.	7a	Tiex a mout le cuer hardi
2.	7b	En quidier et en penser,
3.	7a	Qui l'a couart et failli,
4.	7b	Quant ce vient au demoustrer.
5.	7b	Ce voit on bien esprouver
6.	7a	En amor, por moi le di,
7.	6b	Qui sospris sui d'amer
8.	7a	Cele, qui onques ne vi
9.	7b	Ses ieuz envers moi torner.
10.	7b	Si ne la puis oblier,
11.	6a	Par Diu, ce poise mi,
12.	7a	Car je l'aim tant et criem si,
13.	7a	Que ne sai, comment a li
14.	4b	Voise parler.
15.	6b	*Diex, je n'i os aler!*
16.	6a	*Coment avrai merci?*

As far as we can tell, this piece is not based on a pre-existent discant clausula. The tenor melisma is taken from the Christmas gradual *Viderunt omnes*, rhythmicised into four-measure phrases. Each tenor phrase, or *ordo*, is articulated by a double bar-line in the edition. Although most of the upper-voice parts are newly constructed, they both make use of a refrain, in perfections 33–40 of the triplum and 52–8 of the motetus. In Example 3.8, the text-lines of the refrain are italicised. This piece is an example of two common practices: placing a single refrain at the end of a voice-part and positioning one somewhere in the middle. Both refrains also survive separately in other compositions in addition to this motet and do not therefore raise problems of identification. It is an ideal composition in which to see how refrains function within a reasonably well-controlled environment. But as we investigate this piece in a little more detail, complexities arise that are typical of the use of refrains in the motet repertory, and which tend to be marginalised both in accounts of compositional process[18] and in matters as ostensibly mundane as editorial procedure.[19]

The motetus refrain: '*Diex, je n'i os aler! / Coment avrai merci?*' appears at the end of the voice-part, and also survives in a chanson avec des refrains: *Quant je voi esté* (RS 459). Its composer is Perrot de Douai. The refrain does not occur in the first stanza of the song so we cannot be sure whether the music was the same as that found in the motet. The refrain also occurs in two other motets – both in the fifth fascicle of the Montpellier Codex.

The motetus poem in which the refrain is found uses three line-lengths and two rhymes only. Both rhymes are found in the refrain. Here, the control exerted by the refrain is even greater than in the case of the triplum poem. It does seem to

---

[18] See, for example, Klaus Hofmann, *Untersuchungen zur Kompositionstechnik der Motette im 13. Jahrhundert dargeführt an den Motetten mit dem Tenor IN SECULUM*, Tübinger Beiträge zur Musikwissenschaft 2 (Neuhausen and Stuttgart: Hänssler-Verlag, 1972).

[19] All the editions cited in the notes to Chapter 1 italicise so-called refrains. Nowhere, however, is there any attempt to define criteria for their identification.

argue for the priority of the refrain over the rest of the voice-part, since this piece is an example of the practice, which may also be seen in the triplum, where the changing rhymes and line-lengths of the poem are dictated by the occurrence of refrains using different rhymes and length of lines. In the motetus, the question of line-length is a more potent force in the interpretation of this particular composition. The two principal line-lengths at work in this poem are those of six and seven syllables. Of these, the heptasyllabic line is the more common. However, it is the six-syllable line that is found in the refrain; this line-length only occurs in two other places, lines 7 and 11. The four-syllable line just before the refrain is hardly surprising. The distortion to either rhyme or, as here, line-length just before the appearance of a refrain is common. It is not unusual in monophonic chansons, where regular line-length and rhyme-scheme are distorted by a refrain at the end of the stanza, to find a line between the stanza and the refrain with a length or rhyme that fails to correspond to the refrain or the rest of the stanza. It is known as a *vers de liaison*, and this well illustrates its function.

It is however the relationship between the six- and seven-syllable lines that is of most interest in the motetus of this composition. At the beginning of the piece the heptasyllabic lines are articulated in four-perfection groups, in the third *ordo* of Mode I. This can easily be seen from the paradigmatic analysis of the motetus of this piece (Example 3.9).[20] The paradigms are those of length of text-line. The analysis is read from top left to top right ignoring all spaces, and then continues to the second line, and so on. Reading from top to bottom displays all occurrences of text-lines of similar length. The treatment of text-lines 7 and 11, two hexasyllabic lines, calls for comment. The music for these is not separated from the previous line by a *brevis* rest, as it had been in the case of the heptasyllabic lines. They are run into the previous line to create a musical phrase of seven perfections followed by a *brevis* rest. This is crucial when we look at the refrain, which also consists of hexasyllabic lines preceded by the four-line *vers de liaison*. In the same way as the hexasyllabic lines are run into the heptasyllabic ones, the four-syllable line is joined both to the previous seven-syllable line and to the two following hexasyllabic lines. This may be observed at the end of the analysis of this voice-part in Example 3.9 where the music that goes with text-lines 13 to 16 (the last four stave segments) proceeds without a break.

The refrain found in the motetus of this composition also appears in two other motet sources. They are both found in the fifth fascicle of Montpellier. Example 3.10 gives the refrain as it appears in the motet with which we are concerned and, underneath, as it appears in the two other motet voices: (554) *Dieus, je n'i os aler* and (288) *Si come aloie*. In *Dieus, je n'i os aler*, the refrain is divided into two and placed at beginning and end in what, for the moment, may be termed a *motet enté*. *Si come aloie* simply presents the refrain in the middle of the voice-part. However, Example 3.10 shows that in both *Dieus, je n'i os aler* and *Si come aloie* extra words or lines, and their

20   The analytical basis of this interpretation is outlined in Nicolas Ruwet, 'Methodes d'analyse en musicologie', *Revue belge de musicologie* 20 (1966) 65–90, translated with introduction by Mark Everist as 'Methods of Analysis in Musicology', *Music Analysis* 6 (1987) 3–36.

Example 3.9 (11) *Je m'en vois* – (12) *Tiex a mout le cuer hardi* – *Omnes* (M1); paradigmatic analysis of motetus

music, are present between the two lines of the refrain: *Aimi* in *Dieus, je n'i os aler,*
and *A mon ami* in *Si come aloie.* These are included in square brackets in Example
3.10. A *motet enté* would seem to depend on the pre-existence of a refrain. One
might therefore assume that this composition represents a later branch of the refrain
tradition. The use of the *conjunctura tangendo disiunctim* at the beginning of the
versions of the refrain in both *Dieus, je n'i os aler* and *Si come aloie* might further
suggest a collateral relationship between these two pieces,[21] perhaps an attempt to
adjust the idiosyncratic rhythmic treatment of the beginning of the refrain in the
motet currently under discussion.

Example 3.10 Three versions of refrain 532

The two hexasyllabic refrain lines behave exactly the same way as the two newly
composed hexasyllabic lines in the motetus poem. If we assume for the moment that
the refrain is borrowed from elsewhere, then a logical conclusion is that the way in
which the six-syllable refrain lines were handled dictated the way in which the six-
syllable lines in the rest of the voice-part were managed. Conversely, the refrain
lines may have been handled in this particular way because of the manner in which
other hexasyllabic lines in the composition had been manipulated. In this case, the
answer as to why this voice-part consists of hexasyllabic refrain lines and mostly
heptasyllabic text-lines would lie presumably with the fantasy of the composer. He
would have been responsible for the construction of the poetry and the music in

[21] For a discussion of the *conjunctura tangendo disiunctim,* see Everist, *French 13th-Century Polyphony,* 15 note 69
and the sources cited there.

which the characteristics outlined above would have constituted at least part of the idea of the composition.

The refrain in the triplum: *'J'aim la bele, la blonde, la sage, / Si li ai mon cuer doné'* exists also in a chanson avec des refrains: *Quant la flour de l'espinete* (RS 979); the refrain appears at the end of its second stanza. Each stanza in a chanson avec des refrains therefore ends with different music. Unfortunately, the chanson sources for our refrain[22] do not preserve its music, since, in common with most trouvère manuscripts, they only provide notation for the first stanza. It is difficult therefore to make any statement about the musical origin of the refrain. However, the musical profile of the refrain is of much interest here. In the triplum, the text is declaimed very clearly in alternating crotchets and quavers according to a Mode I pattern. The only exceptions to this are three of the five lines that end with feminine rhymes. In those, the penultimate syllable lasts a complete perfection (text-lines 4, 5 and 8). Of course, a much wider range of rhythmic values is used here, but that does not mask the essential rhythmic movement of the text. Those perfections where the refrain appears, then, 33–40, stand out as being different in two ways. First, they introduce a new manner of text declamation on every quaver (i.e. Mode VI). Second, they present an irregular declamatory style not found elsewhere in the voice-part (i.e. a *mixture* of Mode I and Mode VI). This interpretation of the particular irregularity in perfections 35–6 assumes that the melody of this refrain was the one used in the chanson avec des refrains in which it also appears. The first line of the triplum refrain is the only nine-syllable line in the poem. It is in this line that the new irregular declamation is found. However, the poem also accommodates lines of three, four, five, six and seven syllables. Writing music to a nine-syllable line should therefore have posed no particular problem to the composer of the work. This strongly suggests that the irregular declamation was a feature of the original refrain.

The triplum poem makes use of four rhymes, labelled a to d in the second column of the edition of the text. The first line of the refrain uses a rhyme which occurs only once, and is labelled d in the analysis. This corresponds to the unique nine-syllable line. More important, however, is the rhyme of the second line of the refrain. Labelled c in the edition, it is also found in the poem before the refrain – lines 6, 7 and 9. However, it also controls the rest of the poem, lines 11 (the second line of the refrain) to 16, and sets up an explicit contrast with the *rimes croisées* of the opening pairs of lines. We might also observe that, of the last five lines after the refrain, four make use of the same line-length of seven syllables. Elements of the refrain again control the line-length of at least part of the rest of the poem. Furthermore, the first line of the poem *after* the refrain is self-evidently dependent on the content and syntax of the refrain itself. Lines 10 and 11 read in translation: 'I love the fair one, the blond one, the wise one, and I have given my heart to her'. The next line continues: 'And I consider it the right thing to do'. However significant the musical dimension of this refrain, its poetic qualities have a very powerful influence on the structure of the triplum poem.

22   The chansonniers: Paris, Bibliothèque Nationale, fonds français 846, nouvelles acquisitions françaises 1050, français 1591, français 845, and Paris, Bibliothèque de l'Arsenal, 5198.

The form of the motet (11) *Je m'en vois* – (12) *Tiex a mout le cuer hardi* – *Omnes* (M1) depends both on its borrowed tenor and on its use of refrains. In the ways in which the refrain controls the structure of the poem and the relationship between word and note, it is an important element in the composition.

Refrain and clausula

In the fourth volume of her monumental study of the Montpellier Codex, Yvonne Rokseth drew attention to some of the problems associated with refrains discussed in this chapter.[23] She was intrigued by a group of motets that seemed both to make use of refrains and to be derived from clausulae. Instinctively, one might assume that these two attributes were mutually contradictory. However, a consideration of some of the implications of these motets will not only enrich our understanding of the ways in which refrains and motets interact, but will also suggest that refrains may have originated in the motets themselves, and then have been quoted in other genres. The works to which Rokseth drew attention were as follows:

1. (652) *Plus bele que flor* – (650) *Quant revient et fuelle* – (651) *L'autrier joer* – *Flos filius eius* (O16)
2. (396) *Se j'ai servi longuement* – (397) *Trop longuement* – *Pro patribus* (M30)
3. (419) *Li pluiseur se plaignent* – *Virgo* (M32)
4. (62) *En mai, que neist* – *Domine* (M3)
5. (754) *Ne m'oubliez mie* – *Domino* (BD I)
6. (250) *Quant voi la fleur* – *Et tenuerunt* (M17).

We have already agreed to postpone discussion of motets whose refrains occur in that one location only. The third and the sixth pieces fall into this category, and we may therefore omit them from our discussion. The remaining works will be discussed in turn.

1. (652) *Plus bele que flor* – (650) *Quant revient et fuelle* – (651) *L'autrier joer* – *Flos filius eius* (O16)

This is a work whose earlier Latin history has already been discussed. The refrain '*C'est la fin, la fin, que que nus die, j'amerai*' (vdB 338) occurs at the end of the motetus. The refrain is also found at the end of the third stanza of a chanson avec des refrains (RS 1197.III), at the end of the first stanza of another chanson avec des refrains (RS 2072.I), and also in a rondeau by Guillaume d'Amiens, *C'est la fins koi que nus die*.[24] The motet and the rondeau are preserved with music. The music of the rondeau by Guillaume d'Amiens, *C'est la fins*, is therefore of some significance, and an edition of the piece is given as Example 3.11.

---

[23] Rokseth, *Polyphonies du treizième siècle*, 4: 209 note 1.
[24] The first of the two chansons avec des refrains is found only in the Douce chansonnier, which only records the poetry. The second chanson survives in the manuscript Berne, Staats- und Universitäts- bibliothek, MS 389; although there are stave-lines in this manuscript, the music was never copied.

Example 3.11 Guillaume d'Amiens: rondeau, *C'est la fins*; *I-Rvat* Reg. Lat. 1490, fol. 119v

This rondeau differs from most other thirteenth-century specimens in three respects. First, the music of lines 3 and 4 does not match the first line of the refrain. Although the last four pitches are the same, the first two notes and the first ligature are completely different. Second, the text of line 4 might be expected to duplicate that of the first line of the refrain. Certainly, the first three words are the same, but they continue differently. Coupled with the musical differences just outlined, this can hardly be said to constitute a standard internal refrain line. Finally, although lines 5 and 6 mirror the music of the refrain, as is usual, the musical phrases and lines of poetry are made to overlap. In the new text added to the music of the refrain, we might also expect the line-lengths of the poem to be maintained. But, as can be seen from Example 3.11, line 5 loses its feminine rhyme, and line 6 appropriates the single pitch *d* for its first syllable.[25]

More striking is the fact that the refrain in the rondeau has two words fewer than that of the motet: '*C'est la fins koi que nus die*' instead of '*C'est la fin, la fin, que que nus die*'. This points up one of the two important characteristics in the transmission of this refrain. All four versions, two with music and two without, are given as Example 3.12. The motetus under consideration shares the repetition of the words 'la fin' with the chanson *Amours me sermont* (RS 1197). The rondeau omits this repetition, as does the other chanson *Bele m'est la revenue* (RS 2072). However, this pairing is contradicted by the fact that both the refrain in the motet and in *Bele m'est la revenue* (RS 2072) are prefaced by exactly the same line of poetry: 'K'en ferai?'. This might suggest some similarity of origin for these two versions of the refrain.

25 The poem is discussed further in Chapter 5, in the context of the *C'est la jus type-cadre*.

Example 3.12 Four versions of refrain 338

2. (396) *Se j'ai servi longuement* – (397) *Trop longuement* – *Pro patribus* (M30)

Van den Boogaard identifies two refrains in the motetus of this composition. The first, 'Je l'avrai / L'amor a la bele / Girondele / S'amor, je l'avrai' (vdB 1054), is only found in this one motet, and thus requires treatment with care. The second, '*Dame, iert il toz jors ainsi / Que j'amerai sans guerredon?*' (vdB 411), occurs at the end of the motetus. It is also found in an anonymous rondeau appended to a *salut d'amours* in the manuscript Paris, Bibliothèque Nationale, fonds français 837, unfortunately without music. The texts of the versions in Montpellier and the *salut d'amours* match very closely apart from small orthographical variants, but the range of textual variants in the concordances for the motet suggest little.

3. Excluded for reasons given above

4. (62) *En mai, que neist* – *Domine* (M3)

En mai, que neist is a two-part motet from the sixth fascicle of Montpellier whose motetus ends with the refrain: '*Cele m'a s'amor douné, / Qui mon cuer et mon cors a*' (vdB 314). This is a refrain that has excited interest for various reasons since 1924 when Ludwig tabulated most of its occurrences in his contribution to Adler's *Handbuch der Musikgeschichte*.[26] There are six presentations of the music of this refrain: the original clausula, a chanson (RS 2041), the motet under discussion, where it occurs at the end of the motetus, two other motet voices and a rondeau-motet. The music to all these presentations is in essence the same, although differing transposition levels separate the chanson and one of the motets from the rest of the complex. Ludwig's opinion was that the clausula served as the model for all these presentations. The piece will discussed in the context of the rondeau-motet in Chapter 5.

---

[26] 'Die geistliche nichtliturgische und weltliche einstimmige und die mehrstimmige Musik des Mittelalters bis zum Anfang des 15. Jahrhunderts', *Handbuch der Musikgeschichte*, ed. Guido Adler (Frankfurt am Main: Anstalt, 1924) 206.

5. (754) *Ne m'oubliez mie – Domino (BD I)*

Like *En mai, quant neist, Ne m'oubliez mie* is a two-part motet found in the sixth fascicle
of the Montpellier Codex. However, it includes two refrains that each occur elsewhere. Interestingly, the circulation of both is entirely restricted to the motet repertory.
Example 3.13 is an edition of those parts of the piece in which refrains are found.
One refrain, '*Ne m'oubliez mie / Bele et avenant / Quant je ne voz voi / S'en sui plus
dolens*' (vdB 1361), opens the motet and another, '*Bone amour ai qui m'agree*' (vdB
287), closes it. The first refrain is found at the end of the motetus of another two-
part motet from the sixth fascicle of Montpellier, (567) *La plus bele – Pacem* (M72).

Example 3.13 (754) *Ne m'oubliez mie – Domino* (BD I), perfections 1–12 and 33–48; *F-MO* H 196,
fols. 261v–2r

The only differences concern tiny variations in spelling and one small change in ornamentation, and need not concern us here. The second refrain is only slightly more widely distributed: it is found, as in *Ne m'oubliez mie*, at the end of the motetus, in two other motets: (342) *Quant voi yver* – (343) *Au douz tans pleisant* – *Hodie perlustravit* (M25) and (393) *Mainte dame* – *Han* (M29). The first of these two is found in the fifth fascicle of the Montpellier Codex (because it is in three parts) and in the Munich fragments. The second survives in Roi and Noailles, two chansonniers with large motet collections. Again the differences between the version of the refrain in *Ne m'oubliez mie* and the other two motets are minimal.

Rokseth limited her enquiry to the motets found in Montpellier; but there are two further pieces that make use of refrains and that include a clausula in their compositional history. They are (402) *L'autrier quant me chevauchoie* – *Pro patribus* (M30), and (515a) *Quant l'alouete saut* – *Qui conservaret* (M50). Both pieces are based on clausulae in the Florence manuscript, and in each, a textual and musical fragment finds its way into another motet: respectively (406) *Se longuement* – *Benedicta* (M32), and (83) *L'autrier m'esbatoie* – (84) *Demenant grant joie* – *Manere* (M5). The pieces add little in the way of evidence to our discussion of the question of refrain and clausula.

Two explanations have been offered for the presence of a refrain in a motet based on a clausula.[27] Either a composer took the text only of a refrain and applied it to the music of a phrase of a clausula, or the refrain originated in the process of adding a French text to a clausula (and thereby creating a motet) and was subsequently cited or quoted in a variety of other genres. The first of these alternatives is difficult to sustain on the basis of the surviving evidence. One would want to see evidence of a refrain whose melody had been abandoned and whose poetry had been reused to text a clausula as part of the process of creating a motet. Such evidence is not forthcoming, and this hypothesis remains only a theoretical possibility. Rokseth's second alternative is the more attractive, as the preceding discussion has suggested.

These refrains originate in polyphony and circulate subsequently in monophonic and perhaps non-musical contexts. This is really not surprising, since we can see many examples of a similar procedure whereby entire motet voices, originally derived from clausulae, are divorced from their polyphonic context. The resulting monodies are then copied into manuscripts of trouvère song in a notation that makes them almost unrecognisable.[28] This is analogous to the creation of refrains out of motets derived from clausulae. Two examples may be instructive here.

The motet (415) *Pour conforter* – *Go* (M32) is based on a clausula. But the motetus of this motet also functions as the complete first stanza of a chanson avec des refrains (RS 19.I). The last two lines of the motetus: 'Je voi venir Emmelot / Par mi le vert bois' therefore become the refrain at the end of the first stanza. The remaining two stanzas, as is always the case in a chanson avec des refrains, make use of different refrains. Similar is the motet (764) *Hyer matin a l'enjornee* – *Domino* (BD VI) in which the motetus of the clausula-derived motet becomes the entire first stanza of a

[27] Rokseth, *Polyphonies du treizième siècle*, 4: 209.

[28] Ernest Sanders, 'Motet, Medieval, Ars Antiqua', *The New Grove Dictionary of Music and Musicians*, 20 vols, ed. Stanley Sadie (London: Macmillan, 1980) 12: 621.

chanson à refrain embedded in the *Miracles* of Gautier de Coinci.[29] Here the last eight lines of the motetus become not only the refrain at the end of the first stanza but end all the stanzas of the song.

To return to Rokseth's group of clausula-derived motets with refrains, four pieces are of interest. One, (396) *Se j'ai servi longuement* – (397) *Trop longuement* – *Pro patribus* (M30), is equivocal. The only other occurrence of the refrain either survives without music or was never intended to include it. The three other pieces demonstrate a series of musical and lyric relationships that support the idea that the music of the refrain originated in the clausula. The lyric of the refrain arose out of the process of writing a vernacular text to the clausula. The refrain subsequently circulated in the same way as refrains that originated in chansons or rondeaux. The origins of the refrain '*C'est la fin, la fin*' (vdB 338) may be even more complex. It may also affect our view of the origins of the entire family of 'Flos filius' motets. It is possible that the presence of the refrain in (652) *Plus bele que flor* – (650) *Quant revient et fuelle* – (651) *L'autrier joer* – *Flos filius eius* (O16) may be the result of texting a clausula with a Latin text and only subsequently creating a French contrafactum. The music of the refrain would then have undergone two textings before reaching the form in which it circulated as a refrain.

The foregoing comments would be concrete evidence that could be set against the traditional view of motets quoting or borrowing refrains were it not for one complicating factor: the clausulae that form part of the compositional history of the pieces that we have just been investigating were not embedded in organa in their original sources. They may be clausulae that were conceived not to enrich the musical fabric of organa but as notational models for motets. A compositional scenario in which a 'normal' borrowing of a refrain takes place in a newly composed motet and in which a clausula is created to act as a notational prop is entirely believable. Whatever interpretation one might want to place on these pieces does not contradict the 'borrowing' or 'quotation' hypothesis but demonstrates again how these compositions need to be assessed individually.

---

[29] The most reliable edition of the *Miracles* is Vernon Frederick Koenig, ed., *Les Miracles de Nostre Dame par Gautier de Coinci*, 4 vols, Textes littéraires français 62 [vols 1 and 3], 92 [vol. 2] and 176 [vol. 4] (Geneva: Librairie Droz; Lille: Librairie Giard, 1955–70). See also Jacques Chailley, ed., *Les chansons à la Vierge de Gautier de Coinci 1177 [78]–1236: édition musicale critique avec introduction et commentaires*, Publications de la Société Française de Musicologie 1: 15 (Paris: Heugel et Cie, 1959).

Part Two

Genre

4

The *motet enté*

Introduction: taxonomy

The legacy of a hundred years of scholarship is a perplexing array of classifications for the motet. The taxonomy of the genre seems to be based on widely different criteria. Such subgenres as Franconian and Petronian motets, for example, are named after individuals. Both men composed motets and contributed to the theoretical literature of polyphonic music. The modern view of the motets that bear their names assigns a rhythmic impulse to the Petronian motet and a notational one, presumably, to the Franconian. Petronian motets are those in which the *brevis* is divided into more than three *semibreves*. Two works are known to be attributed in medieval sources to Petrus, and this has encouraged modern scholars to posit Petronian authorship to some or all pieces that exhibit this rhythmic characteristic.[1] If Franconian motets are those that make use of Franconian notation, this poses problems for the interpretation of those pieces whose sources are written partly in Franconian, and partly in earlier or later forms of mensural notation.[2] Exactly how one would distinguish between the musical and poetic styles of the Franconian and non-Franconian motet is far from clear.

Other current classifications of the thirteenth-century motet depend on the language of the texts. Latin motets and French motets are terms already familiar from the earlier chapters in this book. The bilingual motet is a type that also depends for its classification on the language of its texts. Such categorisations are implicit in the codicological organisation of the Montpellier Codex. However, subgenres are also determined by the number of voice-parts. The organisation of Montpellier is controlled by number of voices and language of texts, and this must have lain behind Ludwig's decisions concerning the identification of subgenre.

---

[1] Thirteenth-century attributions of motets to Petrus are based on comments in Jacques de Liège's *Speculum musicae* (Coussemaker, *Scriptores*, 2: 401).

[2] A good example of a source copied in Franconian notation is Paris, Bibliothèque Nationale, fonds latin 11266, much of whose contents derives from earlier sources. See Mark Everist, 'Music and Theory in Late Thirteenth-Century Paris: The Manuscript Paris, Bibliothèque Nationale, *fonds lat.* 11266', *Royal Musical Association Research Chronicle* 17 (1981) 58–9. Franco's position as a composer is tantalising. Jacques de Liège attributed a motet that he heard to Franco (Coussemaker, *Scriptores*, 2: 402). See also Michel Huglo, 'De Francon de Cologne à Jacques de Liège', *Revue belge de musicologie* 34–5 (1980–1) 44–60.

Some of these, double motet and triple motet (that describe three- and four-part works respectively), are labels that obscure more than they illuminate.

Many classifications of thirteenth-century motets rely on the presence of certain stylistic characteristics. Perhaps the most interesting is the so-called conductus-motet. Here, a subgeneric classification is given precision by reference to another genre. Indeed, until fairly recently, 'conductus-style' was a term that was employed to discuss music as widely diverse as fourteenth-century Mass music and the fifteenth-century chanson.

For our present purposes, it is the generic classifications within the domain of the vernacular motet that depend on the use of refrains that are of interest. Five may claim our attention here: *Kurzmotette*, refrain-motet, refrain cento, rondeau-motet and *motet enté*.[3] There is a variety, perhaps even a caprice, in the criteria employed in the classifications of the motets discussed so far. Those grouping vernacular motets are less various but equally inconsistent. The first two of these classifications are the most problematic because they are the least well focused. These two types of motet both consist of one or two refrains over a tenor: the refrain-motet always only employs one, the *Kurzmotette* sometimes more than one. The labels refer to the occurrence of borrowed material in one case and to duration in the other. Rondeau-motets are so-called because of the structures of their upper voices, in which the function of refrains is obligatory. The refrain cento and *motet enté* are classified according to the presence and functioning of refrains. The former is a motet, one of whose voice-parts consists of a chain of refrains; the latter, as we saw in the previous chapter, takes a refrain, divides it into two sections, and places them at the beginning and end of the voice-part. We will see that none of these classifications is particularly meaningful, and they are best treated with suspicion – or ignored. This is especially true of those taxonomies that depend on the identification of refrains. These conclusions form the background to an alternative view of genre to be given in Chapter 8.

Definitions

The *motet enté* assumes a central position in our thinking both about the French thirteenth-century motet, and about medieval music in general. There are two ways in which a *motet enté* is understood or defined today, and these two points of view are outlined first. We may then examine two specific cases where the word 'enter' can be associated with unequivocal musical repertories. One of these suggests that a *motet enté* may in fact be something very different to either of the two current views.

The broader of the two current descriptions of the *motet enté* simply proposes a thirteenth-century motet with French texts in which one of the upper voice-parts makes use of a refrain. Such a usage does not mean that the motet voice necessarily cites or quotes a refrain, but that the piece simply shares a poetic or musical content

---

[3]   These terms are found throughout Gennrich, *Bibliographie*.

with another lyric or narrative work.[4] The second, more specific, definition involves the process of splitting a refrain into two sections, and placing it at the beginning and end of a voice-part in a motet.[5] So, for example, a two-line refrain might appear in a variety of sources intact, but occur divided into two in what Ludwig and his followers would call a *motet enté*. The two elements of the refrain would effectively 'frame' the rest of the voice-part. The motet (459) *Navrés sui au cuer* – (460) *Navrés sui pres du cuer* – *Veritatem* (M37) may serve as an illustration (Example 4.1).

[4] Two examples are Hoppin, *Medieval Music*, 338–40, and Jeremy Yudkin, *Music in Medieval Europe*, Prentice Hall History of Music (Englewood Cliffs, N.J., 1989) 402.

[5] This usage is common among those who have worked more exclusively on the thirteenth-century motet: Ludwig, Gennrich, and especially Rokseth and Anderson. It is found *passim* in Ludwig, *Repertorium*; Gennrich, *Bibliographie*; Rokseth, *Polyphonies du treizième sicèle*. The commentaries to the editions by Anderson listed in the bibliography also use the term in this more restricted sense.

Example 4.1 (459) *Navrés sui au cuer* – (460) *Navrés sui pres du cuer* – *Veritatem* (M37); *F-MO* H 196, fols. 155v–7r

The refrain (vdB 1350) occurs in the motetus. Its first line, '*Navrés sui pres du cuer sans plaie*', occurs at the beginning of the motetus, and its second, '*Diex, si ne sai, qui le fer m'entraie*', comes at the end. The refrain also appears in another motet, of which unfortunately only the text is preserved, in a rondeau appended to the end of a stanza of a *salut d'amours*, and in the narrative poem *Le Tournoi de Chauvenchi*.[6]

The rondeau reads as follows:

> *Navrez sui prés du cuer sanz plaie,*
> *Las! Si ne sai qui le fer m'en traie.*
> Je croi bien ne garirai mie,
> *Navrez sui, ne sai qui m'aie;*
> Se pitié ma dame ne prie
> De moi aidier, por rien ne gariroie.
> *Navrez sui prés du sanz plaie,*
> *Las! Si ne sai qui le fer m'en traie.*

---

6   Motet: (1092) *Navrés sui pres.* The *salut d'amours* is preserved in Paris, Bibliothèque Nationale, fonds français 837, fols 253v–5r; the rondeau under discussion is edited in Nico H. J. van den Boogaard, *Rondeaux et refrains du xiie siècle au début du xive: collationnement, introduction, et notes*, Bibliothèque française et romane, D: 3 (Paris: Editions Klincksieck, 1969) 38. The last citation is found in Maurice Delbouille, ed., *Jacques Bretel: Le Tournoi de Chauvency*, Bibliothèque de la Faculté Philosophique et Lettres de l'Université de Liège 49 (Paris and Liège: Société de l'Edition 'Les Belles Lettres', 1932).

The rondeau is appended to a stanza from a *salut d'amours*. In this case, the *salut* consists of fourteen stanzas, each of which ends either with a refrain or, as here, with a rondeau. The context is slightly broader than a simple eight-line rondeau might suggest. Usually in the rondeaux that end the stanzas of these pieces, the internal repetition of the first line of the refrain is exact. Here of course is an exception. There are other differences between this rondeau and those appended to other stanzas. Most are isosyllabic; the refrain here consists of lines of different lengths: 8' and 9' respectively. This seems, at least in part, to govern the functioning of the rondeau. Perhaps the refrain originated somewhere other than in the rondeau, and the structure of the rondeau is determined by the refrain. It may have originated in a context where irregular line-lengths were more part of the stylistic constraints of the genre, perhaps even the motet currently under discussion. Complicated though it is, this rondeau does at least give us a simple presentation of our refrain intact. The only textual variant is the appearance of 'Las!' in the second line instead of 'Dieus!'

The presence of the refrain in *Le Tournoi de Chauvenchi* is the other case of unbroken occurrence.

> *Navrez sui prés du cuer sanz plaie,*
> *Diex! Si ne truis qui le fer m'en traie.*

In this presentation of the refrain, the selection of vocabulary is similar to that in the *Salut d'amours*, but its use of the word 'Diex' at the beginning of the second line of the refrain allies it with our so-called *motet enté*. The fourth occurrence of the refrain is in a motet text that, like the one in Example 4.1, divides the refrain into two parts and places them at the beginning and end of the text.

> *Navreis suix prés dou cuer san plaie*
> Dont li fers est moult bien agueis
> Ke par mi les dous cousteis
> M'ait ferut an regardant,
> Dont li cousteis ne se sant
> Mai li cuers an est mal mis,
> Se celle a cui suix amis
> Ne lou prant an se menaie,
> *Deus! Je ne truis ki lou fer m'an traie.*

This poem, and the citation in *Le Tournoi de Chauvenchi*, both replace parts of the verb 'savoir' in the second line with parts of the verb 'trover'. Both the motet text and one of the versions of *Le Tournoi de Chauvenchi* appear in the same manuscript: Oxford, Bodleian Library, Douce MS 308. Similar wording in the two poems is perhaps not therefore surprising, but raises a host of questions concerning the parallel distribution of refrains in different genres but identical sources.[7]

Two questions arise out of these comments. First, what did a medieval *musicus*, *cantor* or poet mean when he referred to a *motet enté*? Second, and more elusive, of

---

[7]   An analogous case is the appearance of a redaction of the romance *Renart le nouvel*, replete with refrains, in the same manuscript as the collected works of Adam de la Halle: Paris, Bibliothèque Nationale, fonds français 25566.

what value is the identification of such a process or genre to our modern under-standing and interpretation of the thirteenth-century motet in French?

Terminology

Two examples of the use of the word 'enter' describe surviving poetry and music. These two examples could be seen as the obvious starting points for an answer to the question of defining a *motet enté*. The word 'enter' is found in two sources: in the chansons of Jehan de L'Escurel and in a collection of works found at the end of the trouvère chansonnier Paris, Bibliothèque Nationale, fonds français 845.

The index of the manuscript that preserves L'Escurel's collected chansons – Paris, Bibliothèque Nationale, fonds français 146 – ends with Escurel's works headed 'Balades, rondeaux et diz entez sur les refroiz de rondeaux'.[8] We may take the word 'entez' here to refer to the 'diz' only, since if one were to permit it to refer to anything else we would have to account for 'rondeaux entez sur les refroiz de rondeaux' which makes little sense. The two 'diz entez sur les refroiz de rondeaux' attributed to L'Escurel consist of twenty-four and twenty-eight stanzas respectively.[9] The structure of the stanza is consistent: nine lines with a regular line-length and rhyme-scheme ($A^8A^8B^4B^8B^8C^4C^8C^8D^8$). Each stanza is then followed by a refrain which can be of anything between one and four lines long. The final rhyme of the refrain corresponds to the D rhyme of the stanza – the last line immediately before the refrain. In some cases where the refrain is of more than one line, the rhymes correspond not only to the D rhyme but also to the C rhyme. The most recent editor of the 'diz entez', Nigel Wilkins, in fact speaks of the C and D rhymes being 'dictated' by the rhymes of the refrain.[10] This is a moot point since, as Wilkins himself observes, 'it seems likely, considering the thematic relationships which are to be observed between certain of the interpolated refrains, that some of them were not genuine but were especially composed for that occasion'.[11] This raises questions broader than it is appropriate to discuss here, but one could just add to Wilkins's observations the comment that the other locations in which refrains that are used in the 'diz entez' appear are highly restricted. In any case only about 20 per cent occur in other places at all. In terms of 'grafting' pre-existent material on to a lyric, the 'diz entez' seem to be rather doubtful examples.

The 'grafting' in the 'diz entez sur les refroiz de rondeaux' of L'Escurel is a simple process of adding pre-existent refrains to a series of stanzas. In these cases one might indeed argue that the rhymes of the refrain 'dictate' the rhymes of the last lines of the stanza. On the basis of this evidence, then, we might be tempted to agree that a *motet enté* is simply a motet in which a refrain, either borrowed or composed,

---

[8] Fol. br–v.

[9] They are edited in Nigel Wilkins, ed., *The Works of Jehan de Lescurel*, Corpus mensurabilis musicae 30 (n.p.: American Institute of Musicology, 1966) pp. 21–36.

[10] *Ibid.*, p. vi.

[11] *Ibid.*

appears at some point in one or more of the voice-parts.[12] But that would be to ignore the important collection of *motets entés* in the manuscript français 845.

Motet enté

The correlation of the term '*motet enté*' with a group of pieces could not be clearer. At the beginning of a sequence of compositions in français 845 there is the rubric 'Here begin the *motets entés*'.[13] This manuscript is one of the so-called KNPX group of chansonniers[14] and is closely allied with the Arsenal chansonnier, Paris, Bibliothèque de l'Arsenal, 5198.[15] Both books must have been copied around 1270–80. Therefore the collection of *motets entés* in français 845 is more or less contemporary with the motet collections in Bamberg and the *corpus ancien* of Montpellier, rather younger than the French motets in W₂ and older than the later fascicles of Montpellier and the motets in Turin. There are fifteen works called *motet enté* in français 845, but they are compositions that relate only tangentially to the mainstream of motet composition preserved in the other sources. First of all, the works are monophonic. Despite the fact that Gennrich describes them all as two-part motets with the tenor missing, neither their manuscript presentation nor their concordant versions support such a view. Like the music in the rest of the manuscript, the works are notated successively in two columns. Of the fifteen works preserved there, twelve are unique. Two works have concordances in the chansonnier Douce 308 but without music. A final piece is also preserved not only in Douce 308 but also in a romance entitled *Méliacin* or *Le Conte du Cheval de Fust*. This itself is preserved in four contemporary sources.[16] Again, however, none of these records any music.

Information about the corpus of *motets entés* in français 845 is given in Table 4.1. Reading from left to right, there are two numbering systems: one from Gennrich's *Bibliographie*, and the other from Tischler's *Earliest Motets* where the pieces are edited. Two columns giving information about the refrains in these pieces are followed by a textual incipit. The information about the refrains is divided into two columns; the numbers all refer to the inventory by Nico van den Boogaard. On the left are attested refrains and on the right unattested ones. This allows us to maintain a distinction between refrains which survive in locations other than these motets, and those that do not, during the course of the following discussion.

[12]   This is also the sense in which Johannes de Grocheio appears to use the Latin term '*cantilena entata*'. See Christopher Page, 'Johannes de Grocheio on Secular Music: A Corrected Text and a New Translation', *Plainsong and Medieval Music* 2 (1993) 27 and note 41.

[13]   Paris, Bibliothèque Nationale, fonds français 845, fol. 184r.

[14]   The structure of the KNPX group is explained in Hans Spanke, ed., *Eine altfranzösische Liedersammlung: der anonyme Teil der Liederhandschriften KNPX*, Romanische Bibliothek 20 (Halle: Verlag von Max Niemeyer, 1925).

[15]   The close relationship between the manuscript français 845 and the Arsenal chansonnier is demonstrated in Mark Everist, 'The Sources of Trouvère Song' (unpublished paper).

[16]   *Méliacin* is unedited, and survives in four manuscripts: Florence, Biblioteca Riccardiana, 2757; Paris, Bibliothèque Nationale, fonds français 1455, 1589 and 1633. The lyric insertions are however edited in Edmund Stengel, 'Die altfranzösische Liederzitate aus Girardin d'Amiens *Conte du cheval de fust*', *Zeitschrift für romanische Philologie* 10 (1886) 460–76.

Table 4.1 *Motets entés* in *F-Pn* fr. 845

Gennrich, *Biblio-graphie*	Tischler, *Earliest Motets*	Van den Boogaard (attested)	Van den Boogaard (unattested)	Incipit
1077	345	604		*Douce dame debonaire*
1078	346	796		*Hé amors, morrai je*
1079	347		1807	*Tres haute amor jolie*
1080	348		832	*Hé Deus, tant doucement*
1081	349		455	*D'amors vient et de ma dame*
1082	350	1322		*Mesdisans creveront*
1083	351	1432		*Or ai je trop demoré*
1084	352	487		*De vos vient li maus*
1085	353		51	*Aimi, li maus que j'ai*
1086	354		1557	*Quant plus sui*
1087	355		825	*Hé Dex, que ferai*
1088	356		460	*D'amours vient toute ma joie*
1089	357		818	*Hé Dex, je ni puis durer*
1090	358	144		*Amoureusement languis por joie avoir*
1091	359	538		*Biaus Dieus, la reverré je ja*

Of the fifteen refrains that are supposed to form part of these fifteen pieces, seven occur in other contexts (and are in the 'attested' column), while eight do not. In other words, this is the only appearance that these eight make in the entire repertory of lyric and narrative verse and music. Of these fifteen works, only six behave like *motets entés* as described by Ludwig: their refrains are divided into two portions and placed at the beginning and end of the piece. But of these, only four have refrains that appear elsewhere. We cannot make any judgement on the validity of the two works whose refrains do not survive elsewhere. Their texts certainly behave like the ones whose refrains do have concordances. We simply cannot be certain whether to include six works of this sort in our discussion, or to assume that two are fictions.

Figure 4.1 represents graphically some of the relationships between the refrains of the pieces in this subgroup.

There are only three other works involved in this complex of pieces. This is a strikingly narrow circulation for the four refrains. The three locations of the refrain are a motetus from a three-part motet in the fifth fascicle of Montpellier,[17] both upper voice-parts of a further motet again from the fifth fascicle of Montpellier but also preserved in other manuscripts,[18] and two stanzas of a chanson avec des refrains (RS 1148). This latter song is preserved in the KNPX chansonnier group, and of course therefore in français 845. Two refrains go into the first and fifth stanzas of the chanson. One refrain simply appears at the end of a voice-part, marked 'terminal' in Figure 4.1, but refrains 796 and 144 occupy a rather more complex position in

---

[17]   (471) *Mesdisant par leur envie* – (472) *Biau cors qui a tot doit plaire* – *Veritatem* (M37).
[18]   (9) *Amoureusement me tient* – (10) *Hé, Amours* – *Omnes* (M1).

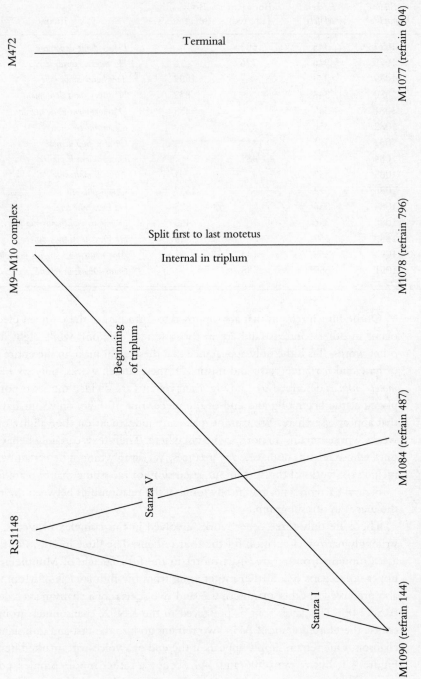

Figure 4.1 Diagrammatic representation of relationships between refrains of four *motets entés* in *F-Pn* fr. 845

another motet. (9) *Amoureusement me tient* – (10) *Hé, Amours* – Omnes (M1), identified as 'M9–M10 complex' in Figure 4.1, is a piece whose use of refrains will be
discussed in Chapter 6. What can be said is that its presence within this group of
pieces yet again breaks down the idea that it conforms to the neat picture usually
painted of the ways in which refrains function in motets: that the refrain is taken from
a chanson or rondeau and then *quoted* within the context of the motet. Although
there are four or perhaps six works that seem on the surface to behave very much
according to the description offered and used by Ludwig, Anderson and Rokseth,
the highly restricted distribution of the refrains in those pieces, where they are
attested, immediately sets them apart from the ones which those authors were in
fact seeking to explain.

There are three other compositions in français 845 that make use of refrains that
are known from other sources. The version of the last piece in Table 4.1 survives in
too fragmentary a form to make any particular statement about the way in which it
works. The two other pieces, (1082) *Mesdisans creveront* and (1083) '*Or ai je trop
demoré*, are worth closer examination. *Mesdisans creveront* uses a three-line refrain that
it splits into three sections and disposes at the beginning, middle and end of the
piece. Unfortunately, none of the other versions of the refrain is preserved with
music. *Or, ai je trop demoré*, no. 1083, is of interest for rather different reasons
(Examples 4.2.1 and 4.2.2).

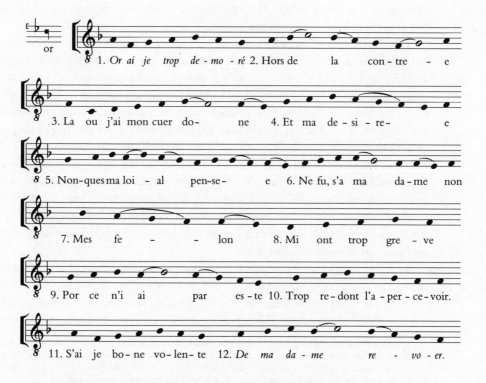

Example 4.2.1 (1083) *Or ai je trop demoré*; F-Pn fr. 845, fol. 190r

This piece exhibits characteristics that are found consistently in this repertory of *motets entés* in français 845. These characteristics will form the basis of conclusions concerning this music.[19]

In Example 4.2.1, the refrain can be seen divided into two and placed at the beginning and end in exactly the same way as in the group of four pieces discussed before. These are text-lines 1 and 12 and are here italicised. The music to each of the two limbs of the refrain is different. However, in the penultimate line of the text (line 11) the music is exactly the same as the first line of the refrain – at the beginning of the piece. It is difficult to stress sufficiently how important – and how rare – this sort of repetition is. Previous discussion has demonstrated the absence of melodic repetition in the newly composed sections, excluding the occasional refrains, of the thirteenth-century motet. Phrases may begin like the one two before it, for example, but it can be guaranteed that it will not continue in the same way. Such a self-conscious avoidance of melodic repetition has much to do with the fact that both the rhythmic and harmonic vocabulary of the music is highly restricted, and the skill in creating variety depends on the constant melodic permutation of a limited number of pitches. To repeat: the pieces in français 845 exploit musical parallelisms, and an exploration of the differences between these pieces and the rest of the motet repertory really stands at the core of the current argument. Such relationships between individual compositions in français 845 have not gone unnoticed, but they have not however been used to reassess the *motet enté*. In his editions of this music in *The Earliest Motets*, Tischler was not only aware of them, but used them instead to interfere editorially with some textual problems.[20]

The repetition that can be witnessed in *Or ai je trop demoré* then represents a rather special approach to melodic construction. It stands apart from more common melodic practices in the motet, and for that matter in other species of discantus: clausula and *cauda* (in conductus) and also in organum triplum and quadruplum. Once we have observed that the penultimate line of text is set to the same music as the first line of the refrain, we are then alerted to other more thoroughgoing series of melodic repetitions in this piece. These are indicated in Example 4.2.2. The music to text-lines 4 and 10 is more or less identical; the only exception is a single ornamental note in the cadence. In addition, one could argue that the music to text-line 8 represents an 'open' form, transposed, of the more closed lines 4 and 10. One might also give serious thought to considering the music to text-lines 5 and 9 in a similar fashion. Much is the same except that line 5 is longer than line 9, and the music is correspondingly elongated.

Such a process of internal musical repetition is one of the most striking features of the fifteen works appended to français 845. It is present in *Or ai je trop demoré* which we have just been examining, but it is also present, to a greater or lesser extent, in ten out the fifteen works in this repertory. Four out of the five that do not exhibit

---

[19] In editing this composition, standard practice is followed in treating the unmeasured notation as it is found in the primary sources. It is therefore transcribed in unstemmed black noteheads. Tischler, however, has treated the pieces as if they were subject to principles of modal rhythm (*Earliest Motets*, 2: 1550). It should not be forgotten that these rhythmic versions are conjectural and therefore contentious.

[20] *Ibid.*, 2: 1546–56.

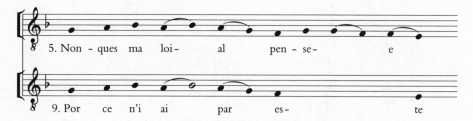

Example 4.2.2 Extract from (1083) *Or ai je trop demoré*; F-Pn fr. 845, fol. 190r

this characteristic are the works discussed and graphed in Figure 4.1: those pieces that employ a refrain found in other sources, and that divide it neatly into two halves and place it at the beginning and end of the composition. The one remaining piece is (1091) *Biaus dieus* where the textual disturbance is too great to make any incontrovertible judgement.

A discussion of one further work from this repertory will investigate the nature of such repetition in slightly more detail. The piece is *Hé Dieus, tant doucement,* and Example 4.3 presents a paradigmatic analysis of the composition based on a new unmeasured edition. The organisation of this analysis follows that of the one in the previous chapter. The primary criteria for segmenting the work are the divisions into line-length and musical phrase. It may be seen how lines 11 and 12 articulate smaller units. Initially, paradigms B and C offer full repetitions (lines 10 and 5 respectively) after which the repetitions dissolve into fragments. Line 13 is here described as two units under paradigm B.[21] Similarly paradigm C breaks down after the initial repetition of line 5 with a fragment that equals the whole of line 9. That same fragment reappears at the beginning of line 11. Its continuation is quite new, and therefore stands well to the right of the graph. The immediate continuity is indicated with a slur. Again the same fragment occurs at the end of line 12. It functions as the inverse of line 11 because its beginning is new and again lies to the right of the graph.

Much of this piece does not form part of a pattern of repetitions. Lines 6–8 lie outside the scheme as outlined in Example 4.3, but would fall inside a structure based on a more systematic analysis of the subunits of lines. Nevertheless, the analysis, as it stands here, does demonstrate a substantial degree of melodic repetition much in line with the rest of the repertory of *motets entés* in français 845. Again, it needs to

---

21 A stricter distributional analysis might make the interpretation of paradigm B more complex. It would not however change the reading of the melody offered here.

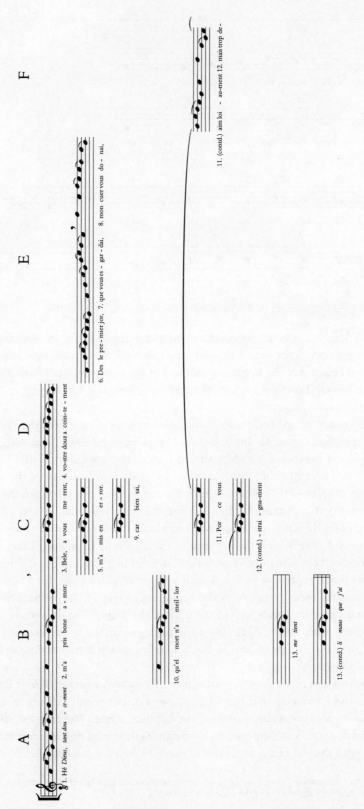

Example 4.3 Paradigmatic analysis of (1080) *Hé Dieus, tant doucement; F-Pn* fr. 845, fol. 184v

be stressed that this piece and the one previously examined behave in a radically different fashion to the major part of the thirteenth-century motet repertory.

This specific musical characteristic – complex patterns of internal repetition – is found in ten out of fifteen compositions in the manuscript français 845. We may wonder if, when the scribe of français 845 labelled these pieces *motets entés*, he was pointing out this specifically musical characteristic of 'grafting' the same musical units on to the rest of the text. There is a difference between these pieces exhibiting characteristics of melodic repetition and those that simply borrow a refrain, divide it into two and place it at beginning and end of a voice-part. While the latter is found more commonly in the motet repertory at large, the former is unique to the collection of pieces we have just been examining. Furthermore, twice as many pieces in this group employ the sort of melodic repetition which we have observed than behave as a *motet enté* in the sense that Ludwig understood it. It will not be out of place to restate the fact that, first, all the *motets entés* in français 845 are mono-phonic, and, second, they are preserved in a notation markedly different to that found in such contemporary motet books as Montpellier, Bamberg or even W_2.[22] There is the very strong possibility that early twentieth-century scholarship developed the wrong element in this collection to support the designation *motet enté*. Reasons for suggesting this are clear: that this group of works functions on a self-referential basis in terms of their melodic organisation. There is one further piece of evidence that reinforces this view of these pieces as self-referential. That is the high degree of intertextual reference in the poems themselves, and this may be seen from the incipits of the poems given on Table 4.1.

When we distance ourselves from the *motets entés* in français 845 and return to the mainstream motet repertory, we find that there are very good grounds for suggesting that we stop calling pieces *motets entés* that simply divide a refrain into two and place it at the beginning and end of a voice-part. We could then suggest that this music should be considered alongside all the other motets that employ such a variety of refrain usages. It is just this variety that will be stressed in Chapter 8 by abandoning the term '*motet enté*', but continuing to work with a compositional premiss that includes such a division of a refrain.

At the beginning of this discussion of the *motet enté*, we considered two sorts of motet: one that simply used a refrain anywhere in a voice-part, and one that divided a refrain into two. One experiences some difficulty in finding straightforward examples of the latter that are not confused with other processes. In other words, when the repertory is considered as a whole, the range and variety of procedures is much greater than using the term '*motet enté*' suggests.

---

[22]   The differences between notational styles found in français 845 and W_2 lie in their interpretation. Both are superficially 'unmeasured' (in that the graphic shapes give no clues to rhythm), but while W_2's 'unmeasured' notation masks a strictly 'measured' rhythmic style – unequivocal because of the unambiguous notation of their clausula models – the notation of français 845 is highly equivocal and may very well reflect an unmeasured style of delivery, as previous remarks above have suggested.

5

Rondeau–motet

Introduction and repertory

The rondeau-motet is a familiar landmark in the history of thirteenth-century polyphony.[1] It is one of the few subgenres that has been proposed for the motet, and therefore commands our attention. In this type of motet, one of the upper voices is written as a six- or eight-line rondeau. As in the monophonic rondeau, both types use a refrain which appears at the beginning and end, and partially in the middle, of the eight-line rondeau-motet. In the six-line version, there is no occurrence of the refrain at the beginning of the piece. Beyond these general observations, many of the dozen or so rondeau-motets behave rather differently. Of these works, listed in Table 5.1, a small number will be seen to share similar characteristics. They are also found in the same manuscripts, and may be tentatively classified as a subgenre.[2] The remainder have only general features in common.

Distinctions between the first eight items and the remaining works in Table 5.1 are fundamental to any enquiry into this subject. All the first group survive in the Noailles chansonnier and in the index to Roi. The second group are all found in Montpellier with concordances in manuscripts related to it geographically, chrono-logically and in terms of repertory and distribution. It is unfortunate that, in recent discussions of the vernacular motet, this distinction was lost and that all the compo-sitions in Table 5.1 have subsequently been grouped together as rondeau-motets.[3]

---

[1] Friedrich Gennrich made the first attempt to collect together all rondeau-motets (*Rondeaux, Virelais und Balladen*). See also his 'Trouvèrelieder und Motettenrepertoire', *Zeitschrift für Musikwissenschaft* 9 (1926) 10–11. Thirty-one years later, in his *Bibliographie* of 1957, he listed twelve compositions whose upper voices were in the form of a rondeau (*Bibliographie*, 2, 18, 27, 44 and *passim*). His terminology now seems inconsistent; the use of such terms as *rondel, rondeau, Rondeau-motette* and such expressions as *Mot[etus] ist ein Rondeau* or *Rondeau von Adam de la Halle* seems to point to indecision concerning subgenre.

[2] Gennrich was systematic, however, in the use of the term *Rondeau-motette* to apply exclusively to these two-part compositions copied in the two chansonniers Noailles and Roi.

[3] Gordon A. Anderson, 'A Unique Notre-Dame Motet Tenor Relationship', *Music and Letters* 55 (1974) 398–409; Tischler, *Style and Evolution of the Earliest Motets*, 1: 79–80.

Table 5.1 Distribution of rondeau-motets

No.	Incipit	Manuscript sources	
		fr. 12615	*fr. 844*
(1)	*(824) Mes cuers est emprisonés – Et pro suo (O9a)*	22. fol. 184r	[12. fol. 198v]
(2)	*(161) Ja n'avrez deduit – In seculum (M13)*	23. fol. 184r	[13. fol. 198v]
(3)	*(502) J'ai mon cuer – Letabitur (M49)*	24. fol. 184r–v	[14. fol. 198v]
(4)	*(503) Ja n'iert nus bien – Justus (M49)*	25. fol. 184v	[15. fol. 198v]
(5)	*(504) Bien doit joie – In Domino (M49)*	26. fol. 184v	[16. fol. 198v]
(6)	*(482) C'est la jus par desous* *– Quia concupivit rex (M37)*	61. fol. 191r–v	—
(7)	*(1035) Aimi, aimi, aimmi – [U.I.]*	68. fol. 192r	—
(8)	*(403) C'est la jus en la roi – Pro patribus (M30)*	82. fol. 195r	—
		H 196	*n. a. f. 13521*
(9)	*(188) J'ai les biens d'amours* *– (189) Que ferai, biau sire Dieus?* *– In seculum (M13)*	129. fols. 189v–90r	42. fol. 386v
(10)	*(467) Li jalous par tout sunt fustat* *– (468) Tuit cil qui sunt enamourat* *– Veritatem (M37)*	157. fols. 218v–19r	—
(11)	*(19) Ci mi tient li maus d'amer* *– (20) Haro! Je n'i puis durer – Omnes (M1)*	150. fols. 212v–13r	—
			Lit. 115
(12)	*(297) Mout me fu grief* *– (298) Robin m'aime – Portare (M22)*	248. fols. 292r–3v	81. fol. 52v
			Plut. 29.1
(13)	*(754) Ne m'oubliés mie – In Domino* *(BD I)*	220. fols. 261v–2r	clausula fol. 88v

Noailles rondeau-motets

The idiosyncratic nature of the works in the Noailles manuscript was recognised by Gennrich in 1921 when he observed that not only were the upper voice-parts in the form of a rondeau but that the tenors were similarly constructed. His primary concern was to use this information for the accurate reconstruction of polyphony in which the tenors had suffered severe textual disturbance. The scribal confusion which created such inaccuracy was a result of the fact that the tenors, all derived from plainsong, were not only subject to structural modification to conform to the pattern of the upper parts but were also notated in the same musical and textual shorthand as the motetus parts. In notating the eight-line rondeau-motet, the scribe mostly attempted to write out lines 1–6 and then to provide an incipit for the terminal refrain. Without a text to serve as a guide, he was faced with insurmountable problems when he came to the tenor. The upper parts of the two six-line rondeau-motets (Table 5.1, nos. 6 and 8) are written out in full, as is the scribe's first attempt at an eight-line rondeau (no. 1). No. 2 is exceptional and is discussed below. Nos. 3, 4 and 5 establish the basic pattern of abbreviating the final refrain. The further abbreviation of lines 3–4 of no. 5 is a direct result of the close association of its text with those of the two preceding poems. The monody, no. 7, is fully notated. The only tenor part written out in full is that for no. 2. The remainder either provide notation for the first two lines (the refrain of the upper voice) or are an attempt to write a longer tenor, the results of which are corrupt. The tenors of the two six-line rondeau-motets presented a similar challenge which the scribe failed to overcome. Understanding this paleographical model is a crucial first step in identifying the musico-poetic structures at work in these pieces. This is not only a question of drawing a distinction between six- and eight-line rondeaux, but also of acknowledging the possibility of the existence of other types of *rondet de carole* in this repertory.

The tenor structure of the rondeau-motet is determined by that of the upper parts. This is almost unique in the field of thirteenth-century chant-derived polyphony. In general, the structure of the tenor is usually independent of the structure of the motetus and triplum. In structuring the tenor of the rondeau-motet, as in the case of any motet, the composer was required to supply a contrapuntal voice-part derived from plainsong. Because of the brevity of the pieces, a Gregorian melisma of between eight and twenty pitches was needed. In Table 5.1, nos. 1, 3, 4, 5 and 6 all use a short melisma unique in the motet repertory, whereas nos. 2 and 8 use fragments of much longer ones: *In seculum* and *Pro patribus*, well known and widely distributed.

To judge from Gennrich and Tischler, there would appear to be two types of structure used in the upper voice-parts of these compositions: the six-line and the eight-line rondeau. In the former case Anderson suggested that the 'original' form of the eight-line rondeau-motet should be reconstructed by expanding six-line structures, placing the refrain not just at the end of the lyric but also at the beginning. This accorded with the observations made by Marcel Françon five years earlier.[4]

Anderson and Françon shared the concept of a 'regular' rondeau structure in the thirteenth century from which all other presentations are deviations. Françon worked to this from his view of the fifteenth-century rondeau,[5] and Anderson's point of departure was the tradition of coaxing thirteenth-century song into *formes fixes* which had begun with Gennrich.[6] A better perspective of these rondeau-motets is

---

4   'Sur la structure du rondeau', *Romance Notes* 10 (1968–9) 147–9. Françon assumes, for example, that a six-line rondeau is not a 'precursor' of the eight-line type but simply the result of scribal inaccuracy.

5   See Françon, *Leçons et notes sur la littérature française au xvi siècle*, 3rd edn with additional notes (Cambridge, Mass.: Harvard University Press, 1965) 26–7.

6   The standard critique of Gennrich's theories as expressed in his *Rondeaux, Virelais und Balladen* is Willi Apel, 'Rondeaux, Virelais, and Ballades in French 13th-Century Song', *Journal of the American Musicological Society* 7 (1954) 121–30. For a view of Gennrich's standardisation of the refrain forms in a single narrative poem see Pierre Le Gentil, 'A propos de Guillaume de Dole', *Mélanges de linguistique romane et de philologie médiévale offerts à M. Maurice Delbouille*, 2 vols, ed. Madeleine Tyssens (Gembloux: Editions J. Duclout, 1964) 2: 389–97.

obtained by viewing them within the context of the thirteenth-century tradition of the rondet de carole.[7] This, as is well known, first appeared as a written tradition in Jean Renart's *Roman de Guillaume de Dole*. It survived largely unchallenged at least up to the works of Adam de la Halle, Guillaume d'Amiens and Jean Acart d'Hesdin.[8] The corpus of rondets de carole encompasses a vast range of lyric and musico-poetic types. The six- and eight-line rondeaux are two of the most common. In the context of this more fluid repertory, a six-line rondeau or rondeau-motet requires no alteration.

There is paleographical support for this view from the scribe of Noailles. He differentiated between six- and eight-line rondeaux. The eight-line rondeau-motets on fol. 184r–v of this manuscript were subjected to greater and greater consistent abbreviation. The two six-line rondeau-motets, however, are characterised by the fact that both upper voices are written out in full and both tenors are corrupt.[9] The textual disturbance in the tenors of both begins at the same place: between the end of the first phrase and the beginning of the second. The structure of the six-line rondeau-motet requires the first phrase to be repeated twice before proceeding to the second musical element. The scribe failed to fulfil this task. In the case of no. 6, he created an ABAB' structure which is obviously an attempt to imitate the beginning of the tenor pattern of an eight-line rondeau but, for no. 8, he simply notated the A and B sections and then organised the now-redundant remainder of the melisma in a similar fashion.[10]

In a footnote to his remarks concerning the 'reconstruction' of eight-line rondeau-motets, Anderson suggested that no. 2 in Table 5.1 should 'not be "restored to full form" without further manuscript evidence'.[11] Ever since Gennrich first published this piece, it has been assumed that it is an abbreviated copy of an eight-line rondeau-motet and has usually been reconstructed with two untexted editorial insertions before the final refrain. Anderson's caution went unheeded.[12] But this is one of only two pieces in Table 5.1 (the other is the monody) which are notated without abbreviation. As it stands in the manuscript, its structure is ABaAB and the piece in this form makes no less musical and textual sense than does its 'reconstructed' eight-line version. There are no surviving thirteenth-century rondets de carole, monophonic or polyphonic, which exactly mirror this scheme. There are however two rondets de carole in Henri d'Andeli's *Le Lai d'Aristote* with the structure AabAB. They are similar to the notated version of no. 2 but slightly more regular.[13] The differences found in the five manuscript versions of the *Lai d'Aristote* are all variations on the same type of rondet de carole: a text enclosed by a refrain line at the beginning and a full statement of the refrain at the end. Furthermore, there exists at least one example of a rondet de carole[14] which, as in this rondeau-motet,

---

7 Bec, *Lyrique française*, 1: 220–8.
8 The texts of all surviving thirteenth- and early fourteenth-century rondets de carole are edited in van den Boogaard, *Rondeaux et refrains*, 27–92.
9 See above, 91–2.
10 Noted in Tischler, *Earliest Motets*, 3: 218.
11 Anderson, 'Motet Tenor Relationship', 407 note 45.
12 Gennrich, *Rondeaux, Virelais und Balladen*, 1: 16–17; Tischler, *Earliest Motets*, 2: 1464.
13 Van den Boogaard, *Rondeaux et refrains*, 32–3.
14 *Nus ne set qu'est douce dolors* (ibid., 39).

uses a complete refrain at the beginning and end, although with four narrative lines separating them. Anderson was partially correct in this instance that the notated form of (161) *Ja n'avrez deduit* – *In seculum* (M13) might not need any 'reconstruction'.

Rondeau-motet cycle

The three pieces which follow *Ja n'avrez deduit* in Noailles (nos. 3–5 in Table 5.1) share similar specific characteristics. Choice of tenor melisma, musico-poetic structure, text, compositional procedure, and distribution are all analogous. These three rondeau-motets constitute a cycle. The tenor melismas on which these motets are based are all taken from the same liturgical item: the verse of *Alleluya. Letabitur iustus in Domino* for the Common of Martyrs.[15] The relevant part of the alleluya verse is given as Example 5.1. Since it is impossible as yet to identify the precise source from which the plainsong was derived, it is given in several versions – from (5.1.1) the modern Vatican gradual,[16] (5.1.2) a twelfth-century gradual from the Auvergne,[17] (5.1.3) a thirteenth-century Parisian missal[18] and (5.1.4) a thirteenth-century Parisian missal and gradual combined.[19] The tenors of the motets are given as Example 5.1.5. The three tenor melismas are not only taken from the same liturgical composition, they also follow each other in order and without a break. Taken together, then, the motets can be viewed as a cyclic polyphonic setting of the first three melismas of the alleluya verse. Figure 5.1 shows the correlation between the plainsong (given in the version shown as Example 5.1.3) and the texts of the three rondeau-motets.[20]

Each of the three plainsong melismas has to be of approximately the same length if all the corresponding upper parts are to be eight-line rondeaux, and this is exactly the result achieved by the composer. As can be seen from Example 5.1, the three tenor melismas consist of nine, twelve and fourteen pitches which are organised into *ordines* of nine, eight and ten perfections. All the relevant sections of the plainsong are used. The poems used for upper voices are similar not only in structure but also in much of their content.[21] While the refrain in each poem is different, the remaining

15 Rokseth, *Polyphonies du treizième siècle*, 4: 181 observes that 'ce n'est certainement pas hasard si ces trois motets, fondés sur trois melismes successifs du verset "Letabitur", sont placés dans [Noailles] à la suite l'un de l'autre'.

16 *Graduale sacrosanctae romanae ecclesiae de tempore et de sanctis primum sancti Pii X iussu restitutum et editum Pauli VI pontificis maximi cura nunc recognitum ad exemplar 'Ordinis cantus missae' dispositum et rhythmicis signis a Solesmensibus monachis diligenter ornatum* (Solesmes: Abbaye Saint-Pierre; Tournai: Desclée, 1979) 479.

17 Brussels, Bibliothèque royale Albert 1er, MS II 3823, fol. 10r. See Karlheinz Schlager, ed., *Alleluya-Melodien I bis 1100*, Monumenta monodica medii aevi 7 (Kassel etc.: Barenreiter, 1968) 277–8. The tenth-century date, advanced in *Catalogue de la bibliothèque de F. J. Fétis acquise par l'état Belge* (Paris: Firmin Didot; Brussels: C. Muquardt, 1877) 135, is misleading. See John A. Emerson, 'Sources, MS, II, 5: Western Plainchant, 12th Century', *The New Grove Dictionary of Music and Musicians*, 20 vols, ed. Stanley Sadie (London: Macmillan, 1980) 17: 621.

18 Paris, Bibliothèque Nationale, fonds latin 9441, fol. 192v; see Victor Leroquais, *Les Sacramentaires et les missels manuscrits des bibliothèques publiques de France*, 4 vols. (Paris: n.p., 1924) 2: 114.

19 London, British Library, Add. 38723, fols. 159v–60r.

20 The three texts are edited in Raynaud, *Recueil de motets*, 2: 75–6. See also Ludwig, *Repertorium*, 1/1: 290, where the pieces are summarily dismissed as 'textlich gleich oder ähnlich'.

21 Noted by Tischler (*Style and Evolution of the Earliest Motets*, 4: unpaginated commentary to nos. 283–5).

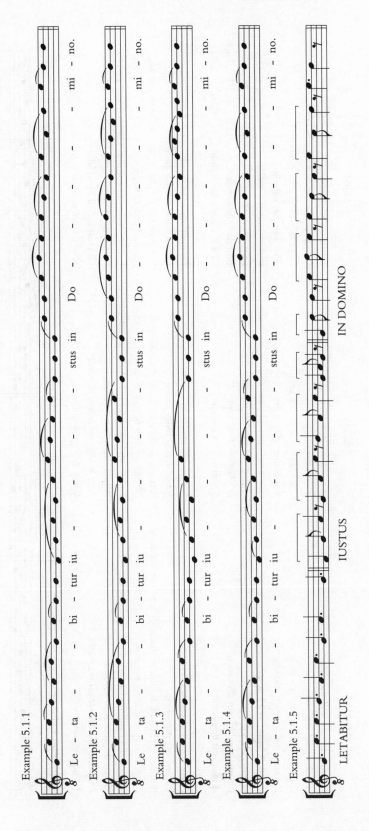

Example 5.1 Four versions of *Letabitur iustus in Domino* melisma and derivative tenor segments

Figure 5.1 Correspondence between tenor chant and motetus texts in (502) *J'ai mon cuer*, (503) *Ja n'iert nus bien* and (504) *Bien doit joie*

M502

J'ai mon cuer del tout abandouné
A vous, ma douce amie;
C'est la jus c'on dist ens mi le pré,
J'ai mon cuer del tou[t] abandouné.
Gieus et baus i avoit assamblé,
Quant rose est espanie.
J'ai mon cuer del tout abandouné
A vous, ma douce amie.

I have entirely abandoned my heart
To you, my sweet love;
It is down there, it is said, in the middle of the meadow,
I have entirely abandoned my heart.
Games and pastimes had been arranged there,
When the rose is in bloom.
I have entirely abandoned my heart
To you, my sweet love.

M503

Ja n'iert nus bien assenés,
S'amours ne li font aïe;
C'est la jus ens mi les prés;
Ja n'iert nus bien assenés.
Gieus et baus i a levés
Quant [la] rose est espanie:
Ja n'iert nus bien assenés,
S'amours ne li font aïe.

No one will ever be well advised,
If love does not help him;
It is down there amongst the meadows;
No one will ever be well advised.
Games and pastimes have been set up there
When the rose is in bloom:
No one will ever be well advised,
If love does not help him.

M504

Bien doit joie demener
Chi[l] ki a son voloir a amie:
C'est la jus [qu'on dist en pré];
Bien doit [joie demener].
Jeus et baus [i a levé],
J'aim bien, et s'est ma joie faillie.
Bien doit joie demener
Chil ki a son voloir a amie

He must indeed be joyful
Who has a love to his liking:
It is down there, [they say, in the meadow];
He must [indeed be joyful].
Games and pastimes [have been set up there],
I am indeed in love, yet I am bereft of joy.
He must indeed be joyful
Who has a love to his liking.

Le - ta - bi - tur iu - stus in Do - mi - no

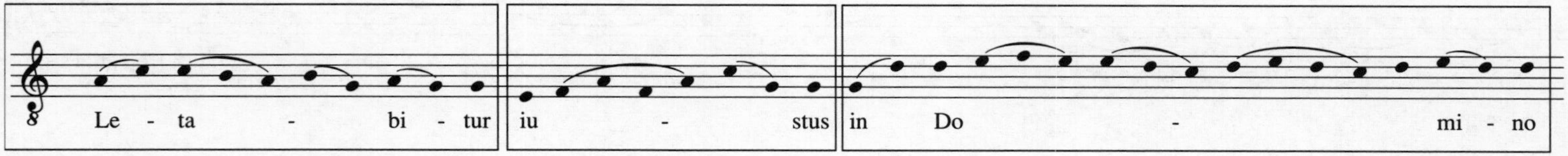

lines – what Johannes de Grocheio would have described as the 'additamenta'[22] – are strikingly similar in all three poems. Apart from line 6 of the third poem, the very slight changes in the non-refrain lines are a result of the structure of the refrain, which determines the musico-poetic structure of the rest of the poem. The refrain in the first poem consists of nine- and six-syllable lines, in the second of seven-syllable lines and in the third of seven- and nine-syllable lines. This is the reason for the difference between *assamblé* and a pluperfect in the first poem and *levés* and a perfect in the second. The erratic sequence of tenses here is quite typical of much French lyric poetry of the period. By the time the scribe reached the third poem, he gave up writing the same line for a second time and simply gave incipits as indicated by the editorial expansions in square brackets.[23] Since the music for each of the refrains is different, identical or near–identical, non-refrain lines in the three poems receive different musical treatments. There is a curious contradiction here between the mobility of the lyric refrain among the three poems and the stasis of the narrative *additamenta*. The fact that the narrative elements are similar suggests a community of thought and intention between the three poems. This is irrespective of, but congruent with, the relationship between the tenors of the three motets.

Type-cadre

The three texts that constitute this cycle of rondeau-motets are not simply closely related to each other. They are three poems representative of what Paul Zumthor has termed a *type-cadre*[24] which, in total, comprises the twenty-four texts listed in Table 5.2.

Furthermore, two other motets in Table 5.1 – nos. 6 and 8 – participate in this *type-cadre* even though they play no part in the cyclic organisation of items 3–5. Of the first eight compositions in Table 5.1, then, five share the characteristics of this *type-cadre*.

A *type-cadre* is derived from the segmentation of a repertory of poems according to their shared vocabulary, content and rhetorical technique. For Zumthor, the predominant *type-cadre* is that of the *rencontre*, familiar from *pastourelle* poetry.[25] Two lesser *type-cadres* are those of *Bele Aeliz* and *C'est la jus*.[26] The appearances of these

---

22 Johannes de Grocheio's description of the component parts of the *rondellus* (*responsorium* and *additamenta*) has received sufficient comment to make further discussion here redundant: see Ernst Rohloff, ed., *Der Musiktraktat des Johannes de Grocheio nach dem Quellen neu herausgegeben mit Übersetzung ins Deutsche und Revisionsbericht*, Media latinitas musica 2 (Leipzig: Komissionsverlag Gebruder Reinecke, 1943) 50–1, and Rohloff, ed., *Die Quellenhandschriften zum Musiktraktat des Johannes de Grocheio im Faksimile herausgegeben nebst Übertragung des Textes und Übersetzung ins Deutsche, dazu Bericht, Literaturschau, Tabellen und Indices* (Leipzig: VEB Deutscher Verlag für Musik, [1972]) 74–5; Doss-Quinby, *Les Refrains chez les trouvères*, 63–5; Bec, *Lyrique française*, 1: 226. The reading 'addimenta', favoured by Bec, is supported by only one of the two sources for the treatise (Darmstadt, Hessische Landes- und Hochschulbibliothek, MS 2663, fol. 61r, and is suppressed in Rohloff's editions.

23 See Figure 5.1.

24 *Essai de poétique médiévale*, Collection Poétique (Paris: Editions de Seuil, 1972) 289–306.

25 *Ibid.*, 298–301.

26 *Ibid.*, 86–8. See also Maurice Delbouille, 'Sur les traces de Bele Aëlis', *Mélanges de philologie romane dédiés à la mémoire de Jean Boutière (1899–1967)* 2 vols, ed. Irénée Cluzel and François Pirot (Liège: Editions Soledi, 1971) 1: 200–18.

Table 5.2 *C'est la jus*: poems participating in the *type-cadre*

No.	First line	Reference to Boogaard, *Rondeaux et refrains*
(1)	*Ainsi doit entrer en ville*	47
(2)	*Bien doit joie demener*	161
(3)	*C'est la fins, koi que nus die*	93
(4)	*C'est la gieus, en mi les prez*	16
(5)	*C'est la gieus, la gieus, q'en dit*	15
(6)	*C'est la jus c'on dist au lai*	(ii.7★)
(7)	*C'est la jus c'on dit es prés*	44
(8)	*C'est la jus desouz l'olive*	17
(9)	*C'est la jus, desoz l'olive*	6
(10)	*C'est la jus en la praele*	10
(11)	*C'est la jus en la ramée*	111
(12)	*C'est la jus en la roi prée*	164
(13)	*C'est la jus, la jus desouz la coudroie*	165
(14)	*C'est la jus par desous l'olive*	162
(15)	*C'est tot la gieus, el glaioloi*	4
(16)	*C'est tot la gieus, en mi les prez*	5
(17)	*Diex, vez les ci, les douz braz*	180
(18)	*J'ai mon cuer del tout abandouné*	159
(19)	*Ja n'iert nus bien assenés*	160
(20)	*La jus, desouz l'olive*	11
(21)	*La jus, desoz la raime*	1
(22)	*Prendé si garde, s'on me regarde*	93
(23)	*Sor la rive de mer*	13
(24)	*Tout la gieus, sor rive mer*	14

last two configurations are restricted almost exclusively to the rondet de carole. The *type-cadre C'est la jus* generates two subspecies which could be labelled respectively 'well-spring' (as a translation of *fontaine*) and 'pastime'. Table 5.3 illustrates the basic formula of the *type-cadre*, with its two subspecies.[27]

At the simplest level, the first line of the two (which is common to nearly all the examples of the *type-cadre*), consists of an indicative element ('It is down there . . .') followed by an adverbial clause of place which gives rise to a large number of variations. Many of these are simply the result of the metrical exigencies of the poem in which they are found. For example, the first line of *C'est la jus par desous l'olive* (Table 5.2, no. 14) differs from the third line of *Ainsi doit entrer en ville* (Table 5.2, no. 1; the line in question reads: 'C'est la jus, desous l'olive') only by the addition of a single preposition. This is caused by the differences in line-length between octosyllables and lines of seven syllables, both with feminine end-rhymes. There is a tripartite distinction between *pré* (meadow), *olive* (olive-tree) and miscellaneous scenarios within the second element of this *type-cadre*. About half the poems use a

---

[27] Superscript numbers indicate the number of times that each of the formulations occurs.

Table 5.3 The *type-cadre* C'est la jus

		'Well-spring'			'Pastime'	
C'EST LA JUS[14]	EN MI LES PRES[5]	LA FONTAINNE[5]	Y SORT[6]	SERIE[6]	JEUS ET BAUS[5]	I A LEVES[3]
la gieus, la gieus[2]	q'en dit en ces prez[1]	fontenele[4]	sordoit[3]	clere[2]		sont criés[1]
tot la gieus[4]	desous l'olive[4]	Une fontaine[1]	couroit[1]	coie[1]	Un baut[1]	avoit assamblé[1]
La jus[2]	en la ramée[1]					ot levez[1]
Tot la jus[1]	q'en dist au lai praielle[1]					
	en la praele[1]					
	en la roi prée[1]				DAMES I ONT BAUS LEVEZ[2]	
	desouz la coudroie[1]				vont por caroler[1]	
	par desous l'olive[1]					
	c'om dist souz l'olive[1]				LA PASTOURELLE U GARDOIT VACHES[1]	
	c'on dist ens mi le pré[1]					
	desouz la raime[1]					
	en cel boschiage[1]					
	sor rive mer[1]					
	el glaioloi[1]					
	c'on dit es prés[1]					

formulation involving *pré*, while the other two groups are each used in a quarter of the texts. Of the two dozen poems in this *type-cadre* listed in Table 5.2, ten each fall into the two subspecies of 'well-spring' and 'pastime'. Four texts make a limited use only of the range of linguistic possibilities represented by these groupings.

In general, texts which use the formulation '*olive*' are followed by the subspecies 'well-spring', and those which employ the expression '*pré*' are followed by the 'pastime' subspecies. There are, however, sufficient examples of interference between these two pairs of elements not to regard '*olive*' and '*pré*' as parts of the same sub-species. The following upper-voice text from the motet listed in Table 5.1 as no. 8 is an example of such interference:

> C'est la jus en la roi prée,
> *Cele m'a s'amour dounée.*
> La fontenele i sort clere.
> Faus vilains traiés en la!
> *Cele m'a s'amour dounée*
> *Ki mon cuer et mon cors a.*
>
> It is over there in the steeply-sloping meadow,
> *She has given me her love.*
> The little well-spring runs clear there.
> False knaves, go away!
> *She has given me her love*
> *Who possesses my heart and soul.*

Other examples are not so clear. *C'est la jus, la jus desouz la coudroie* (Table 5.2, no. 13) might very well be considered among that group of '*pré*' texts. Its subsequent use of the 'well-spring' formulation would therefore represent a further interference. The two texts which use formulations involving *glaioloi* and *raime* pose a serious problem.[28] It might be argued that *Prendés i garde* only just qualifies for consideration here since the line which is supposed to take on the 'pastime' formulation is only very loosely related: '*La pastourelle u gardoit vaches*'.[29] In short, then, there are two pairs of variables within the *C'est la jus type-cadre*: '*pré*' – '*olive*' and 'well-spring' – 'pastime'. The two non-cyclic rondeau-motets which fall into this *type-cadre* occupy a rather different position to the three cyclic pieces. Comparison of these two groups of poems shows how the bonds between the texts of the three cyclic pieces are stronger than those between the five texts as a whole. There is a further distinction in terms of structure. The cyclic poems are eight-line rondeaux; the other two pieces are six-line rondeaux. The former all fall into the 'pastimes' subdivision; the latter are both examples of the 'well-spring' motif. The three cyclic poems consistently pair off 'pastime' with '*pré*': this consistency is absent from the other two texts, where, in one case, '*olive*' is followed by 'well-spring' (the normal sequence) and, in the other case, '*pré*' is

---

[28]   The problem concerns the botanical interpretation of 'a place where gladioli are grown' and 'under the branches'; an attempted correlation of either of these with the two groupings '*olive*' and '*pré*' yields inconclusive results.

[29]   An example of such interference, in this case between two different *type-cadres*, is discussed in Delbouille, 'Bele Aëlis', 212–13: *C'est la gieus, la gieus, qu'en dit en ces prez* (Table 5.2, no. 5).

followed by 'pastime'. This latter text has already been given as an example of this type of interference between successive lexical choices.[30] In other words, the three cyclic compositions behave in a tightly controlled fashion, and share a maximum number of characteristics. The other two pieces function within the *type-cadre* in exactly the same variable way that might distinguish any two of the remaining nineteen poems in the group.

It is an established fact that, within the *Bele Aeliz type-cadre*, rondets de carole are put together in cycles to create a multi-strophic *chanson à carole*. Both Delbouille and Bec suggest that the *C'est la jus type-cadre* also participates in this function but fail to offer any evidence beyond the circumstantial.[31] Indeed, there is no evidence that *C'est la jus* was ever put together in this way. However, the similarity of treatment between the two *type-cadres* is significant, and it comes as no surprise, therefore, that it is these types of texts that are used in the cycle of rondeau-motets (Table 5.1, nos. 3–5).

Refrains

The refrains of monophonic rondeaux and rondets de carole often appear in other contexts as parts of motets, chansons à refrain, chansons avec des refrains and verse narratives.[32] Either text only, or both text and notation, can function in this way. Of the eight rondeau-motets in the first part of Table 5.1, only one – the six-line motet (403) *C'est la jus en la roi – Pro patribus* (M30) – has a refrain which is used elsewhere. This raises the possibility of isolating some trends in compositional practice among this group of works. Moreover, the refrain used in this motet, '*Cele m'a s'amour donée / Qui mon cuer et mon cors a*',[33] is unusual in suggesting a good deal about the balance between borrowed and original material in the composition.

Example 5.2 gives the music for all known occurrences of the refrain. Example 5.2.1 is a paradigmatic analysis of the six lines of the motet (403) *C'est la jus*, all of which are set to variants of the music of the refrain. Only three, lines 2, 5 and 6, employ its text. All except one of the remaining untexted phrases are settings of the text shown at the head of the example. The exception is the appearance of the refrain in Florence (Example 5.2.7), where it occurs as part of a clausula melisma.

In the case of the refrain '*Cele m'a s'amour donée / Qui mon cuer et mon cors a*', the music to all appearances of the refrain is essentially identical. The clausula from Florence serves as a model for the two-part French motet (62) *En mai que neist – Domine* (M3). Near-identical text and music then found their way into three other

---

[30] Above, p. 100.

[31] Delbouille, 'Bele Aëlis', 202; Bec, *Lyrique française*, 1: 224.

[32] The most recent study of the refrain is Doss-Quinby, *Les Refrains chez les trouvères*. The bias of this study is towards the lyrics whilst the music of the refrains, especially in the motet and verse narrative, awaits similar treatment notwithstanding Maria V. Fowler, 'Musical Interpolations in Thirteenth- and Fourteenth-Century French Narratives', 2 vols (Ph.D. diss., Yale University, 1979); Maria V. Coldwell (*née* Fowler), '*Guillaume de Dole* and Medieval Romances with Musical Interpolations', *Musica disciplina* 35 (1981) 55–86; and Maureen B. McC. Boulton, 'Lyric Insertion in French Narrative Fiction in the Thirteenth and Fourteenth Centuries' (M.Litt. diss., University of Oxford, 1979).

[33] *Refrain* vdB 314.

Example 5.2 Versions of refrain 314

French motets, one of which was the rondeau-motet (403) *C'est la jus en la roi – Pro patribus* (M30). Concerning this group of pieces which share the same musico-textual fragment, Ludwig was in no doubt that they all sprang originally from the clausula.[34]

The text-critical differences between the various appearances of the 'refrain' are problematic. For example, there are significant differences in pitch, at the beginning of the passage, between the clausula and the motet ostensibly modelled on it. At the same place in the phrase, the rondeau-motet (lines 1–4 of Example 5.2) and the Noailles reading of the chanson (line 8) agree on a version which is different both from the clausula (line 10) and the motet derived from it (line 5). This particular agreement is understandable. The differences between clausula and derived motet cannot be explained so convincingly on contrapuntal grounds as pitch differences in motets based on different tenors.

In the context of the many variations in the different presentations of the same 'refrain', both in melodic structure and decoration, the internal inconsistencies in the upper voice of (403) *C'est la jus en la roi – Pro patribus* (M30) (visible in lines 1–4 of Example 5.2) recede into insignificance. Almost all the differences in the rondeau-motet are found, on at least one occasion, in the other examples given in Example 5.2. Whether this implies that the composer of (403) *C'est la jus en la roi – Pro patribus* (M30) was aware of the other versions, or whether the rondeau-motet was known to the composer, is a question whose answer depends on many unsupported assumptions concerning compositional method in the period. There are, however, two facts that are relatively certain. The music of the refrain used in the rondeau-motet (403) *C'est la jus en la roi – Pro patribus* (M30) originated in a Notre-Dame clausula, and the text of the same refrain was first composed to this music in the motet (62) *En mai que neist la rosée – Ne* (M3). The structure of both voice-parts in the rondeau-motets listed in the top part of Table 5.1 is borrowed. In all cases except (403) *C'est la jus en la roi – Pro patribus* (M30), it is impossible to say how much of the music of the upper parts is newly composed and how much is appropriated from other sources. The foregoing evidence allows the reconstruction of the composer's working methods in this piece alone. Previous general remarks are still valid except for those relating to the question of the choice of tenor melisma. In this case, the pitches of the upper part are already determined. Simply choosing a melisma or melisma-segment of the right length would not have been sufficient here since the selection of the melody to serve as the tenor had to agree contrapuntally with the pre-existing upper voice. The composition of this particular piece is therefore rather the process of fitting two types of borrowed material together. It is the non-refrain lines of text which are actually newly composed, and this, coupled with the skill of matching disparate types of borrowed material, represents one of the principal points of interest in the work. It is certainly fortunate that the only rondeau-motet whose refrain survives in more than one source yields so much information on this subject.

[34] Ludwig, 'Die geistliche nichtliturgische und weltliche einstimmige und die mehrstimmige Musik des Mittelalters, 205–7. Ludwig also includes (*ibid.*, 206) a table indicating the various appearances of refrain no. 314 in each contrapuntal context. However, he ignores the textual variants of the upper voice of (403) *C'est la jus en la roi – Pro patribus* (M30). His table and Example 5.2 of the present study are therefore complementary. See also Gennrich, *Rondeaux, Virelais und Balladen*, 2: 26–8.

On the other hand, its idiosyncratic nature makes it very difficult to suggest how general this compositional process was. In other words, is it possible to make any statement about the balance of borrowed and original material in the remaining rondeau-motets in the first part of Table 5.1? Any of the remaining rondeau-motets of this kind may well have functioned in the same way. They may also have had refrains which originated in secular songs, subsequently lost, or the refrains may have been newly composed as part of the motet. The absence of any concordances could, in this case, be explained either by the fact that the refrain became detached from its context, or by the loss of evidence indicating further use.

In summary, the motets in the first part of Table 5.1 are broadly similar in style. Their upper parts are in the shape of a rondeau or a rondet de carole, and their tenors mirror this structure. There is a logic in the choice of the tenor chant, and their upper-voice texts are all typical of the type of dance-song on which they are modelled. Five of these texts borrow elements of the same *type-cadre* and three of those are even more closely related: they form a cycle. The distribution of the compositions is also of significance. The first five pieces succeed each other in Noailles, and the index of Roi suggests that they were preserved there in a similar fashion. The remaining three pieces are unica in Noailles. The distribution of all eight pieces is therefore restricted to two manuscripts which have long been acknowledged to be closely related. Such a restricted distribution might imply that the origin of the compositions and that of the manuscripts might be the same. This, however, is an assumption that relies on the absence of concordances in unrelated manuscripts with different origins. In this case, however, to ignore such a relationship between concordance-base and manuscript origin would be to deny the compositions their probable origin.

Distribution and technique

On the basis of an examination of script, decoration, contents, heraldry and phonology, there is compelling evidence that Noailles was copied in Artois, and perhaps even in Arras, and that Roi dates from between 1253 and 1277.[35] In general, the two manuscripts are of the type that preserves lyric and narrative vernacular verse and originated in the north-eastern counties of modern France. Given that the distribution of these compositions is restricted to these manuscripts, there seems to be a good case for considering Artois as the place of origin of the rondeau-motets. Further weight is given to this argument by the stylistic division that separates these 'Artesian' rondeau-motets from putative examples in the other sources listed in the second part of Table 5.1 and discussed below.[36] Whether the dates of the manuscripts likewise suggest a date of composition in the third quarter of the century is a difficult question; this date, however, is only shortly before the dates currently accepted for the sources of the remaining motets in Table 5.1.[37]

---

[35]   For a discussion of provenance and date in these two manuscripts as well as the relationship between them, see Everist, *Polyphonic Music*, 176–86 and the references cited there.

[36]   Pp. 105–8.   [37]   See above, pp. 11–12.

The first eight pieces in Table 5.1 are a repertory limited both by style and by distribution. We might then consider only these compositions as rondeau-motets. Other works which have been labelled *rondel*, rondeau, etc. (nos. 9–13 in Table 5.1) are characterised by very different distributions, styles and compositional aspirations. Each of the latter either meets the challenge of combining a rondeau upper voice with a tenor in a radically different manner to that of the Artesian repertory, or does not face up to that compositional problem at all. Since there are so few similarities between the compositions in the second half of Table 5.1, they will be discussed one at a time.

(188) *J'ai les biens d'amours* – (189) *Que ferai, biau sire Dieus?* – *In seculum* (M13) [Table 5.1, no. 9].

Of all the pieces in the second part of Table 5.1, this motet is the clearest example of the use of a rondeau in the motetus. The poem is of six lines and fully regular.[38] There are problems with the interpretation of the melody both in the versions in Montpellier and La Clayette manuscripts. Comparative examination of both versions suggests that both are corrupt redactions of what, musically speaking, was originally a perfect six-line rondeau.[39] The tenor of this composition consists of a single *cursus* of the *In seculum* melisma and not, as was the case with the Artesian pieces discussed above, a piece of plainsong adapted to the structure of the rondeau.[40] The compositional challenge in this piece was therefore to match a repetitious upper-voice rondeau structure with a plainsong melisma which possessed no internal pattern of repetition. One of the characteristics of the *In seculum* melisma is its concentration on the pitches *a* and *c*. The pitches of the rondeau-structured motetus, *c*, *g*, *e* and *f* predominantly, call for counterpoint based around C8–5, A8–5 and F6–3 sonorities. A careful rhythmic organisation of the pitches *a* and *c* to coincide with these sonorities creates a satisfactory contrapuntal line. It also results in a tenor with an irregular rhythmic structure. The phrases do not match the *ordines* of the first rhythmic mode found in the motetus.[41]

---

[38] Ludwig, *Repertorium*, 1/2: 373 notes that '*der Mot[etus] ist rondeauartig gebaut*'.

[39] Anderson ('Motet Tenor Relationship', 407 note 51) is not, therefore, entirely accurate when he claims that La Clayette offers 'an earlier and better reading'. It is difficult to justify the labelling of the piece as a 'Rondeau motet enté' in Richard Hoppin, ed., *Anthology of Medieval Music*, Norton Introduction to Music History (New York: W. W. Norton; Toronto: R. J. Mcloed, 1978) 116–17.

[40] Ludwig's usual term to describe an unpatterned tenor – '*unregelmässig*' – describes this voice-part (*Repertorium*, 1/2: 373). Hofmann (*Untersuchungen zur Kompositionstechnik der Motette im 13. Jahrhundert*, 46 note 75) assumes that it is only the refrain which determines the 'unruly' nature of the tenor, but gives insufficient weight to the overall structure of the motetus; he then confuses the issue (*ibid.*, 49) by considering the triplum as a refrain cento, an assertion which is by no means proved (see below, pp. 113–14).

[41] Rokseth, *Polyphonies du treizième siècle*, 4: 274; Gennrich, *Florilegium motetorum: ein Querschnitt durch das Motettenschaffen des 13. Jahrhunderts*, Summa musicae medii aevi 17 (Langen bei Frankfurt: n.p., 1966) 172.

(467) *Li jalous par tout sunt fustat* – (468) *Tuit cil qui sunt enamourat* – *Veritatem* (M37) [Table 5.1, no. 10].

This composition was originally recognised as a work which 'appartient à la *langue d'oc*, bien que le copiste l'ait un peu françisé'[42] by Paul Meyer. He went on to suggest an alternative interpretation of the piece: 'le motet en question a pu être composé par un homme du Nord à l'imitation des motets méridionaux'.[43]

For Meyer, the motetus was, as Gennrich later proposed, a rondeau.[44] Although there have never been any claims for southern provenance for compositions preserved in central motet sources, Meyer was claiming an artificial use of some aspects of Provençal syntax and orthography by a northerner. István Frank,[45] supported by Terence Newcombe,[46] more accurately described the text of *Tuit cil qui sunt enamourat* as a Franco-Occitanian imitation of a Provençal *ballada* which, in terms of its textual structure, he regarded as the same as the French rondeau. Frank's analysis of the musico-poetic relationships in this voice-part showed that the musical structure was a *schéma libre*. He also tried to show how the reverse was the case of the triplum (i.e., that the text was a *schéma libre*, with rhymes in a rondeau pattern, but the melody was that of the rondeau). There are other possible interpretations of this 'pastiche littéraire'. Its fundamental nature and purpose are still slightly obscure. Nevertheless, such a parody of Provençal music and verse structures is well outside the orbit of the Artesian rondeau-motet. The double *cursus* of the tenor (which, in combination with the repeating pattern of the upper voices, results, in at least one place – perfections 25–6 – in a control of dissonance inconsistent with the rest of the motet) also sets it apart from that group of compositions.[47] The composition is unique, and, although the piece contains stylistic elements of the Artesian rondeau-motet, it can hardly be classed as a member of the same genre.

(19) *Ci mi tient li maus d'amer* – (20) *Haro! Je n'i puis durer* – *Omnes* (M1) [Table 5.1, no. 11].

The issues raised by this motet are of a different nature. The principal area of doubt concerns the musico-poetic structure of the motetus. Ludwig had suggested that the motetus was 'balletenartig gebaut'. Gennrich's suggestion of a virelai structure involved positing repeats in the music which do not exist.[48] This view was accepted without comment by Rokseth in 1939.[49] By 1957, Gennrich had revised his opinion and he now stated that the structure was that of a rondeau.[50] Twelve years later, Boogaard listed the voice as a *motet enté*.[51] The least defensible of these suggestions is Gennrich's

---

[42] 'Mélanges de littérature provençale 2: motets à trois parties', *Romania* 1 (1872) 404.
[43] *Ibid.*
[44] Meyer's view was supported by Ludwig (*Repertorium*, 1/2: 377–8).
[45] István Frank, '*Tuit cil qui sunt enamourat*: notes de philologie pour l'étude des origines lyriques 2', *Romania* 75 (1954) 101.
[46] Terence Newcombe, 'The Refrain in Troubadour Lyric Poetry', *Nottingham Medieval Studies* 19 (1975) 7.
[47] Tischler, *Montpellier Codex*, 2: 188.
[48] Ludwig, *Repertorium*, 1/2: 376; Gennrich, *Rondeaux, Virelais und Balladen*, 2: 40–1.
[49] Rokseth, *Polyphonies du treizième siècle*, 4: 277.
[50] *Bibliographie*, 2.
[51] *Rondeaux et refrains*, 140.

view of the piece as a virelai, a view which in any case had been effectively challenged by Apel in 1954.[52] There are many questions surrounding these musico-poetic structures,[53] but an examination of the text[54] and music shows that inter-pretations of the piece as a rondeau and as a *motet enté* both have a degree of validity. The presence of the same refrain[55] at the beginning and end of the text obviously suggests a rondeau. However, the repetition of the first element of the refrain in the middle of the poem is missing. Van den Boogaard, however, gives an example of just such an eight-line rondeau from the anonymous *salut d'amours* preserved in Paris, Bibliothèque Nationale, fonds français 837.[56] It is therefore perhaps inconsistent to label one a rondeau and another a *motet enté*. The interpretation of the piece as a *motet enté* of course poses problems. This work makes use of a complete refrain both at its beginning and end. Neither the metre nor the rhyme-scheme of either poem is particularly regular. Examples exist where parts of a refrain appear at the beginning of a text and then occur complete at the end. One is (796) *En mai, quant rosier florist* – (795) *J'ai trouvé qui m'amera* – *Fiat* (O50). In (565) *J'amaisse mais je n'os amer* – *Mansuetudinem* (M71), the complete refrain again appears at both ends of the motetus text. No case has been made, however, for viewing these pieces as rondeaux, and Boogaard's consideration of *Ci mi tient* as a *motet enté* gets closer to its compo-sitional strategy than Gennrich's view of the piece as a rondeau. One would still want to take issue with the term '*motet enté*'. Whatever conclusion is reached concerning genre in the motetus of *Ci mi tient*, the complexity of the relationship between the voices is not in doubt.

(297) *Mout me fu grief* – (298) *Robin m'aime* – *Portare* (M22) [Table 5.1, no. 12].

This motet, which includes the complete chanson *Robin m'aime* as its motetus, is the only example outside the Artesian repertory of a piece with a tenor structure that exactly mirrors that of its motetus. However, the upper voice here does not match the six- or eight-line patterns of the rondeau-motets in Table 5.1. The seven-line musico-poetic structure is ABaabAB. Neither does its metric and rhyme structure concur with the pattern of one or two line-lengths coupled with two rhymes that is typical both of the rondet de carole and of the rondeau. Furthermore, it is the only work to be considered in this study where the text and music of the motetus are borrowed entirely from elsewhere. The constraints on the composer are very different to those of either the Artesian rondeau-motet or any of the other pieces here discussed.[57]

52 'Rondeaux, Virelais, and Ballades', 128.
53 Many of these are discussed in Ernest Hoepffner, 'Virelais et Ballades dans le Chansonnier d'Oxford', *Archivum romanicum: nuova rivista di filologia romanza* 4 (1920) 20–40, esp. 38–9.
54 Raynaud, *Recueil de motets*, 1: 143.
55 Van den Boogaard, *Rondeaux et refrains*, 140.
56 *Ibid.*, 39; see also Paul Meyer, 'Le Salut d'amour dans les littératures provençale et française', *Bibliothèque de l'Ecole des Chartes* 28 (1867) 154–62.
57 The use of the chanson from *Li gieus de Robin et de Marion* is discussed in Ludwig, *Repertorium*, 1/2: 432–4.

(754) *Ne m'oubliez mie – Domino* (BD I) [Table 5.1, no. 13].

Van den Boogaard published the last five lines of the motetus text of this composition as a rondeau.[58] He implied that a line was missing after 'Marions i est aleé'. This was not implied by Gennrich in his attempt to reconstruct a rondeau from the last two lines of the poem;[59] these constitute a refrain, and are not only musically identical to each other but also appear in two other sources which are also musically and textually the same. However, neither Gennrich nor Rokseth[60] gave due weight to the fact that this motet is based on a surviving clausula in Florence. The repeated phrases which suggested a reconstructable rondeau to Gennrich are a characteristic of the clausula's duplum. There seems little likelihood of this phrase being borrowed from either of the other two motets which use this refrain,[61] on text-critical grounds. Neither does there seem any cause to assume a reversal of the normal sequence whereby the motet is derived from the clausula. The new text written to the clausula duplum reflected, in its use of heptasyllables with feminine rhymes, the parallel phrases of the music. Both music and text then circulated as a refrain. There is no question of the music and text originating as a rondeau (or even as a refrain). Van den Boogaard's positing a lost fourth line is unsupported by the source. These lines do touch on the genre of the rondet de carole in the use of elements of the *C'est la jus type-cadre* (the poem has already been listed in Table 5.2). It is as if, when the composer of the text saw a repeating phrase in his melismatic model, he responded by using a text which imitated the repetitious poetry of the rondet de carole.

Of the five compositions contained in the second half of Table 5.1, nos. 11 and 13 can be eliminated from this investigation on the grounds that their so-called rondeau upper voices are the result of creative reconstruction or misinterpretation. Although the three remaining pieces can be shown to incorporate elements of rondeau composition in their upper parts, they are very different from the rondeau-motets discussed earlier. One of the three consists of a lyrico-choreographic monody subsumed into a three-part complex, and another is an attempt to construct a pastiche of Provençal dance-songs. Only no. 9 attempts to combine a motetus in the form of a rondeau with a plainsong tenor. This is the only motet that is worth comparing with the Artesian compositions. The most telling contrast here is that of the tenor usage in the three-part piece. Rhythmic manipulation is used to accommodate the upper voice, rather than the structural resequencing of the pieces from Artois.

58   *Rondeaux et refrains*, 65.
59   *Rondeaux, Virelais und Balladen*, 2: 39.
60   *Polyphonies du treizième siècle*, 4: 285.
61   vdB 287. Motets which also use this refrain are listed in van den Boogaard, *Rondeaux et refrains*, 117.

6

Refrain cento

Repertory and function

The term 'refrain cento' was originally coined to explain motets, found in the Bamberg manuscript, whose upper voices were thought to be completely made up of refrains.[1] This basic assumption has been repeated with little or no disagreement,[2] and indeed a small industry[3] has recently been excavating more putative refrain centos to the extent that nineteen works have been proposed as examples of this genre.[4] On closer inspection, however, many of these works do not really fulfil the conditions laid down for them. The few pieces that do assemble voice-parts out of a chain of refrains do so in such different ways that to consider the refrain cento a subgenre of the motet is misleading.

All the works that have at one time been considered refrain centos are listed in Table 6.1.

[1] Rudolf Adelbert Meyer, 'Die in unseren Motetten enthaltenen Refrains', Albert Stimming, *Die altfranzösischen Motette der Bamberger Handschrift nebst einem Anhang, enthaltend altfranzösische Motette aus anderen deutschen Handschriften mit Anmerkungen und Glossar*, Gesellschaft für romanische Literatur 13 (Dresden: Gesellschaft für romanische Literatur, 1906) 143. Meyer's work appeared during the final stages of the preparation of Friedrich Ludwig's *Repertorium*, and Meyer's ideas were given a much wider currency. See, for example, Ludwig, *Repertorium*, 1/1: 292 and 297.

[2] 'Well-known refrains . . . become woven into the motet in various ways. Some pieces consist almost entirely of them . . . .' (Gustave Reese, *Music in the Middle Ages with an Introduction on the Music of Ancient Times* (London: J. M. Dent, 1941) 317); 'There are even a few motet texts . . . that consist entirely of refrains . . . in the manner of a *cento*' (Willi Apel, 'Refrain', *Harvard Dictionary of Music*, ed. Willi Apel (Cambridge, Mass.: Harvard University Press, 1944) 633); 'In a few cases, the entire text of a motet appears to consist of nothing but refrains' (Hoppin, *Medieval Music*, 338).

[3] Gennrich included a large number of so-called refrain centos in his *Bibliographie* of 1957 largely without comment. It is in his article entitled 'Refrain-Studien' of 1955 where his philosophy concerning these pieces can be recovered: 'Moreover, there are refrain centos, i.e., pieces which consist exclusively of a sequence of refrains and which are used as motet voices' (*ibid.*, 376–7). He then proceeds to give examples. Klaus Hofmann leaned very heavily on Gennrich's view of genre in refrain compositions – too heavily in some cases. In his examination of compositional practice in those motets built on the *In seculum* melisma, he took some pieces which Gennrich had suggested might possibly (*vielleicht*) be refrain centos and described them as probably (*wahrscheinlich*) refrain centos (Hofmann, *Untersuchungen zur Kompositionstechnik der Motette im 13. Jahrhundert*, 122). He identified (166) *La bele m'ocit, Dieus!* (see below Table 6.1) as a refrain cento (*ibid.*, 46).

[4] Hans Tischler, Gordon Anderson and Eglal Doss-Quinby have been the three most active in these archaeological exercises. Tischler's position is most clearly established in his *Style and Evolution of the Earliest Motets*, 1: 63, 77–9 and 152. Anderson's views are scattered amongst the commentaries to his editions of this repertory: *Latin Compositions*; *Motets of the Manuscript La Clayette: Paris, Bibliothèque Nationale, nouv. acq. f. fr. 13521*, Corpus mensurabilis musicae 68 (n.p.: American Institute of Musicology, 1975);

n. 4 continued on p. 110

Table 6.1 Distribution of refrain centos

Gennrich no.	Incipit	Status
(9)	*Amoureusement me tient li maus que j'ai*	Triplum, three-part French motet
(46)	*Tout leis enmi les prés*	Motetus, two-part French motet
(54)	*Ja pour longue demouree*	Motetus, two-part French motet
(166)	*La bele m'ocit, Dieus!*	Motetus, two-part French motet
(173)	*Brunete, a cui j'ai mon cuer doné*	Motetus, three-part French motet
(188)	*J'ai les biens d'amours*	Triplum, three-part French motet
(208)	*Hé cuer joli*	Motetus, three-part French motet
(253a)	*Endurez, endurez les maus d'amer*	Motetus, two-part French motet
(335)	*Amors vaint tout fors*	Triplum, four-part French motet; Triplum, three-part French motet
(367)	*Ja ne mi marierai*	Triplum, three-part French motet
(433)	*Cele m'a s'amour donée*	Motetus, two-part French motet
(435)	*Renvoisiement i vois a mon ami*	Motetus, two-part French motet
(436)	*J'ai fait ami a mon chois*	Motetus, two-part French motet
(445)	*Nus ne sait mes maus s'il n'aime*	Motetus, two-part French motet
(457)	*A vous pens, bele, douce amie*	Motetus, two-part French motet
(570)	*Ne puet faillir*	Motetus, three-part French motet
([706b] 823)	'Hé! monnier	Motetus, two-part French motet
(880T)	*Cis a cui je sui amie*	Tenor, three-part French motet
(1117)	*'Je l'avrai ou j'i morrai'*	Text

There is a lack of consistency in the appearance of these so-called refrain centos. They always seem to be complete voice-parts, but they can appear in a variety of contexts: the motetus or triplum in a double motet, the motetus in a two-part motet, either upper voice in a bilingual motet, or even as the tenor of a double motet. One refrain cento apparently survives only as a text. There is furthermore no obvious concordance-base for this group of compositions. Some works turn up in the *corpus ancien* of Montpellier and in such loosely related sources as Bamberg. Others, however, are preserved in sources that are usually presumed (but only on notational grounds) to be fractionally earlier – W$_2$ and the Munich fragments, for example. Again, a significant proportion appear in two manuscripts which, it has been argued, originate in north-eastern France: the Roi and Noailles chansonniers.[5]

Compositions of the Bamberg Manuscript: Bamberg, Staatsbibliothek, Lit.115 (olim Ed.IV.6), Corpus mensurabilis musicae 75 (Neuhausen and Stuttgart: Hänssler-Verlag; American Institute of Musicology, 1977). Doss-Quinby's observations are confined to a single list, *Les Refrains chez les trouvères*, 263 note 61, a discussion of (433) *Cele m'a s'amour donée* and some selective comments on the classical background to the cento. Leo Treitler and van den Boogaard have also reinforced this view. See Leo Treitler, '"Centonate Chant": *Übles Flickwerk* or *E pluribus unus?*' *Journal of the American Musicological Society* 28 (1975) 14 and van den Boogaard, *Rondeaux and refrains*, 23 note 21. Treitler's statement to the effect that 'Sometimes, various late medieval practices in which melodic material from here and there is combined (the *motet enté*, for example), have been referred to under the heading of cento' apparently fails to distinguish between a refrain cento and a *motet enté*, and seems to assume that the latter represents a subset of the former. For the critique of this position, see above pp. 82–9.

5   Everist, *Polyphonic Music*, 175–87.

More confusing still are those pieces whose concordance-base seems to cross over these very loosely defined boundaries. Finally, one piece which will loom large in the discussion of this pseudo-genre appears in the seventh fascicle of Montpellier, in Turin, in Bamberg and in the index that survives in Besançon of a lost manuscript.

Technique: refrain and cento

Two works listed in Table 6.1, (570) *Ne puet faillir* and (173) *Brunete, a cui j'ai mon cuer doné* have been described as refrain centos. These upper voices are supposed to be completely made up of refrains, that is, entirely constituted from borrowed material. The text of *Ne puet faillir* is as follows.

> Ne puet faillir a honour
> Fins cuers, qui bien amera.
> D'amours vient sens et honors:
> Qui bien la sert, joie avra.
> Haute chose a en amour;
> Bien la doit garder qui l'a.
> Amours fait tous biens douner:
> Cuer renvoisier et tous maus oblier.
> Fins cuers ne s'en doit repentir de bien amer,
> De bien amer.

In *Ne puet faillir*, a ten-line text is supposed to be made up of five two-line refrains.[6] It is the identification of these on which the interpretation of this piece as a refrain cento stands or falls. It is therefore slightly perplexing to find that only one of these refrains in fact survives with any concordances. The last two lines of the poem, 'Fins cuers ne s'en doit repentir de bien amer / De bien amer' appear in a rondeau, in an anonymous *salut d'amours*,[7] and at the end of the first stanza of a chanson preserved in the KNPX group of sources.[8] In fact, the refrain as it appears in its concordant sources only consists of one line: 'Fins cuers ne s'en doit repentir de bien amer', and the repetition of the last three words is a compositional modification found only in the motet voice *Ne puet faillir*. Nevertheless, this is clearly a refrain. Is it to be assumed that the four remaining refrains, so called, once circulated in more than one source each and that all the others have been lost? A large number of sources for the repertory of refrains may have existed – and many may not have been written down. The detail of the rest of this piece may enhance our answer to the problem. On musical grounds, two points need to be made. The music of the first and third pairs of lines (lines 1–2 and 5–6) is constructed in a similar fashion. The first and second lines of each stand in an *ouvert–clos* relationship to each other. This, coupled to the fact that some of the musical phrases articulate the pairs of lines with rests,

---

6   These are van den Boogaard (hereafter vdB) 1364/Gennrich (hereafter G) 1287; vdB 457/G 1290; vdB 785/G 1285; vdB 158/G 1464; vdB 755/G 458.

7   Paris, Bibliothèque Nationale, fonds français 837, fols. 253v–5r. Edited in Meyer, 'Salut d'amour', 154–62. The rondeau itself is edited in van den Boogaard, *Rondeaux et refrains*, 37.

8   No. 1449 in Raynaud's listing. See Spanke, ed., *G. Raynauds Bibliographie des altfranzösischen Liedes*, 206.

might suggest some sort of separate origin for each of these pairs. A consideration of textual elements, however, suggests the opposite.

The first six lines of the poem consist of heptasyllables which rhyme alternately: *rimes croisées*.[9] This alone is a quite extraordinary feature for a motet text, and an even more extraordinary one for a voice-part which is supposed to be made up of pre-existent material. This regularity is rendered even more striking when the last two lines, which are known from concordant sources and must be a refrain, are considered. Here, any sense of regularity of metre or rhyme collapses. Indeed, editors of this piece have found it difficult to reach any conclusion regarding either the number of lines in this part of the poem or where lines begin and end.[10] These differences scarcely matter since the line-lengths of the refrain are very different to the regular heptasyllables of the rest of the poem,[11] and the rhymes of the refrain bear no relation to the preceding *rimes croisées*. The fourth pair of lines: 'Amours fait tous biens douner / Cuer renvoisier et tous maus oblier' is of crucial importance in the interpretation of this voice-part. It breaks the pattern of heptasyllabic lines,[12] and it introduces a new rhyme. Such *vers de liaisons* have already been noted. They mark the boundary between newly composed material (the body of the poem) and the refrain which it introduces. Hence, it seems very doubtful indeed that the previous lines of the poem are themselves refrains. It is furthermore unlikely that an interpretation of the pieces as a chain of refrains has any validity. The sense of the poem has a potential value in interpreting this text. Certainly, each of the pairs of lines makes grammatical sense on its own. But there is a consistency here. All the sentences are of a similar construction. They are all simple epithets. The use of the first or second person, so common in refrains, is absent. Furthermore, the overall logic and tone of the poem are similarly consistent. In the three pieces that will be seriously considered as examples of the refrain cento, such inconsistencies are of great importance.

Ne puet faillir is an example of a motetus voice-part which ends, as so many do, with a single refrain. There is very little evidence to suggest that any of the rest of the voice-part is compiled from refrains. The correspondences between coherence and line-length first suggested this piece as a possible candidate.[13] Many of the characteristics of this unique piece argue that it could only have been conceived as a single entity with a single refrain.

In many respects, *Ne puet faillir* is a rarity. Its rhyme-scheme and line-length, so regular for the most part, are not typical of the motet repertory in general. A work that poses similar problems is (173) *Brunete, a cui j'ai mon cuer doné*. Its text is given below.

---

9   Theodor Wilhelm Elwert, *Traité de versification française des origines à nos jours*, Bibliothèque française et romane, série A: manuels et études linguistiques 8 (Paris: Editions Klincksieck, 1965) 106.

10   The edition of these lines follows the suggestions made in Raynaud, *Recueil de motets*, 1: 52 and Stimming, *Die altfranzösischen Motette der Bamberger Handschrift*, 61. The line is divided as follows: 'Fins cuers ne s'en doit repentir / De bien amer, de bien amer' in Tischler, *Montpellier Codex*, 4: 31.

11   Either a pair of lines of twelve and four syllables respectively or of two octosyllabic lines.

12   Again, the edition follows Raynaud and Stimming. Tischler splits this single line into two lines of four and six syllables.

13   Meyer, 'Refrains', 161–2.

> Brunete, a cui j'ai mon cuer doné,
> Por voz ai maint grief mal enduré;
> Por Deu, pregne voz de moi pité,
> Fins cuers amorous [et douz!]
> De deboinaireté
> Vient amors.

This is a six-line poem which behaves very much like *Ne puet faillir*. The last two lines, 'De deboinaireté / Vient amors' are well known as a refrain.[14] They also appear in an anonymous *salut d'amours*,[15] as well as in a chanson[16] and in the *salut à refrains* by Philippe de Rémi.[17] Also like *Ne puet faillir*, the earlier parts of the poem are regular. In this case, all octosyllables share a single rhyme. However, the first four lines of the poem are not known from any other sources. Again, the *vers de liaison*, 'Fins cuers amourous', divides the core of the poem from its refrain. We might reach the same conclusion concerning this piece as for *Ne puet faillir*. It would be wrong to consider this piece a refrain cento. A more accurate interpretation is as a voice-part with a single terminal refrain.

Another putative refrain cento raises further questions. This is the text of (188) *J'ai les biens d'amours*:

> J'ai les biens d'amours sans dolour,
> Car cele m'a s'amour donee,
> Qui mon cuer et m'amour a;
> Et puisqu'el l'a,
> Bien sai, qu'ele m'amera.

The second and third text-lines of this piece, 'Cele m'a s'amour donee / Qui mon cuer et m'amour a', with their music, constitute a widely distributed refrain.[18] The remaining lines of the poem create a variety of problems. For example, it is difficult to view the last two lines of the voice-part as a refrain when, quite clearly, their sense is dependent on what precedes them. It is a characteristic of the refrain that its sense is complete. These last two lines are related to the previous two (a genuine refrain) not only by additive and explanatory conjunctions, *et* and *puisque*, but by a pronoun which also refers back to the refrain. The problems surrounding the issues of line-length and rhyme are here very large. As was the case with *Ne puet faillir*, editors cannot agree on where the lines exactly divide. Gaston Raynaud, for example, attempted to make the second line end with the word *amour* so as to rhyme with *dolour* in the previous line.[19] Concordances of the refrain make this interpretation

---

14   vdB 468/G 1204.
15   Paris, Bibliothèque Nationale, fonds français 837, fols. 271r–2v. Edited in Oscar Schultz-Gora, 'Ein ungedruckter *Salu d'amors* nebst Antwort', *Zeitschrift für romanische Philologie* 24 (1900) 358–69.
16   Raynaud/Spanke no. 459.
17   Paris, Bibliothèque Nationale, fonds français 1558, fol. 114v. Edited in Hermann Suchier, ed., *Œuvres poétiques de Philippe de Rémi, Sire de Beaumanoir*, 2 vols., Société des anciens textes français (Paris: Firmin Didot, 1884–5) 2: 313–16.
18   vdB 314/ G 2. For concordances see van den Boogaard, *Rondeaux et refrains*, 121. Note however that the version of this refrain begins with the word 'car' which does not appear in any of the other sources for this refrain. This type of modification, made for the purposes of continuity, is different to the cross-relations which exist between the last two lines of the poem and the refrain itself.
19   Raynaud, *Recueil de motets*, 1: 123.

unlikely, especially since the musical phrase ends after *donee*. A judgement about the relationship between the line-length and rhyme of the refrain and that of the rest of the poem would be very difficult. Very similar problems exist in (445) *Nus ne sait mes maus s'il n'aime*, (54) *Ja pour longue demouree* and (208) *Hé cuer joli*. This question of coherence and structure may, for the moment, be left on one side. It will be developed later.

Two so-called refrain centos can be discounted almost without comment. These are ([706b] 823) *Hé! monnier* and (1117) *Je l'avrai ou j'i morrai*, and are two fairly recent additions to this corpus. Van den Boogaard and Gennrich both call the second, *Je l'avrai ou j'i morrai*, a *motet enté*.[20] There is no doubt that the refrain is divided into two and placed at beginning and end of the voice-part.[21] *Hé! monnier* is included here because of its listing in Hans Tischler's recent *The Style and Evolution of the Earliest Motets*.[22] There are no refrains listed for this motet either by van den Boogaard or by Gennrich. The obscene story-line is very strong. Despite musical correspondences, which are probably related to the dialogue form of the text, none of these suggests the presence of any borrowed material and certainly not the existence of a refrain.

In his *Style and Evolution of the Earliest Motets*, Tischler associated a group of pieces that he called refrain centos with two other groups of compositions: *Kurzmotetten* and refrain-motets.[23] The distinguishing characteristics of these motets have already been outlined, and some will be discussed later in another context. The compositional emphases in these works need to be distinguished and differentiated from the refrain cento. The term 'refrain-motet' should be reserved for works that consist solely of a single refrain over a tenor. (253a) *Endurez, endurez* is a good example. The *Kurzmotette* simply presents a short text over an unpatterned tenor. The upper voice is sometimes two or more refrains, as in (435) *Renvoisiement i vois a mon ami*. Some pieces may or may not have refrains as their upper voices, and the question of identifying these is just as fraught as in the case of the so-called refrain cento. But the very brevity of these pieces marks them out from the idea of a cento. They are polyphonic settings of two refrains, or of short newly composed texts, not attempts at putting together a sequence of borrowed material over a single tenor. These are fascinating pieces, and, even if one were to disagree with Ludwig's view that they were associated with the earliest stages of motet composition,[24] their position in the history of the French motet is surely critical and still to be assessed.[25]

Two more works, which should also probably be ruled out of consideration as refrain centos, raise some issues which may be productive not only for the interpretation of these pieces but also for a view of the larger corpus of French-texted motets.

---

[20] Van den Boogaard, *Rondeaux et refrains*, 187 and *passim*; Gennrich, *Bibliographie*, 100.

[21] Doss-Quinby is alone in her assertion that the piece is a refrain cento (*Les Refrains chez les trouvères*, 263 note 61).

[22] *Style and Evolution of the Earliest Motets*, 1: 79.

[23] *Ibid.*

[24] Ludwig, *Repertorium*, 1/1: 304–5.

[25] Three other works fall into this category: (367) *Ja ne mi marierai*; (436) *J'ai fait ami a mon chois*; (457) *A vous pens, bele, douce amie*.

The first of these pieces is (46) *Tout leis enmi*, whose text follows.

> Tout leis enmi les prez,
> *Amors ai a mon volenté.*   vdB 912,
> Jeus et baus i ot levez,
> Träi m'ont mi oill,
> Mis cuers dort
> En la violete,
> Einsint me debrisent amors,
> Et si ne senti onques mes
> Hé! amors, froiches noveles,
> Trop vos esloigniez de moi!
> *Onques ne soi amer a gas,*
> *N'oncor ne m'en repen ge pas.*   vdB 1428
> *Or la, or la voi, or la voi, la voi, la voi,*
> *Por deu salüez la moi!*   vdB 1448
> Je vi Robin ou boais aler,
> Einsint s'en vet le biaus Robin
> Et bele Marion ausint,
> *Se je n'ai s'amer, la mort m'est dounee,*
> *Je n'i puis faillir.*   vdB 1685

Those refrains which have concordances have been italicized and the numbers which they receive in van den Boogaard's bibliography appear on the right of the text. Both van den Boogaard (implicitly) and Gennrich (explicitly)[26] claimed that this piece is a refrain cento. However, they failed to offer any explanation for lines 1, 3 and 4. It was suggested that the rest of the poem consisted of 'refrains', and that any concordances had been lost. Even in those lines which are supposed to make use of known refrains, there is a substantial degree of recomposition. For example, the second line of the piece (vdB 912) is preserved not just in this motet voice but also apparently in a rondeau. This survives, without music, as an interpolation in the *Roman de la Poire*. It is also found in another motet.[27] But the refrain in all concordant sources consists of two lines as follows: '*J'ai amours a ma volenté / Teles com ge voel*'. The motet seems to use only the first line of this refrain. The simple inversion of the first couple of words, on the other hand, is a commonplace in the transmission of this genre.

There are more curiosities. The first three lines of the poem employ exactly the same melodic fragment three times over. The tune for the fourth line of the text bears a striking resemblance to the tune of the second line of the refrain in concordant sources. These relationships are demonstrated in Example 6.1. Furthermore, the text of the first four lines of the motet poem looks suspiciously as if it contains elements of the 'pastime' *type-cadre*.[28] Indeed, one might even go as far as to say that the first four lines could very well even have been borrowed from a rondet de carole whose text depended on the *type-cadre*. The refrain 912 also appeared in a rondeau without music. Its text follows.[29]

[26] Van den Boogaard assigned a number to most so-called refrains in the composition and Gennrich, *Bibliographie*, 4, gave it the label 'Refrain-Cento'.

[27] Van den Boogaard, *Rondeaux et refrains*, 174.

[28] For a discussion of the definition of the *type-cadre*, ultimately derived from Zumthor, see above, pp. 97–100.

[29] Van den Boogaard, *Rondeaux et refrains*, 31.

Example 6.1 Comparison between (46) *Tout leis enmi* (perfections 1–22 motetus), *D-W* 1099, fol. 247v, and end of (153) *Tout adés mi trouverés*, *D-W* 1099, fol. 222r

> C'est la gieus, en mi les prez,
> *J'ai amors a ma volenté,*
> Dames i ont baus levez.
> Gari m'ont mi oel.
> *J'ai amors a ma volenté*
> *Teles com ge voel*

Three things are striking about the relationship between this poem and the first four lines of the motet *Tout leis enmi*. First is the astonishing range of shared images: the scenario – 'les prez'; the action – 'Jeus et baus i ot levez' as opposed to 'Dames i ont baus levez'; and the first person response – 'Träi m'ont mi oill' as opposed to 'Gari m'ont mi oel'. Second is the identity of rhyme-scheme and structure of line-length in the two poems. Third is the identical musico-poetic structure, and all that entails for a musical reconstruction of the rondet de carole. It can safely be assumed that the musical structure of the rondet de carole would have been aAabAB. It is surely no accident that the music of the first four lines of the motet *Tout leis enmi* follows exactly the same structure: AAAB. The first four lines of this piece have nothing to do with the process of stringing together a sequence of refrains. They are a fragment of a rondet de carole, either borrowed, or written in strict imitation of such a genre. In addition, there are very close poetic links between the first four lines of this motet and the particular rondet de carole which shares the same refrain.

Of the three other refrains which apparently exist in this piece, none behaves exactly as if it were the result of borrowing. Refrain 1428 has a different melody here to the versions which survive in its two concordances: a chanson and a *motet enté*.[30] Refrain 1448 only appears elsewhere in a chanson without music; but the structure of the refrain is different. In the current motet, the text is '*Or la, or la voi, or*

---

30   The chanson and motet which share this refrain are given in van den Boogaard, *Rondeaux et refrains*, 219.

la voi, la voi, la voi / Por deu salüez la moi' whereas the chanson has a truncated form of the refrain: '*Or la voi, la voi / Por Dieu, salués de moi*'. Given the internal musical repetitions in the motet voice, it is difficult to avoid the conclusion that the shorter chanson form of the refrain is in a sense more 'original' than the motet version. The composer of the motet substantially altered the structure of the borrowed refrain to suit his own purposes. In this case, these changes were almost certainly caused by the nature of the tenor at that particular point in the piece.

The final refrain in this composition (vdB 1685) appears in a variety of other sources. Whereas the melody in this motet is in Mode VI, the melodies in concordant sources are in Mode II. These may be two independent views of the same 'unmeasured' original or as one version depending directly on the other.

There can be no question of the motet *Tout leis enmi* participating in what might be called a 'normal' process of refrain borrowing. There are other lines of this text which Gennrich and van den Boogaard also considered refrains. Some points must be conceded. The pair of lines 'Einsint me debrisent amors / Et si ne senti onques mes' has a melody in which each of the two lines is set to an *ouvert* or *clos* form of the same melodic fragment. This is certainly a characteristic of some refrains. It is difficult to be conclusive until some type of systematic catalogue and analysis of both the musical and literary qualities of the complete corpus of refrains has been drawn up. *Tout leis enmi* is a motet whose construction is inseparably bound up with its use of refrains. But it is not a refrain cento, and to assume the contrary is a serious barrier to its interpretation.

The second piece which poses its own set of problems is (9) *Amoureusement me tient*. The problems associated with this piece involve not only this voice-part but

Example 6.2 (9) *Amoureusement me tient* – (10) *Hé, Amours – Omnes* (M1); *F-MO* H 196, fols. 114v–15r

also the motetus in this double motet. Example 6.2 is an edition of the motet followed by an edition of the triplum text.

> Amoureusement me tient li maus que j'ai;
> Por ce chanterai: Aimi!
> Hé, Amors morrai je
> Sans avoir merci?
> Aimi, las, aimi! Je muir por li
> Et ne por quant voel je chanter
> Pour moi deduire et por moi deporter.
> Las, que porrai je devenir?
> Nule riens tant ne desir.
> Or me di:
> Diex d'amors, vivrai je
> Longuement ainsi?

The triplum of this voice-part has been described as a refrain cento.[31] Although there are clearly three known refrains present, of the twelve lines of the poem with their accompanying music, four do not figure at all in the Gennrich or van den Boogaard bibliographies. These are lines 2, 7 and 8, and 10. The first refrain appears in a chanson and in another motet. All three versions use the same melody.[32] The other two refrains are rather more interesting. Both appear in both the triplum and motetus of this very motet. In the edition of the piece, refrain 796 appears in the triplum, perfections 12–17, and in the motetus, divided between perfections 1–3 and 40–2. Likewise, refrain 504 can be seen at the end of the triplum, perfections 37–42, and in the motetus, perfections 29–34. Elements of refrain 796 are marked with a solid bracket and those of refrain 504 with a broken one. Refrain 796 also appears in another motet in the collection at the end of the chansonnier français 845, and was discussed in Chapter 4.[33]

The distribution of these two refrains is very limited. Are they examples of borrowing from elsewhere or are they examples of newly composed pseudo-refrains? In either case, they represent a significant level of intratextuality between the two motet voices of this piece. However, in the case of refrain 504 there is no trace of the refrain outside this piece. Other concordances may have been lost. The possibility has to be acknowledged that these sorts of compositional processes take place largely independently of thoroughgoing refrain usage. In other words, the shared notes and words are here the result of compositional choice and not of borrowing from an external body of material.[34]

---

[31] Doss-Quinby, *Les Refrains chez les trouvères*, 263 note 61.

[32] '*Amoureusement me tient li max que j'ai*', vdB 144/G 85. For concordances see van den Boogaard, *Rondeaux et refrains*, 105.

[33] Fols. 184, 190 and 189 (the last leaves of this manuscript are misbound).

[34] (335) *Amors vaint tout fors* has been signalled as a refrain cento by Doss-Quinby and, only slightly less incorrectly, as 'partly' a refrain cento by Tischler. The text of the second half of the voice-part consists of direct speech enclosing passages of indirect speech. Gennrich and van den Boogaard claim that all this material consists of refrains. Of the seven so-called refrains, only three (vdB 587, 900, 664) appear in other sources. Significantly, the first two of these both appear in the motetus of (286) *Nus ne set les biens d'amors* – (287) *Ja Dieus ne me doinst corage* – *Portare* (M22), although the transposition levels are different (respectively a fifth and a *second* higher) in both cases.

Perhaps the most pressing problems concerning the identification of refrains have been the questions of concordance-base and distribution. Furthermore, the criteria hypothesising lost concordances for refrains are contentious. The ways in which refrains with irregular rhyme-schemes and line-lengths could distort a more regularly structured poem may be valuable for establishing criteria. Some motets may very well have been witnesses more to a sophisticated sort of intratextuality than to the creation of a string of refrains. The differences between *Kurzmotette*, refrain-motet and putative refrain cento are further important elements. Questions of coherence and continuity between text and refrain are clearly important in challenging the generic status of the refrain cento. They also begin to emerge as important factors in a more general critical appraisal of the motet.

Examples

There are three motets that require serious consideration as refrain centos. They are the following, all listed in Table 6.1: (166) *La bele m'ocit, Dieus!*, (433) *Cele m'a s'amour donée* and (880T) *Cis a cui je sui amie*. In these pieces, the proportion of refrains with concordances is very high: between two-thirds and three-quarters. In those cases where the remaining refrains do not have concordances, the evidence to suggest that they are genuine refrains is very good. There are obvious distinctions of coherence. There are many instances of switching rhythmic mode between one refrain and the next. Where concordances with music exist, these in large part agree with the melody in the motet in question. Doss-Quinby expressed the idea that the presence of refrains is often indicated in the sources by the relevant text-lines beginning with an upper-case letter.[35] Of all the pieces discussed in this chapter, only two mark out their refrains with upper-case letters. Significantly, they are two of the three pieces which are under consideration as refrain centos: *Cis a cui je sui amie* and *Cele m'a s'amour donée*.[36] Nevertheless, there is a clear justification for beginning to consider these pieces in the same artistic terms.

To qualify for any kind of status as genre, these three pieces should exhibit a range of characteristics that separated them, as a group, from the rest of the repertory. Such a group could then be placed alongside the clausula, conductus *cum cauda* or *jeu parti*. But distribution and concordance-base vary greatly. The motet to which *Cis a cui* is the tenor is found in the seventh fascicle of Montpellier, in Bamberg, in Turin and in the Besançon index. *Cele m'a s'amour donée* is found in W$_2$ and Noailles whereas *La bele m'ocit, Dieus!* was viewed by the scribe of Montpellier as so important that it opens the sixth fascicle of the manuscript.

---

[35] Doss-Quinby, *Les Refrains chez les trouvères*, 107–8 and note 18.

[36] Of the three sources for *Cis a cui*, Montpellier capitalises the first letter of the text of every refrain except for the last, but also capitalises the initial letters of both the first and second lines of refrain vdB 636/G 1377. Bamberg, however, only capitalises three of the first letters of its refrains and Turin only two. For (433) *Cele m'a s'amour donée*, the picture is clearer: Noailles capitalises all first letters of refrains except the last. W$_2$ does the same but leaves out the initial letters of the second, eighth and last refrains. It is doubtful, however, whether the use of upper-case letters can be considered a general guide to the presence of a refrain.

The two centos which form *moteti* in two-part works are themselves very different from each other. The difference lies in questions of tenor usage and the nature of the relationship between the motetus and the tenor. *La bele m'ocit, Dieus!* consists of a motetus voice which is fitted to one of the most well-known and widely used tenor fragments in this repertory: *In seculum.* The ways in which this particular fragment can be manipulated have been discussed by Klaus Hofmann[37] and others. Ludwig would have described the organisation of this piece's tenor as unpatterned – as opposed to the patterned tenors which consist of repeating *ordines* superimposed over one or more statements of a chant melody. Here, the melody is presented three times. It receives a different rhythmic profile on each occasion. The reasons are straightforward. Changing rhythmic mode, irregular phrase-lengths and differing melodic profiles of independent refrains are characteristics of this motet. They force the composer into an irregular rhythmic organisation of the tenor. There is an analogous situation in a three-part piece whose motetus is cast in the form of a rondeau over the *In seculum* tenor: (188) *J'ai les biens d'amours* – (189) *Que ferai, biau sire Dieus?* – *In seculum* (M13). There, we have already observed that this particular melisma lends itself well to this sort of procedure. It concentrates on a very limited range of pitches: a large proportion of this melisma focuses on the tetrachord *g* to *c*.[38]

The two-part motet that opens the sixth fascicle of Montpellier, (166) *La bele m'ocit, Dieus!* – *In seculum* (M13), is singular in the construction of its motetus and traditional in its tenor structure. The nature of the rhythm imposed on the tenor is exceptional. The other refrain cento, *Cele m'a s'amour donée,* behaves differently. Its tenor is not based on a chant melisma, but on the *Alleluya. Hodie Maria virgo celos ascendit,* using almost the entire first half of the alleluya and all of the verse as far as the end of the melisma on the word 'Regnat'. The last two words of the chant, 'in eternum', are not set in polyphony.[39] This sets the piece aside from conventional tenor treatment in the thirteenth-century motet and from the treatment that was found in *La bele m'ocit, Dieus!* – *In seculum.* The *Alleluya* tenor is more consistently organised in terms of rhythmic mode than that of the *In seculum* tenor of *La bele m'ocit.* The former is cast in the first rhythmic mode throughout, but is not organised into *ordines.* Both tenors are inconsistent but in different ways.

Of the nine putative refrains in *Cis a cui je sui amie,* six have unequivocal concordances. Of these, three occur in one other place only: the *roman* entitled *La Cour d'amour* by Mathieu le Poirier. Indeed, two of the refrains which appear consecutively in the motet tenor are found in contiguity, although reversed, in *La Cour d'amour.*[40] In addition, two of the other refrains appear fairly close together in the *roman* by Jacquemart Giélée: *Renart le nouvel.*[41] Although the refrains in *Renart le nouvel* are

---

[37] Hofmann, *Untersuchungen*, 7–51.

[38] See above p. 105.

[39] This is entirely in keeping with the general principle that solo sections only of the chant were set in polyphony.

[40] Paris, Bibliothèque Nationale, fonds français 1731, fols. 36–72.

[41] *Renart le nouvel* is preserved in four manuscripts: Paris, Bibliothèque Nationale, fonds français 25566 fols. 119–79; *ibid.*, 372, fols. 1–60; *ibid.*, 1593; *ibid.*, 1581 fols. 1–57. See the edition in Henri Roussel, ed., *Renart le nouvel par Jacquemart Gielee publié d'après le manuscrit La Vallière,* Société des anciens textes français (Paris: Editions A. and J. Picard, 1961).

furnished with music in three of the four versions of the poem,[42] there are so many refrains in that part of the story that their appearance both there and in the motet may well be fortuitous. Unfortunately, the sole manuscript of *La Cour d'amour* – Paris, Bibliothèque Nationale, n. a. f. 1731 – does not include notation, so it is impossible to compare anything more than the texts.[43] A clear relationship exists between this motet voice and the one specific *roman*. Until we have a wider view of these sorts of relationships, it is difficult to make any kind of realistic interpretation of this correspondence. Explanations might range from the purely accidental to common authorship.[44]

Two further types of such intertextual relationships are found in the two other refrain centos. The first concerns the density of refrain concordances between *La bele m'ocit, Dieus!* and a group of motets in the fifth fascicle of Montpellier. Four works share exactly the same refrains as *La bele m'ocit, Dieus!*[45] Of these, three behave in an uncomplicated fashion. The same text and melody appear both in *La bele m'ocit* and in one or even two of the others. In the motet (184) *En son service amourous* – (185) *Tant est plesant* – *In seculum* (M13), the final refrain corresponds to that of *La bele m'ocit, Dieus!* Furthermore, it is also presented over the same portion of the tenor melisma: *In seculum*. Although the rhythm of both upper voices and tenors is slightly different in the two motets, the resultant counterpoint is very similar indeed. The two passages are given as Example 6.3.

The motet (433) *Cele m'a s'amour donée* – *Alleluya . . .* (M34) is based on a tenor that uses a liturgical item in its entirety. With the exception of the melisma on the word 'Regnat', which is the basis for many clausulae and Latin motets, the use of the remainder of this liturgical item in polyphony is highly restricted. In addition to this motet which uses the whole item, there survive three French motets on the melismas *Alleluya, Hodie* and *Gaudete* respectively.[46] Three two-part French motets on the *Regnat* melisma survive.[47] This means that of the liturgical item whose text reads as follows, 'Alleluya. Hodie Maria virgo celos ascendit. Gaudete qui cum Christo regnat in eternum', the following parts are used for a layer of motet composition, in addition to (433) *Cele m'a s'amour donée* – *Alleluya . . .* (M34):

---

[42] Even the fourth source, Paris, Bibliothèque Nationale, fonds français 1581, contains blank staves for the notation of the refrains and music for one of them.

[43] However, the scribe may very well have planned to include the music to these refrains since there are gaps between the refrains which may have been intended to carry the stave-lines. This manuscript is more difficult than most in this condition to interpret since there is the possibility that these gaps may be the result of some other method of articulating the text. See above p. 80.

[44] In her discussion of this piece, Evans ('The Unity of Text and Music in the Late Thirteenth-Century French Motet', 230) argues that 'Nothing suggests that the exact textual environment of *refrains* 6, 7, and 9 [of *Cis a cui*] in *La cour d'amour* needs to be taken into account in developing a plausible interpretation of the compositional technique behind the construction of [*Cis a cui*]'. While this seems defensible in Evans's own terms – a reading of the poem which seeks to analyse coherence and compositional technique in terms of a consistent series of lexical choices, rhymes and phonemes – it surely underplays the potential historical and cultural significance of these correlations. See also Evans, 'The Textual Function of a Refrain Cento in a Thirteenth Century French Motet', *Music and Letters* 71 (1990) 187–97.

[45] The works in question are (787) *Grant solaz me fet amors* – (788) *Pleüst Diu* – *Neuma* (Neuma III. Toni); (182) *L'autrier trouvai une plesant tousete* – (183) *L'autrier, les une espinete* – *In seculum* (M13); (172) *Trop souvent me duel et sui en grieté* – (173) *Brunete, a cui j'ai mon cuer doné* – *In seculum* (M13); (184) *En son service amourous* – (185) *Tant est plesant* – *In seculum* (M13).

[46] They are (434) *Mieus voil sentir* – *Alleluya* (M34); (435) *Renvoisiement* – *Hodie* (M34); (436) *J'ai fait ami* – *Gaudete* (M34).

[47] (445) *Nus ne sait* – *Regnat* (M34); (446) *Dusque ci ai* – *Regnat* (M34); (447) *Lonc le rieu* – *Regnat* (M34).

Example 6.3 Lower two parts of (166) *La bele m'ocit, Dieus!*, F-MO H 196, fol. 231v, and (185) *Tant est plesant*; F-MO H 196, fol. 167r. Tenor follows emendations suggested in Rokseth, *Polyphonies du treizième siècle* 2: 232–3

Alleluya, Hodie ('Maria virgo celos ascendit' is omitted) *Gaudete* and *Regnat*. As in the case of *Cele m'a s'amour donée – Alleluya. Hodie*, the last two words, 'in eternum', are left out of consideration.

The compositions on the *Alleluya. Hodie* (M34) melisma clearly behave in a similar fashion to each other, and share similar patterns of distribution. We have already seen how three rondeau-motets function as a cycle. They are all based on the same tenor chant, have identical structures in their upper parts and belong to the same *type-cadre*. Even though they use different refrains, the non-repeating parts of these rondeau voice-parts are very similar. The issues here are not so clear, however, as in the case of the rondeau-motet cycle. First, the motets on the *Alleluya. Hodie* tenor do not occupy the whole chant; in the case of the rondeau-motets, the alleluya verse which was used for this cyclic setting consisted very neatly of three appropriately sized melismas. The *Alleluya. Hodie* does not behave like this, and a polyphonic setting of the melismas on any of the words 'Maria', 'virgo', 'celos' or 'ascendit' is scarcely imaginable. They consist only of six, nine, nine and five pitches respectively. This contrasts with sixteen pitches for 'Alleluya', twenty-three pitches for 'Hodie', twenty-four pitches for 'Gaudete' and over forty for 'Regnat'. Significantly, the texts of the three pieces, *Mieuz aim mourir – Alleluya, Renvoisiement – Hodie* and *J'ai fait ami a mon chois – Gaudete*, have little in common – not even their refrains.

The refrain can, however, help a great deal when it comes to try and interpret the three French-texted motets on the melisma *Regnat*, and to answer the question: which, if any, of these pieces is related to the refrain cento *Cele m'a s'amour donée – Alleluya. Hodie*? The three motets on *Regnat* which need to be considered because of their proximity to *Cele m'a s'amour* (they are all copied in Noailles with rare concordances in related manuscripts) are (445) *Nus ne sait mes maus – Regnat* (M34), (446) *Dusque ci ai – Regnat* (M34) and (447) *Lonc le rieu de la fontaine – Regnat* (M34).

Of the five lines which make up the text of *Nus ne sait mes maus*,[48] the first two are a refrain ('*Nus ne sent les maus, s'il n'aime / Ou s'il n'a amé*' (vdB 1402)), as is the last single line ('*Je les sent, les maus d'amors*' (vdB 1059)). They are here separated by two lines. They are also separated by two lines in the refrain cento *Cele m'a s'amour donée*, and they both appear in that part of the two motets where the tenor is working its way through the melisma *Regnat*. The refrain, '*Nus ne sent les maus, s'il n'aime / Ou s'il n'a amé*', occurs at the beginning of the motet *Nus ne sait* and it also appears at the beginning of the statement of the *Regnat* melisma in *Cele m'a s'amour donée*. What this means is that, except for a few minor changes resulting from the unsuccessful attempts to impose a regular *ordo* on the *Regnat* tenor, the counterpoint in these passages is remarkably similar in both pieces. This is made clear in Example 6.4.

Example 6.4 Comparison between extracts from (433) *Cele m'a s'amour donée*, *D-W* 1099, fol. 228r, and (445) *Nus ne sait mes maus*, *F-Pn* fr.12615, fol. 187v

This very same refrain is also used in the motet *Dusque ci ai – Regnat*. It appears in a different contrapuntal relationship to that seen in *Cele m'a s'amour* or *Nus ne sait*. Only one of these three motets based on *Regnat* may be set alongside the other pieces which are closely related to the refrain cento *Cele m'a s'amour donée*: *Nus ne sait* and not one of the other two. This group of motets is not cyclic in exactly the same way as the group of rondeau-motets mentioned earlier, they are witnesses to a self-referential mode of composition which, on the basis of manuscript preservation and distribution, may well be localised away from Paris and in the north-east of present-day France.

Cele m'a s'amour donée – Alleluya emerges as a very singular work indeed. Its relations are the curious experimental compositions that one finds in Noailles and related sources. The motets themselves are such a great distance removed from what might be considered to be the 'mainstream' of motet composition. It is unrelated to either of the other two works which appear to make use of any technique of centonisation.

48   Discussed above, p. 114.

The two refrain centos that form the upper parts to motets, *Cele m'a s'amour donée* – *Alleluya* and *La bele m'ocit, Dieus!* – *In seculum*, are separated by tenor usage and context. The former is a refrain cento which is constructed over almost a complete liturgical item with no internal repetition. In the latter, the refrain cento is built over one of the most popular tenor melismas. It is not heavily indebted to the concept of *ordo*, but it does go through such familiar motions as presenting the tenor three times, each with a different rhythmic profile. The context for each of the pieces is very different. *La bele m'ocit, Dieus!* is unique in Montpellier. There, it occupies a place of some distinction at the start of the sixth fascicle, and shares significant characteristics with a number of pieces in the fifth fascicle of that manuscript. *Cele m'a s'amour donée* is closely related to a number of pieces in the chansonniers. This re-emphasises the substantial geographical divide which separates Montpellier (Paris) from Noailles and Roi (Artois/Arras), and hence also separates the two motets. *Cis a cui je sui amie*, in contrast to the other two works discussed, is a tenor and also the basis for a piece with a radically different distribution.

Three pieces exist which all attempt to use an unbroken sequence of refrains to construct a voice-part. They do not, however, constitute a genre in the sense implied by Gennrich and others, but a technique which might appear in various subgenres of the motet. It appears here both in the tenors and upper voices of French-texted motets. It also appears in conductus, and no one has yet examined the context and content of the texts of Latin motets from this viewpoint to see whether something broadly analogous is present there. This technique of constructing a cento is comparable to some of the more complex manipulations of tenors – the clausula with the *Nusmido* tenor, for example[49] – or such techniques as modal transmutation.

Two points seem to emerge from the investigation of this music. (1) Only three pieces really fit the received description of refrain cento. (2) The three pieces are so radically different in their musical and poetic characteristics that this phenomenon needs to be considered a technique and not a genre.

---

[49] Ludwig, *Repertorium*, 1/1: 80; see also Ludwig, 'Die mehrstimmige Musik des 14. Jahrhunderts', *Sammelbände der internationalen Musikgesellschaft* 4 (1902–3) 30.

7

Devotional forms

Introduction

It is easy to assume that sacred music of the twelfth and thirteenth centuries was sung in Latin and secular music was sung in a vernacular language. The opposition between sacred and secular, and Latin and vernacular, may be seen at its most focused in plainsong and its accretions, on the one hand, and the chansons of the trouvères and troubadours, on the other. However, the musical and lyric impulse that went into the chansons of the aristocratic poet-musicians was often redirected into sacred, devotional songs in the vernacular. The converse is also found: as may be seen in the conductus repertory or the so-called *Carmina Burana*, Latin may be used in a secular context.

The motet involves, from the very earliest stages in its history, the assimilation of French secular poems and both sacred and secular texts in Latin over tenors derived from plainsong. In the light of this bitextuality, and especially of the intrinsically bilingual nature of the French motet, we should not be surprised to find motets with devotional texts in French. What is perhaps surprising is that there are so few – about two dozen – of them. These motets are scattered among the major sources for the vernacular motet: W$_2$, the Montpellier Codex, the Bamberg manuscript and smaller sources. The musical characteristics of these motets are those of their secular companions. The identification of these forms enables us to place them within both the context of motet composition in the thirteenth century, and that of a vernacular culture in general.

Nineteen voice-parts of motets survive that are furnished with a French devotional text. Two of these are found within a single composition, and this results in a total of eighteen motets. The voice-parts are listed in Table 7.1.

This group of pieces is a small proportion of the vernacular motet repertory, and an even smaller fraction of the corpus of motets with texts either in Latin or French. However, there are almost as many vernacular devotional pieces as there are bilingual motets.[1] Although the latter have been assured of a place in standard histories of music, the type with devotional texts is hardly ever mentioned. It allows

[1] Anderson, 'Notre Dame Bilingual Motets'.

Table 7.1 Motets with devotional texts

1.	(94)	*Virgne glorieuse – Manere* (M5)
2.	(102)	*A la clarté – Et illuminare* (M9)
3.	(105)	*Et illumina – Et illuminare* (M9)
4.	(115)	*Ne quier d'amours – Hec Dies* (M13)
5.	(146)	*Li douz maus –* (147) *Ma loiauté –* (148) *Trop ai lonctens – In seculum* (M13)
6.	(220)	*Qui la vaudroit –* (218) *Qui d'amors velt bien joïr –* (219) *Qui longuement porroit joïr – Nostrum* (M14)
7.	(249)	*Biau sire Dieus – Et tenuerunt* (M17)
8.	(307a)	*Dieu nous a done – Ta* (M23)
9.	(389)	*La bele estoile –* (390) *Celui de cui –* (388) *La bele en cui – Johanne* (M29)
10.	(408)	*Benoïte est et sera – Benedicta* (M32)
11.	[(450)	*Glorieuse Deu –*] (450) *Glorieuse Deu – Veritatem* (M37)
12.	(536)	*De la virge Katerine –* (535) *Quant froidure –* (532) *Agmina milicie – Agmina* (M65)
13.	(652)	*Plus bele que flor –* (650) *Quant revient et fuelle –* (651) *L'autrier joer – Flos filius eius* (O16)
14.	(711)	*Douce Dame –* (712) *Quant voi – Cumque* (O31)
15.	(718)	*Hé! Mere Dieu –* (719) *La virge Marie – Aptatur* (O45)
16.	(760d)	*Duce creature [– Domino* (BD1)]
17.	(926)	*Un chant renvoisie – 'Decantatur'* (U.I)
18.	(1046)	*Virge pucele –* (1047) *De cuer gai – [tenor unidentified]*

us to identify a compositional trend in the poetry of the motet without begging the problematic question of genre.

Latin and French motets are characterised by a level of intertextuality. At its simplest, this consists of nothing more than the borrowing of a tenor chant. Often there is a more subtle relationship between the motet and other material that shares its lyric or melody. The tenors of the earliest Latin motets are based on plainsong filtered through the discant clausulae of the *Magnus liber organi* or its supplements. In addition, the Latin texts of these motets may allude to the tenor incipit, to the text of the entire plainsong from where the melisma is taken, or to other liturgical items for the same feast. In French secular motets, however, the upper voices rarely have anything to do with the verbal content of the tenor, and wholesale glossing is unknown. The intertextual functions in the French motet are taken over by the refrain and its contexts. However, there are rare exceptions where, for example, a tenor incipit, *Hec Dies*, appears in the same motet as a motetus text beginning *Hui main*.[2] Here, an Easter gradual seems to prompt the *exordium* of a *pastourelle*-type motet text.[3]

In comparison with Latin and secular French motets, motets with French devotional texts are something of a hybrid. The tenor incipit or chant is as important as it is in the Latin motet, but the essential building brick of the vernacular motet, the refrain, is almost completely absent. The poetry, however, is animated by a style and register that is analogous to that found in the secular texts of vernacular motets. Investigation of the broader environment of Old-French culture, and of devotional literature in particular, will enable us to establish a context for these pieces.

---

[2] (122) *Hui main – Hec Dies* (M13). The correlation is noted in Tischler, *Montpellier Codex*, 3: 6.

[3] The question is a little more problematic than this summary suggests. There are two other motets that begin with the same motetus incipit. They are (217) *Hui matin a l'ajournée – Nostrum* (M14) and (48a) *Hui matin au point – Nobis* (M2). Clearly, neither motet relates its motetus and tenor incipits. The first piece, *Hui matin a l'ajournée* is a contrafactum of the Latin-texted motet (216) *Nostrum est impletum – Nostrum* (M14).

Cultural background

From a study of the music and poetry of the twelfth and thirteenth centuries, it is easy to form the impression that literature written in French was diverting, entertaining and a relief from technical works written in Latin. But such a view is seriously incomplete. Alongside poetry, both narrative and lyric, there exist three major fields of vernacular literature: devotional, technical and didactic. The last two fields are represented by bestiaries, lapidaries, herbals, algorisms and astronomical treatises. All appeared in French, often adapted from Latin, in the thirteenth century.[4] The appearance of such didactic and technical literature in French was prompted by the needs of those who could not understand Latin.[5]

The history of French literature in the eleventh and early twelfth centuries consists of two parallel traditions represented by saints' lives and *chansons de geste*.[6] The earliest examples of saints' lives are those of Alexis and Eulalie, from the middle of the eleventh century, and Thomas, from the second half of the twelfth. Wace's lives of Margaret and Nicholas are also important. Lives of both the Blessed Virgin Mary and St Francis appear in the thirteenth century. Such works were by then, in addition to appearing in narrative verse or prose, also being written in a dramatic form; Jean Bodel's *Jeu de Saint Nicholas*, for example, dates from around 1200.[7] Given this great interest in hagiography in Old-French literature before 1200, it comes as something of a surprise to find no hagiographical texts in the *chansons pieuses*, the 145 sacred Old-French lyric poems whose poetry and music were written in the late twelfth and thirteenth centuries.[8] St Michael is mentioned in one, but only in its *envoi*, and St Gregory's life is used as an *exemplum* in another. St Gabriel is mentioned but in the context of the Annunciation.[9] One looks in vain among the *chansons pieuses* for a reflection of the tradition of saints' lives or some equivalents to, for example, the hagiographical poems scattered throughout Rutebeuf's sacred output.

Rutebeuf's oeuvre contains a large proportion of poems associated with the Church, the mendicants and the university. In addition to four Marian poems, there are translations of two miracles: *Le Miracle de Théophile* and *Le Sacristain et la femme au chevalier*. There are also two poetic lives of saints: *La Vie de Sainte Marie l'Egyptienne* and *La Vie de Sainte Elysabel*.[10] *Le Miracle de Théophile* and *La Vie de Sainte Elysabel* play an important role in two motets with devotional texts.

---

[4] For a useful introduction to a typology of Old-French sacred and technical literature, see Karl D. Uitti, 'French Literature: Before 1200', *Dictionary of the Middle Ages*, 12 vols, ed. Joseph R. Strayer (New York: Charles Scribner's Sons, 1982–9) 5: 232–54.

[5] This is certainly the argument that has been advanced for the appearance of the Psalter in French, for example. See Victor Leroquais, *Les Livres d'heures manuscrits de la Bibliothèque Nationale*, 3 vols (Paris: n.p., 1927–43) 1: x.

[6] Uitti, 'French Literature', 5: 236.

[7] Paul Meyer, 'Légendes hagiographiques en français', *Histoire littéraire de la France*, 411 vols (Paris: Imprimerie Royale etc., 1733–1981) 33: 328–458. See also Willis H. Bowen, 'Present Status of Studies in Saints' Lives in Old French Verse', *Symposium* 1: 2 (1947) 82–6.

[8] Edward Järnström and Arthur Långfors, eds, *Recueil de chansons pieuses du xiiie siècle*, 2 vols, Annales academiae scientiarum fennicae B.III.1 and B.XX.4 (Helsinki: Imprimerie de la Société de Littérature Finnoise, 1910–27). The songs are scattered widely among the chansonniers of the thirteenth century.

[9] *Ibid.*, 1: 129, 2: 120 and 2: 154, respectively.

[10] See Edmond Faral, and Julia Bastin, eds, *Œuvres complètes de Rutebeuf*, 2 vols (Paris: Picard, 1959–60) 2: 20–234.

In addition to vernacular saints' lives, there exists an octosyllabic verse translation of the Passion story into French, from around the millennium, and a series of Gospel homilies of Maurice de Sully from the second half of the twelfth century.[11] A major innovation, contemporary with Sully, was the appearance of formal biblical translations into French. Walter Map reported that he had seen French translations of the Psalter and other books of the Bible at the Third Lateran Council of 1179.[12] Whether or not this is correct, and Map's claims have led to no small amount of confusion, there certainly existed two translations of the Psalter by *c.* 1200: one of the Hebrew version and one of the Gallican.[13] The thirteenth century saw the piecemeal translation of all the remaining books of the Bible. The so-called 'Bible of the Thirteenth Century' was an amalgam of translations, each with a different origin.[14] Its appearance in at least four different versions before 1300 was further confused by its conflation with Guyart de Moulins' *Bible historiale.*[15]

Whatever the reasons for the growth in activity of biblical translation and hagiography in the last quarter of the twelfth century and onwards, it is clear that accessibility was a major consideration in a world where there existed those who had an interest in the Bible, lives of the saints and liturgy, but who lacked the linguistic skills of the clerk.[16] A similar characteristic is detectable in the devotional needs of those outside clerical orders without the time to recite the canonical hours. Such liturgical tools as the Book of Hours arose to service the devotional needs of those unable to participate in the liturgy. Certainly, by the mid-fourteenth century, the Book of Hours was the standard devotional tool for those outside holy orders. But in the thirteenth century, the prayer-book for the non-clergy was the Psalter.[17] What is now known as a Book of Hours evolved in the late twelfth century but only in combination with the Psalter. The Book of Hours, whose main components in any case are psalms, does not begin to appear separately from the Psalter until *c.* 1300.[18]

---

[11] Raymond C. St-Jacques, 'Bible, French', *Dictionary of the Middle Ages*, 2: 218–19 is a useful summary. A slightly more detailed survey is Guy de Poerck and Rike van Deyck, 'La Bible et l'activité traductrice dans les pays romans avant 1300', *La Littérature didactique, allegorique et satirique*, 2 vols, ed. Jürgen Beyer and Franz Koppe, Grundriss der romanischen Literaturen des Mittelalters 6 (Heidelberg: Winter; Universitäts-verlag, 1968–70) 1: 21–39 and 2: 54–69. Older, but still useful, is Samuel Berger, *La Bible française au moyen âge: étude sur les plus anciennes versions de la bible écrites en prose de langue d'oil* (Paris: H. Champion, 1884).

[12] Berger, *Bible française*, 37.

[13] Both the earliest copies of each are in British libraries. Cambridge, Trinity College, MS R. 17. 1 gives a translation of the complete text of all three versions of the Psalter: Hebrew, Gallican and Roman. The Hebrew version is translated into Anglo-Norman, and all three versions are glossed both in French and Latin. The first French translation of the Gallican Psalter now survives as Oxford, Bodleian Library, Douce 320. See St-Jacques, 'Bible, French', 218, and Berger, *Bible française*, 1–2.

[14] Colin A. Robson, 'Vernacular Scriptures in France', *The West from the Fathers to the Reformation*, The Cambridge History of the Bible 2, ed. Geoffrey William Lampe (Cambridge: Cambridge University Press, 1979) 445–6. See also Clive R. Sneddon, 'A Critical Edition of the Four Gospels in the Thirteenth-Century Old-French Translation of the Bible', 2 vols (D.Phil. diss., University of Oxford, 1978) and Sneddon, 'The *Bible du xiiie siècle*: Its Medieval Public in the Light of its Manuscript Transmission', *The Bible and Medieval Culture*, ed. W. Lourdaux and D. Verhelst, Mediaevalia Lovaniensia Series 1: Studia 7 (Louvain: Louvain University Press, 1979) 127–40.

[15] Berger, *Bible française*, 157–99.

[16] Sneddon, '*Bible du xiiie siècle*', 137.

[17] Leroquais, *Livres d'heures*, 1: x–xii.

[18] Devotional books listed by Leroquais from before 1300 are Paris, Bibliothèque Nationale, lat. 14284, 1073A, 13235, 1077, 13260 and 1328.

The translation of the Psalter into Old French was in the vanguard of vernacular biblical activity from around 1200. However, elements of the Breviary, stripped of their association with the liturgical year, are also of importance in the growth of the Book of Hours. The constituent parts of the Latin Book of Hours rapidly became standard: calendar, Little Office of the Virgin, penitential and gradual psalms, litanies of the saints, suffrages, Gospel excerpts, Hours of the Cross and of the Holy Spirit, and the Office of the Dead.[19] Two Marian prayers were also included: *Obsecro te* and *O intemerata*. Although the main contents of the Book of Hours were in Latin, some vernacular prayers were also included. The most popular of these was *Doulce Dame*. It is difficult to get a clear idea from the surviving material of just how common was the inclusion of vernacular material in thirteenth-century combined Psalter–Hours. Neither is it easy to identify the stage at which completely vernacular Books of Hours appeared, although this must have taken place after 1300. Of the five thirteenth-century Psalter–Hours that now survive in Parisian libraries, for example, only two are exclusively in Latin. The remaining three include either vernacular prayers or verse prefaces to Latin items.[20]

The growth in the cult of the Rosary makes it clear that lay devotion was not restricted to a tradition of reading from Books of Hours. As far back as the millennium, beads had been used to relate prayer to the 150 psalms, but by the thirteenth century they were an essential element of both devotion and dress,[21] and the recitation of the Psalter was abbreviated to a series of Paternosters, Ave Marias and Glorias. This can been seen as an analogy to the abbreviation of the liturgy into the Book of Hours.[22] It also helps to explain such practices as the abbreviation of elaborate prayers into a series of fleeting Marian images in the *chanson pieuse*, or the compression of a saint's *vita* into the epigrammatic text of a motet.

The composition of literature that takes the Virgin Mary as its subject is primarily a Latin phenomenon. Of all the changes in the poetic content of the Latin motet in the thirteenth century, the most striking is the growth in writing Marian texts.[23] But, as we have seen, Marian literature in Old French is a significant parallel to that in Latin, and the texts of vernacular devotional motets are an important subset of Old-French Marian literature. Three types of poetry are analogous to the poetry of these motets: miracles of the Virgin in Old French, such Marian poems as those composed by Rutebeuf, and the so-called *chanson pieuse*. The *chanson pieuse* may be divided into three further groups: the sacred *lai*, the strophic song and the motet.

The sacred *lai* is characterised by its musical and metrical structure. In its use of image, and in its range of vocabulary, its poetry bears comparison both with that of the *chanson pieuse* and the motet.[24] The literary register of the *lai pieuse* is very high.

---

[19] Michael Kwatera, 'Book of Hours', *Dictionary of the Middle Ages*, 12 vols, ed. Joseph R. Strayer (New York: Charles Scribner's Sons, 1982–9) 2: 326.

[20] Of the six books listed in note 18 above, only lat. 13235 and lat. 13260 contain no material in French.

[21] Eithne Wilkins, *The Rose-Garden Game: The Symbolic Background to the European Prayer-Beads* (London: Victor Gollancz, 1969) 26–46.

[22] Mary Josephine Ward, *The Splendour of the Rosary* (London: Sheed and Ward, 1946) 18.

[23] Hans Tischler, 'Classicism and Romanticism in Thirteenth-Century Music', *Revue belge de musicologie* 16 (1962) 10.

[24] Alfred Jeanroy, Louis Brandin and Pierre Aubry, *Lais et descorts français du xiiie siècle: texte et musique*, Mélanges de musicologie critique (Paris: Welter, 1901) 26–42 and 69–73.

Thibaut of Navarre, perhaps the archpoet of the *chanson courtois*, was responsible for one of the *lais pieuses*: *Commencerai a faire un lai* (RS 84).

In terms of its music and its metrical layout, the *chanson pieuse* is a devotional counterpart to the song of the trouvère. This has prompted the suggestion that there exists a *registre pieux* that represents a different response to the *aristocratisant* and *popularisant* drive of non-sacred French verse.[25] A strikingly large proportion of *chansons pieuses* are paraphrases of *chansons courtois*, *chansons de femme* and *chansons d'ami*. All three of these types represent different linguistic registers, and there is substantial registral interference.[26] These sorts of registral interferences are present in the texts of the motet in general, and perhaps suggest why poems of the *registre pieux* might have been attractive to the composers of the motet with French devotional texts.

Although the style and rhetoric of the *chanson pieuse* and the motet with French devotional texts may be similar, there are subtle differences in content. In the *chanson pieuse*, there is an almost complete concentration on songs to the Virgin. This characteristic is shared, to a slightly lesser degree, by the motet with devotional texts in French. However, there may be a great variety of themes or topics treated within the context of a single Marian song. This is especially true in the case of allusion to the Old Testament, and in the use of symbols from Antiquity and legend. Furthermore, most *chansons pieuses* are strophic and allow greater scope for the development of sustained images than do the much shorter motet texts. It is for this reason that those *chansons pieuses* whose texts are about Christ or God – termed here 'Theo-Christological' – are often fused with Mariological poems. In the motets, only one of these subjects is treated in any given piece.

Vernacular devotional poetry, including motet texts, and Latin sacred traditions are related to the issue of *amour courtois*. *Amour courtois* is often viewed as a mediation between Bernardine spirituality and the cult of the Blessed Virgin Mary. It has been effectively argued that the imagery and language both of the cult of the Blessed Virgin and of St Bernard's mysticism were heavily influenced by the lyric tradition of the troubadours.[27] This influence accords well with the idea that trouvère song shares a language and rhetoric with the *chanson pieuse*. Coupled with the ways in which secular motet texts are written and integrated into a polyphonic context, these relationships are important for the composition of devotional polyphony in this period.

---

[25] Bec, *Lyrique française*, 1: 142–50. He attempts a graphic presentation of the *registre pieux* (ibid., 150).

[26] Perhaps Bec gives insufficient weight to the lowest registral types in his description, the rondets de carole, or perhaps they are of only a local Anglo-Norman interest. The pieces are found in the manuscript Metz, Bibliothèque Municipale, MS 535. See Paul Meyer, 'Notice du MS. 535 de la Bibliothèque Municipale de Metz renfermant diverses compositions pieuses (prose et vers) en français', *Bulletin de la Société des Anciens Textes Français* 12 (1886) 41–76. Such registral interference creates a range of problems that are not solved by Bec's invocation of the *rotrouenge* (Bec, *Lyrique française*, 146–7), that was defined by Gennrich as a purely musical genre (Friedrich Gennrich, *Die altfranzösische Rotrouenge*, Literatur-historisch-musikwissenschaftliche Studien 2 (Halle: Niemeyer, 1925), and Gennrich, 'Zu den altfranzösischen Rotrouenge', *Zeitschrift für romanische Philologie* 46 (1926) 335–41).

[27] Moshé Lazar, *Amour courtois et 'fin'amours' dans la littérature du xiie siècle*, Bibliothèque française et romane; série c: Etudes littéraires 8 (Paris: Klincksieck, 1964) 81–4; Alexander J. Denomy, 'An Inquiry into the Origins of Courtly Love', *Mediaeval Studies* 6 (1944) 257–9.

Register

The foregoing discussion has suggested that the concept of the *registre pieux* is important for coming to terms with the devotional lyric in French. For the motets under discussion, it is useful to probe further the question of textual content and register. For motets with devotional texts, we may propose a simple division according to textual content: hagiographical, Mariological and Theo-Christological – texts that refer to saints, the Blessed Virgin Mary and to God or Christ. In Table 7.2, the incipits of the motet texts are set out under these headings.

The first of the two Theo-Christological texts, (249) *Biau sire Dieus*, is given below as an example of the content and tone of this type of poetry.

> Biau sire Dieus, qe porrai devenir?
> Qe chascun jor veons le mont mourir
> A si grant tort;
> Qe ne pensons a nos ames guerir?
> Vez la la mort,
> Qi nos vient assallir;
> Qar leissons tout si pensons de fouir,
> Alons en fort
> Vers Jesu Crist, qi por nos vout morir;
> Bien li devons ce servise merir,
> Autrement nos soumes mort.

Dear Lord, what can become of me? When each day we see the world die of such great wrong, how can we cure our souls? See, there, death who comes to assail us. Therefore let us abandon everything, let us think of fleeing [the world], let us go boldly to Jesus who wishes to die for us. We must well deserve this service, otherwise we are dead.

The poem points to the failings of the world as a reason for turning to Christ. The presence of only two of this type of text in the devotional motet repertory is commensurate with its rarity in the *chanson pieuse*.

As in the *chanson pieuse*, Mariological texts are clearly in the majority. There are three subdivisions of these Mariological poems in Table 7.2. Of the first two subdivisions, which include nearly all the texts, the simplest distinction is that the observations in the attributive poems are couched in the third person ('Rose est novele et des dames la flor', for example), while the pleas for intercession are made in the first or second person ('Dame, envers ton fil car fai ma pais, ou dampnés serai'). Although the attributive or descriptive texts clearly depend on poetry from other lyric registers, the intercessory poems seem to reach rather further into the Mariological cult for their impetus. These poems still share many characteristics with other vernacular lyrics. However, the idea of the Virgin as *mediatrix*, so important in the intercessory motet poem, is a concept fundamental to Marian literature in French from at least as early as the mid-twelfth century. It had first appeared in Latin in the *Libri miraculorum* of Gregory of Tours written in the second half of the sixth century.[28]

[28] Hilda Graef, *Devotion to the Blessed Virgin*, Faith and Fact Books 45 (London: Burns and Oates, 1963) 25–55.

Table 7.2 Generic classification of devotional motets

Hagiological	Theo–Christological	(1) Attributive/descriptive (3rd)	Mariological (2) Intercessory (1st, 2nd)	(3) Enigmatic
			(94) *Virgne glorieuse*	
		(102) *A la clarté*		
			(105) *Et illumina*	
			(115) *Ne quier d'amours*	
		(148) *Trop ai lonctens*		(220) *Qui la vaudroit*
	(249) *Biau sire Dieus*			
	(307a) *Dieu nous a done*			
			(389) *La bele estoile*	
		(408) *Benoîte est et sera*		
			(450) *Glorieuse Deu*	
(536) *De la virge Katerine*				
		(652) *Plus bele que flor*		
			(711) *Douce Dame*	
			(718) *Hé! Mere Dieu*	
		(719) *La virge Marie*		
			(760d) *Duce creature*	
				(765) *Hui matin* [but only in its Gautier version]
(926) *Un chant renvoisie*				
			(1046) *Virge pucele*	

It is possible to distinguish between attribution and intercession within the repertory of *chansons pieuses*. The multi-strophic nature of the *chanson pieuse* leads to a far greater range of subjects for reasons simply of length. This enables both the intercessory and attributive elements to appear in a single chanson. In the motet, whose texts rarely run to more than twenty lines of poetry, there is a very clear distinction between these two types of poem.

The third type of text is the enigmatic. Susan Stakel writes that 'In some [two] cases the poet even seems to be playing a game with the audience, for the identity of the love-object is not revealed as the Virgin Mary until the very end of the poem'.[29] The following text illustrates this technique.

> Qui la vaudroit lonc tans de fin cuer amer
> Et reclamer
> Et li douter,
> Cele ou maint henours
> Et loiauté
> Et bonté
> Et largece et genté,
> Bien li porroit vanter
> Sans desvanter,
> Qu'ele est la plus bele riens pour amer,
> Qu'on puet trover
> Sanz douter,
> Car c'est la dame des flours
> De toutes odours.

He who would love her loyally for a long time and court her and humble himself before her in whom resides honour and loyalty and goodness and generosity and nobility, he could indeed rightfully boast that she is without a doubt the most beautiful creature one could ever find to love: she is the wondrously perfumed flower among ladies.

Calling this a Marian poem depends on the correspondence of 'La dame des flours / De toutes odours' with the Blessed Virgin Mary. There are other compositions that are unequivocally Marian and that use a similar formulation. It has been assumed that the piece whose text is currently under inspection is indeed Marian.[30] The terms in which the characterisation is couched are vague, and the suggestion that anyone, rather than a single individual, could love the subject seems to suggest the Virgin. On the other hand, there are instances of unquestionably secular women being described in the same terms. Our view of this piece has to be ambiguous. The doubt about this poem's meaning is part of its purpose.

[29]   Tischler, *Montpellier Codex*, 4: xix.
[30]   Anderson, *Motets of the Manuscript La Clayette*, lxxii.

Hagiographical motets

The repertory of devotional motets includes two whose texts are strictly hagio-graphical: *De la virge Katerine* and *Un chant renvoisie*. The text of *De la virge Katerine* offers a summary of the principal events in the saint's life as well as the main elements of her iconography. This twenty-two line text manages to fit in the details of how her sermons led to her martyrdom and how, after her death, angels carried her to Mount Sinai where the Holy Law was received. The usual references to wheels are absent, but are replaced by Catherine's three crowns.[31] The voice-part that refers to St Catherine interacts with the rest of the musical composition in a variety of ways. The voice that carries this text forms part of a four-part motet preserved in the La Clayette manuscript. The entire motet consists of a tenor borrowed from plainsong with three further voice-parts above it. Each one of these carries its own text. Example 7.1 presents the first eight perfections of the work.

Example 7.1 (536) *De la virge Katerine* – (535) *Quant froidure* – (532) *Agmina milicie* – *Agmina* (M65); *F-Pn* n. a. f. 13521, fol. 377r

The texts are very different. First, the tenor is taken from a Marian alleluya, *Alleluya. Corpus beate virginis*. The last word of this plainsong provides the incipit for the tenor: 'Agmina'. The motetus is in Latin and loosely glosses the subject matter of the verse of the plainsong. The triplum is in French, and occupies itself with images of a renewing spring and of the attributes of the beloved. The quadruplum concerns St Catherine.

The original version of this St Catherine motet is very different to the state of the piece presented in Example 7.1. The first eight perfections of probably the oldest surviving form of this work are shown in Example 7.2.

[31] Karl Künstle, *Ikonographie der christlichen Kunst*, 2 vols (Freiburg im Breisgau: Herder, 1926–8) 1: 369–74; P. Assion, 'Katharina (AIKATERINE) von Alexandrien', *Ikonographie der Heiligen*, 4 vols. ed. Karl Georg Kastner, Lexikon der christlichen Ikonographie 5–8 (Rome etc.: Herder, 1973–6) 3: 289–97; Maurice and Wilfrid Drake, *Saints and their Emblems* (London: Werner Laurie, 1916) 24; Herbert Thurston and Donald Attwater, eds, *Butler's Lives of the Saints*, 4 vols (London: Burns and Oates, 1956) 4: 420–1.

AGMINA

Example 7.2 [(532) *Agmina milicie*] – (532) *Agmina milicie* – *Agmina* (M65), perfections 1–8, upper parts reversed; *I-Fl* Plut. 29. 1, fol. 396v

Here, the music is in three parts only. The lowest two are the same as the two lowest parts of the four-part motet from La Clayette. The music of the triplum is also the same, but carries the same text as the motetus. The resulting composition is a purely Latin work. It consists of a Marian tenor and a single Marian upper-voice text that glosses it. There are none of the conflicts between Latin and vernacular, or sacred and secular, that characterise the version from which Example 7.1 is taken. Ultimately, the reading of this motet, and a rationalisation of its two versions, will depend on an understanding of the other four-part works that employ devotional texts in one of their voice-parts.

A further reworking of the motet is found in the Bamberg manuscript. There the music of the tenor and motetus from the versions in Examples 7.1 and 7.2 form the basis of the composition. A triplum is added that shares the music of the La Clayette quadruplum. It now has a new Latin text. This poem begins, like the motetus poem, with an allusion to the 'Agmina' of the tenor chant; it therefore makes its Marian allegiance clear. It does however make a reference to St Catherine in the middle of the verse. This allies this Latin contrafactum closely with our devotional Old-French text. Finally, two English theorists from the early fourteenth century, Robert de Handlo and Walter Odington, cite a version of this motet with a new triplum whose text leans very heavily on the Marian poem of the original motet in this family. Instead of being addressed to the Virgin, however, it is now addressed to St Catherine.[32] Unfortunately, since the piece is included by both theorists to illustrate a specifically musical point, only a few perfections of music and a couple of lines of text survive. Nevertheless, this does seem to enhance the significance of our Old-French motet on St Catherine within this family of pieces. It would be a striking coincidence if the anonymous composer of the Bamberg text, Odington and Handlo had arrived independently at the idea of writing a motet on St Catherine on a

---

[32] Frederick F. Hammond, ed., *Walteri Odington Summa de speculatione musicae*, Corpus scriptorum de musica 14 (Rome: American Institute of Musicology, 1970) 143; Peter Lefferts, ed., *Robertus de Handlo: Regule/Rules and Johannes Hanboys: Summa/The Summa: A New Critical Text and Translation on Facing Pages with an Introduction, Annotations, and indices verborum and nominum et rerum*, Greek and Latin Music Theory (Lincoln and London: University of Nebraska Press, 1991) 174–5.

Marian tenor. It seems therefore plausible that they were aware of the Old-French version of this piece. We may conclude by assuming, therefore, that *De la virge Katerine* exercised a greater influence on the next generation of motet revision than its apparently maverick text might have originally suggested.

The second of the two hagiographical motets is by contrast musically very simple but textually very complex. It is listed in Table 7.1 as item 17. The piece survives in one version only and in a single source. This is the text of the motet:

> Un chant renvoisie et bel
> Dirai de Sainte Ysabel,
> De cui fisent li oisel
> En leur chans feste a sa mort.
> A li servir mes m'acort,
> Car des vertus me recort,
> Qu'a Cambrai fait de nouvel
> La parent si biau jouel
> Oustre revescu troi mort.
> Tort, dame, ai, quant vostre confort
> Requis n'ai par ma folie
> Du mal, qui me contralie,
> Dont sans vous ne vivrai mie;
> Por que vous requier et prie
> De cuer entier et loial:
> *Douz cuers, alegiez mon mal,*
> *Qu'il ne m'ocie!*   [Refrain vdB 623]

I shall sing a merry and beautiful song about St Elizabeth, whom the birds celebrated in their songs at her death. It suits me henceforth to serve her because I remember the miracles: that at Cambrai – such a marvel recently accomplished over there – three raised from the dead. I am wrong, Lady, when, through my folly, I have not requested your solace from the pain that afflicts me and that, without you, I shall never survive. For which reason I beg and beseech you loyally and whole-heartedly: Sweet heart, ease my pain, lest it kill me.

The Sainte Ysabel of the poem must be St Elizabeth of Hungary. She appears regularly in French calendars on 19 November, and is usually described as Ysabel.[33] Born in 1207, she died in 1231 and was canonised four years later.[34] Confirmation that this is the case may come from the poem *Un chant renvoisie* itself. Lines 3 and 4 of the poem describe how birds sang at the saint's death. Both the anonymous verse *Vie de Sainte Ysabel* and Rutebeuf's poetic life describe Ysabel's last hours in more detail. One of her maids heard her singing on her death bed, and since she had only ever heard her singing plainsong asked for explanation. Ysabel's response was that a bird sent from Heaven sat between her and the wall and was responsible for the singing.[35] At this, the maid drew the conclusion that this must have been 'the musique of some Angell from heaven'.[36]

[33] For example, Paris, Bibliothèque Nationale, fonds lat. 1328, fol. 12v.
[34] M. Francis Laughlin, 'Elizabeth of Hungary (Thuringia), St', *New Catholic Encyclopedia*, 17 vols (New York etc.: McGraw-Hill, 1967–79) 5: 282.
[35] *Œuvres complètes de Rutebeuf*, 2: 101–66.
[36] Henry Hawkins, *The History of S. Elizabeth* (n.p.: n.p., 1632; *R* [English Recusant Literature 1558–1640] London: Scolar, 1974) 350.

Singing, both human and ornithological, links these observations to the death of another Ysabel, sister of St Louis and founder of the Abbey of Longchamp. Although she was not beatified until 1521, her cult was of no small importance from the second half of the thirteenth century, and may be of some significance in the interpretation of this motet. Her life was written by Agnes de Harcourt, and describes her death in terms similar to those used for the Ysabel of the motet: Elizabeth of Hungary. She writes that at the time of Ysabel's death was heard sweet and melodious singing. Exactly as in the case of Elizabeth of Hungary, no one knew what it was, but assumed that it was the melody of the Angels taking her soul to Heaven.[37] This may be thought to be nothing more than coincidence were it not for the fact that Rutebeuf's *Vie de Sainte Ysabel* – the life of St Elizabeth of Hungary – was dedicated to Isabelle of France and may even have been commissioned by her.[38]

Matters are complicated by the tenor on which the motet is built. In the manuscript in which it survives,[39] the tenor is written after the motetus and makes excellent contrapuntal sense. But it remains unidentified despite what may be an incipit: the word 'decantantur'. This incipit may be little more than the crudest form of canon but it might of course relate to the almost obsessive attitude towards song on the part of both Isabelle of France and Elizabeth of Hungary. Although it does relate to the wrong Ysabel, it is worth noting that the sequence for Isabelle of France begins 'Ysabellis matris merita / *Decantemus* in ecclesia'.[40] Given that this sequence probably dates from no earlier than Isabelle's beatification in 1521, it may simply be reported here as a loose end in a rather complex and untidy knot.[41] The links between the two saints were, however, clearly acknowledged in the thirteenth century, and in the interpretation of works relating to St Elizabeth of Hungary it is inadvisable to lose sight of St Elizabeth of France.

Hardly any of the voice-parts with devotional texts with which we are dealing make use of refrains in the same way as so many of their secular counterparts. In motets that mix secular and devotional texts, the non-devotional voice-parts may well employ refrains. However, motets with a devotional text occasionally make use of what is essentially a Latin phenomenon: alluding to the incipit of the tenor in the upper-voice texts. A few straightforward examples will suffice. The first word of *Benoîte est et sera* alludes to its tenor incipit: 'Benedicta'; this is taken from the gradual *Benedicta. Virgo Dei genetrix*, for the Assumption of the Blessed Virgin Mary. *A la clarté qui tout enlumina* makes reference to the tenor incipit: 'Et illuminare', taken from the Epiphany gradual *Omnes de Saba*. In this respect, these two motets behave very much like Latin pieces mentioned earlier in the chapter. A third example mimics Latin practices more closely. It is probably best illustrated by examining the beginning of the motetus text. The work's tenor incipit, 'Et illumina', is given below.

37 Charles de Fresne [Ducange], ed., *Histoire de S. Louys IX. du nom Roy de France écrite par Iean Sire de Joinville, Sénechal de Champagne* (Paris: Mabre-Creamoisy, 1668) 169–81.
38 *Œuvres complètes de Rutebeuf*, 2: 60.
39 Paris, Bibliothèque de l'Arsenal, 3517–18, fol. 14r.
40 Oliger Livier, 'Le plus ancien office liturgique de la B.se Isabelle de France (d.1270)', *Miscellanea Giovanni Mercati*, 6 vols, Studi e testi 121–6 (Vatican City: Biblioteca Apostolica Vaticana, 1946) 2: 507.
41 *Ibid.*, 489–90.

Et illumina.

Je vous salu,

Dame, selonc mon savoir.

Porte de salu,

J'en sai bien de voir,

Car mout m'avez valu,

Et pouvez valoir,

Comme mere Jesu.

Cuer recreu

Ai eu

Si m'en doi douloir.

Mal ai, por voir,

En ce siecle vescu!

Sans vostre escu

N'avrai je mes vaincu;

A vous espoir avoir

Bon confort et vertu.

[Tenor]: Et illumina

'Et illumina'. Hail, Lady, according to my knowledge, Gateway to salvation, I well know, for you have been of great value, and shall be of value, as mother of Jesus. I have been of feeble heart; thus I should grieve. Woe indeed that I have lived in this world! Without your protection, I shall never triumph; from you I hope to receive great solace and strength.

Strictly speaking, the motetus text is macaronic. It duplicates the Latin tenor incipit at the beginning of the poem. Although this is a characteristic of the Latin motet from its very earliest years, it is almost unknown in the French repertory. *Et illumina / Je vous salu* is therefore something of a rarity.

In families of motets that include a piece with devotional texts, Latin motets from the same family may trope or duplicate tenor incipits. (248) *Ne sedeas – Et tenuerunt* (M17) is a Latin version of *Biau sire Dieus*, and closes its motetus with the words 'et tenuerunt', for instance. Such correspondences are only very occasionally found in French devotional versions. A good example is a piece at whose core is the two–part work: *O Maria, maris stella* on the tenor *Veritatem*. It survives in a variety of versions, both in two and in three parts. The end of its motetus ('in veritate') alludes to the tenor incipit ('Veritatem'). The French devotional piece that forms part of the same family as *O Maria, maris stella, Glorïeuse deu amie*, ends its motetus with the same sort of allusion: 'La ou vostre fiz est vie / Et voie et veritez'. These correspondences mark off a substantial proportion of vernacular devotional texts from secular French poems, and represent a musico–textual distinction between the two types.

Contrafactum

Contrafactum is important for the repertory of motets with devotional texts. A large number of *chansons pieuses* are modelled on secular originals.[42] Much work remains to be done on the musical relationships between *chansons pieuses* and their models.[43] Similarities in metre and rhyme may for example demonstrate that a particular devotional song is modelled on a secular one. Of the motets listed in Table 7.1, all but two function within a complex of contrafacta and reworkings. It is difficult to assess the significance of the two exceptions simply because we cannot be sure that there were not other versions of these pieces that have not survived the last 700 years.

Of the total of five motets on the tenor melisma *Et illuminare*, two have already been mentioned. The five motets divide into two subgroups in each of which the music of the upper parts is the same. Among the five motets in the two groups, there are two pieces with French devotional texts: one in each group. One text is intercessory, and the other is attributive or descriptive. Two of the remaining three Latin motets also employ Marian texts. Curiously, this concentration on the Virgin Mary in four out of the five motetus poems, two in French and two in Latin, seems not to be prompted by the substance or context of the plainsong. Although a performance context for Latin Marian motets on non-Marian tenors might well have been the commemoration of the Virgin on the day to which the tenor was assigned, such an explanation would hardly suffice for French-texted Marian pieces.[44] The presence of such a large proportion of French Marian texts in this motet complex is startling enough. That they are built on non-Marian tenors is even more striking.

(94) *Virgne glorieuse – Manere* (M5) is preserved uniquely in a manuscript now in Boulogne-sur-Mer. It gives us not just a date of composition but some fascinating data on the process of contrafactum.[45] In the same hand that copied both the poetry and the music of the motet is written the text given below:

Anno Domini Mo CCo lxo quinto fuit littera istius verbuli inventa a quodam canonico istius ecclesie. Si quis eum legerit vel cantaverit dicat Pater noster et Ave Maria pro animabus omnium fidelium defunctum.

The text of this little composition was composed by a certain canon of this church in the year of our Lord 1265. If anybody reads or sings it, let them say *Pater noster* and *Ave Maria* for the souls of the faithful dead.

The text suggests that *quidam canonicus* should be credited with the composition of the text alone, and not the music. This corresponds to what else is known about the composition of the piece. *Virgne glorieuse* is only a tiny offshoot of a large complex of

---

[42] This is perhaps one of the most discussed elements in the repertory of *chansons pieuses*. See Alfred Jeanroy, 'Imitations pieuses de chansons profanes', *Romania* 18 (1889) 477–86; Jeanroy, 'Modèles profanes de chansons pieuses', *Romania* 40 (1911) 84–6.

[43] Friedrich Gennrich, *Cantilenae piae: 31 altfranzösische geistliche Lieder der HS Paris, Bibl. Nat. Nouv. Acq. Fr. 1050*, Musikwissenschaftliche Studienbibliothek 24 (Langen bei Frankfurt: n.p., 1966).

[44] Rebecca Baltzer, 'Performance Practice, the Notre-Dame Calendar, and the Earliest Latin Liturgical Motets'. Paper read at symposium *Das Ereignis Notre-Dame*, Herzog-August-Bibliothek, Wolfenbüttel, 15–20 April 1985.

[45] Boulogne-sur-Mer, Bibliothèque Municipale, MS 119.

motets based on the popular *Manere* tenor. This devotional text is not known else-where, however. To be able to offer a more precise identification of *quidam canonicus* would be very attractive. Unfortunately, there are problems with the provenance of this manuscript. It is supposed to come from the Benedictine Abbey of St Bertin, but the evidence, only a seventeenth-century pressmark for the manuscript, is slight.[46] It is also difficult to see how *quidam canonicus*, a member of a cathedral chapter bound by monastic rule, could have been a member of the Benedictine order. Nevertheless, this text does give one example of the circumstances under which such a contrafactum might have been composed.

The final observation that touches on the question of contrafactum relates both to the motet repertory and the *Miracles* of Gautier de Coinci. This is the clearest link between the repertory of the *chanson pieuse* and the motet. Two texts are instructive.

(764) *Hyer matin a l'enjornee*	(765) *Hui matin a l'ajornee*
Hyer matin a l'enjornee,	Hui matin a l'ajornee,
Toute m'ambleure,	Toute m'ambleure,
Chevauchai aval la pree	Chevauchai par une pree
Querant aventure.	Par bone aventure.
Une pucele ai trovee,	Une florete ai trovee,
Gente de faiture,	Gente de faiture;
Mais de tant me desagree,	En la flor, qui tant m'agree,
Que de moi n'ot cure.	Tornai lues ma cure.
Douz ot ris	Adonc fis
Et simple vis,	Vers jusqu'a six
Vers les ieuz et bien assis;	De la flor de paradis.
Seule estoit	*Chascun lou*
Et si notoit:	*Qui l'aim et lout.*
'O, o, o, o, o, o	O, o, o, o, o,
Dorenlot', si chantot	N'i a tel dorenlot,
Mout li avenoit,	*Por tout a un mot.*
O, o, o, o,	O, o, o, o,
Et a chascun mot	*Sache qui m'ot*
Souvent regretot	*Mar voit, Marot*
Sa compaignete Marot.	*Qui let Marie por Marot*

The poem on the left is the motetus text of a motet unique in W$_2$ on the tenor *Benedicamus Domino*. It is musically identical to two Latin motets: (762) *Alpha bovi et leoni – Domino* (BD VI) and (763) *Larga manum seminatum – Domino* (BD VI). On the right is the first stanza of a monophonic chanson found in the *Miracles* of Gautier de Coinci.[47] The motet on the left is not, however, devotional. Pierre Bec has described the two poems in terms of an *abstract* secular model and devotional derivation.[48] But he understates the reworking of the motet text into this poem. In line 5, Bec sees

[46]   Gilbert Reaney, *Manuscripts of Polyphonic Music (11th – Early 14th Century)*, Répertoire International des Sources Musicales BIV$_1$ (Munich and Duisberg: G. Henle Verlag, 1966) 260–1.

[47]   Bec, *Lyrique française*, 2: 74–7; Chailley, *Les chansons à la Vierge de Gautier de Coinci*.

[48]   Bec, *Lyrique française*, 1: 148–9; Bec, 'L'accès au lieu érotique: motifs et éxorde dans la lyrique popu-larisante du moyen âge à nos jours', *Love and Marriage in the Twelfth Century*, ed. Willy van Hoecke and Andries Welkenhuysen, Medievalia Lovanensia 1: 8 (Louvain: Louvain University Press, 1981) 250–97.

the *pastourelle* origin of the *fleur de paradis* in the motif of the *fleur trouvée*.[49] But the derivation here is registrally more complex. It involves the switch from the *popularisant* term *pucele* to the term *florete* with the implication that it is synonymous with the Blessed Virgin Mary. From line 7 in the poem, much of the syntax changes, although the metre and rhyme-scheme remain the same. The last nine lines function as a refrain in Gautier's multi-strophic poem. Although the two poems are very different, certain points of similarity may be observed beyond those of rhyme and metre. The nonsense syllables, especially typical of *popularisant* poems, and the presence of the near-universal lover, Marot, are common to both. Van den Boogaard does not draw any distinction between these two refrains. The process of adaptation, however, involves taking the secular motet whose last nine lines have nothing to do with refrain technique, and adapting it to the requirements of a multi-strophic *chanson pieuse*. The last nine lines are then repeated as a refrain. In short, the motet has nothing to do with refrains or devotional poetry. These are two elements introduced into the Gautier poem by the process of adaptation.

(307a) *Dieu nous a done*, no. 8 in Table 7.1, survives in the Munich fragments.[50] It is one of two Latin motets that survive there that are based on the tenor melisma *Ta*, from the word 'captivitatem'. This is taken in turn from the *Alleluya. Ascendens Christus* for the Ascension. The two Latin motets are each in two parts and are musically identical; one is a contrafactum of the other. They are also strophic: one stanza of the text is underlaid to the music and the remaining stanzas are copied underneath the motet. Just before the Latin pieces is the text of a devotional French poem whose metre and rhyme match those of the two Latin motets that follow it.[51] It may be assumed that the fragmentary French text is all that survives of the remaining stanzas of a devotional French version of the piece. Immediately, some problems arise. Most would look at the beginning of this text and would say it begins in the middle of a line with the words '. . . que soions net'. Ludwig, however, clearly had access to a source that is not known to us today. He was able to offer the incipit of the stanza: 'Dieu nous a done'. This is however not the beginning of the first stanza of the poem, since it is not accompanied by notation.[52] We know from the way in which the two Latin motets are copied that the first stanza would still have been supplied with music.[53] All the same, this is the only example of a French-texted motet, devotional or secular, that comes down to us in more than one stanza. Strophic structures are almost unknown in the Latin motet repertory, and in the French repertory *Dieu nous a done* is unique.

---

[49] Bec, *Lyrique française*, 1: 76.

[50] Dittmer, *Eine zentrale Quelle der Notre-Dame Musik*, 29; Dittmer, 'The Lost Fragments of a Notre Dame Manuscript in Johannes Wolf's Library', *Aspects of Medieval and Renaissance Music: A Birthday Offering to Gustave Reese*, ed. Jan LaRue (London, Melbourne and Cape Town: Oxford University Press, 1967) plate 9.

[51] Dittmer, *Zentrale Quelle*, 63.

[52] Ludwig, *Repertorium*, 1/1: 279–85.

[53] It is difficult to see why Dittmer thinks that this must be the third or the fourth stanza of the poem and not the second (*Zentrale Quelle*, 64).

Context

Speaking of this music as 'devotional' is fraught with difficulties. If it is possible to describe the texts of individual voice-parts as 'devotional', how may we describe motets where voice-parts with devotional texts are combined with those with non-devotional ones? Of the eighteen compositions listed in Table 7.1, eleven are completely devotional. The composition consists of one or two devotional voice-parts and the tenor. The other seven pieces mix devotional voice-parts and secular material within the same composition. It is to the question of how devotional texts behave contextually that we may now turn.

(718) *Hé! Mere Dieu* – (719) *La virge Marie* – *Aptatur* (O45) is the only vernacular work in which two devotional texts are combined in a three-part motet. The two poems match in terms of register. They both borrow *aristocratisant* elements from trouvère poetry. Feudal imagery, for example, is particularly prominent in both texts. The triplum text alludes to the miracle of Theophilus. References to Old-Testament, New-Testament or Patristic theology are otherwise unknown in the devotional motet repertory, but very common in the *chanson pieuse*. Theophilus, for example, figures in no less than seven such songs. The triplum of the motet, *Hé! Mere Dieu*, is oblique, and alludes to the Theophilus legend. Theophilus gave his soul to the devil in order to secure a post. He later repented and asked the Virgin Mary to obtain forgiveness. She agreed and compelled the devil to tear up the contract with Theophilus. The story has been described as 'the most potent literary influence on the growing trust in Mary's intercessory power'.[54] This simple legend was cited from the fifth century onwards in the East. Its translation by Paul the Deacon in the late ninth century familiarised the West with such concepts as Mary as the *redemptrix* of captives and *mediatrix* between God and Man, and the image of Christ as the implacable judge.[55] Its popularity in Old French is attested by versions by Rutebeuf and Gautier de Coinci. The content of this voice-part's poem is closest of all the pieces discussed here to that of the *chanson pieuse*.

In the account of the motet on St Catherine, it was suggested that it would only be possible to explain this piece in the context of other four-part or 'triple' motets that made use of devotional texts. Motets with devotional texts make up a large proportion of this repertory. The four-part motet is represented by the music in the second fascicle of the Montpellier Codex and by a number of works in the La Clayette manuscript. These two sources share a total of twenty compositions. This is of course a repertory of comparable size to that of the devotional motet itself. It is therefore striking that there is more than a 25 per cent overlap between the two types of compositions. Five of the voice-parts with devotional texts we have been considering here form part of a triple motet. Furthermore, of the seven motets that mix devotional and secular texts, five of these are triple motets. There is a combination of two compositional emphases here: the use of devotional texts and the attempt to write music in four parts. Four-part motets have been described as 'a

---

[54] Graef, *Devotion to the Blessed Virgin*, 30.   [55] *Ibid.*, 30–9.

marginal development destined to remain largely unsuccessful'. A further objection to this repertory was their lack of 'regard for topical correlation of the poems'.[56] This is however a common characteristic of the double motet as well. If we look at the five motets with which we are here concerned, there is plenty of evidence of topical correlation of the poems. Even if most of these pieces are the result of contrafactum technique, there are attempts to establish some sort of connection between the texts. In support of this claim, we may refer back to an example from Chapter 3: (652) *Plus bele que flor* – (650) *Quant revient et fuelle* – (651) *L'autrier joer* – *Flos filius eius* (O16). This piece includes the voice-part with a devotional text listed as no. 13 in Table 7.1. As previous discussion has shown, it is a work whose musical origins lie much earlier in the century. None of the music, except of course for the tenor, was originally composed for the texts given in Chapter 3. Nevertheless, whoever was responsible for the four-part motet allowed the text of the tenor incipit to permeate the texture of the piece. The *flos* of the tenor translates into *flor* in all three voice-parts above it. It is first seen in the quadruplum in perfection 3, second in the triplum in perfection 4, and third in the motetus in perfection 12. The range of interpretations of the image of a flower in this text is wide. In the tenor, it is the flower of the Son (of God). By contrast, in the triplum, the flower is simply part of a springtime *exordium*: 'When the return of leaf and flower signal the arrival of the summer season. . .'. In the motetus, the flower is to be gathered in the context of the *pastourelle* idiom. In the quadruplum it is the flower that is less beautiful than the one to whom the author submits. That this is the Blessed Virgin is made clear in the rest of the poem. In the quadruplum, the flower is the point of comparison with the Blessed Virgin, whereas in the tenor, it is the fruit of the Blessed Virgin herself. This distinction is focused in the quadruplum, whose text is as follows:

> Plus bele que flor
> Est, ce m'est avis,
> Cele a qui m'ator.
> Tant con soie vis,
> N'avrai de m'amor
> Joie ne delis
> Autre mès la flor
> Qu'est de paradis:
> Mere est au Signour,
> Qu'est si noz amis
> Et nos a retor
> Veut avoir tot dis.

The one to whom I submit is, in my opinion, more beautiful than a flower. As long as I am alive, in truth, no one will have the joy and pleasure of my love except for this flower which grows in Paradise: she is the mother of our Lord who wants forever to possess you, friend, and the two of us together.

This twelve-line poem has a consistent rhyme- and metrical scheme. The tenor incipit: 'flos', appears twice during the course of the poem. Its location is striking: at

[56] Sanders, 'Motet, Medieval, Ars Antiqua', 12: 621.

the end of the first line and the end of the seventh; placing the repetition here has the effect of articulating the twelve lines of the poem into two groups of six. The last word of the first of each of these two groups of lines is *flor*. The sense of the poem crosses this division: 'As long as I am alive, in truth, no one will have the joy and pleasure of my love except for this flower which grows in Paradise' (lines 4–8). This occupies the last three lines of the first group of six lines and the first two of the second. It is, furthermore, almost as if the composer of the text was trying to articulate these two groups of lines by reference to the tenor. The repetition of the word 'flor' not only elaborates the structure of the quadruplum poem, it articulates the beginning of the second *cursus* of the tenor. There are two statements of the tenor *cursus* prefaced by a short phrase of five perfections that falls outside the main rhythmic scheme of the tenor. The quadruplum therefore reflects the content of the tenor both implicitly and explicitly, while the triplum and motetus reinterpret the 'flower' in essentially non-devotional and secular terms.

The St Catherine motet, another triple motet – *Qui la vaudroit* – and the motet just discussed seem to have excited a particular interest in the mind of the compiler of the second fascicle of the Montpellier Codex. They are the first three works in the fascicle. Standing apart from this group is the last four-part piece to be discussed. It differs in the ways in which the individual voice-parts interact and in its implications for chronology. This is the triple motet on the *In seculum* tenor, no. 5 in Table 7.1: (146) *Li douz maus* – (147) *Ma loiauté* – (148) *Trop ai lonctens* – *In seculum* (M13). The devotional text is in the triplum.

Although this piece exists in a variety of sources, only the Montpellier Codex preserves all four parts. This is the only version to include the triplum with the Marian text. All other versions of the piece give it either in three parts (quadruplum, motetus and tenor) or in two (motetus and tenor). It will become obvious that either the Marian triplum was added with an astonishing degree of skill, or that at least the bottom three voice-parts of the triple motet were composed as a single entity from which the other versions were abstracted. The triplum and motetus texts of this piece are given below.

> (148) *Trop ai lonctens*
> Trop ai lonctens en folie
> Sejorné.
> Pour ç'a la virge Marie
> Sui tourné
> Et voil amender ma vie
> Sans retour.
> Mout m'agree et mout me plaist la douce amor;
> Or m'otroit Dieus, que je sente sa douçour.
> Car c'est la rose et le lis et la flor
> De bon oudor,
> Pour qu'i fas a li ma voie et mon ator:
> Or sai bien, que j'ai de toutes la mellour.

I have lived foolishly for quite a long time. That is why I have turned to the Virgin Mary and want to mend my ways forever. Her sweet love is ever so agreeable and pleasing to me; may God now grant that I feel her sweetness. For she is the rose and the lily and the sweet-scented blossom; because I make of her my way and my law, I now know well that I have the finest among ladies.

> (147) *Ma loiauté m'a nuisi*
> Ma loiauté m'a nuisi
> Vers amours
> Par un regart de celi
> Qui toz jours
> Est lié de ma dolour
> Sans merci.
> Tartarin m'en vengeront, car Diu en pri,
> Que hastivement vendront pres de ci.
> Las, que pensai, quant l'amai? Quant la vi?
> Bien m'a traï
> Mes cuers, quant onques a li s'abandona.
> *Li dous regars de la bele m'ocirra.*

My loyalty has hurt me in love on account of a glance from her who, ever pitiless, reaps joy from my grief. The Tartars will wreak vengeance for me, for I pray to God that they may quickly come close by. Alas, what was I thinking when I loved her? When I saw her? My heart indeed betrayed me when it abandoned itself to her. The sweet glance of the fair one will kill me.

The two texts share identical metric schemes, and their rhymes mix couplets at the beginning with long sequences of single rhymes towards the end. They are also carefully written antitheses of one another. In at least one place they exploit a lexical correspondence to underline this feature. The two texts are so similar that one could forgive the scribe of Montpellier for accidentally switching the two texts around after the sixth line. The concordances of the piece make it clear how the motetus text, and by implication the triplum text, should behave. The Marian triplum explains how the author repents of his past life and entrusts himself to the Virgin, while the courtly motetus laments the pain and betrayal he suffers as the result of his secular love. The parallel is between the courtly lady – She 'who . . . reaps joy from my grief' – and the Virgin Mary – whose 'love is ever so agreeable and pleasing to me'. The nexus of this antithesis comes at the end of the sixth line in both poems where the word 'Sans' is used to indicate, in the triplum, the eternal commitment to the Virgin – 'sans retour' – and, in the motetus, the absence of pity in the cruelty of the courtly lady – 'sans merci'. Just at the point where these two poems coalesce, the quadruplum, which is otherwise completely unrelated to the two lower texted voices, sings 'En qui j'ai tot mon cuer mis' (In whom I have entrusted my entire heart). It cannot have escaped the notice of the composer of the quadruplum that both the protagonists in the triplum and motetus had indeed entrusted their hearts to a Lady. The very different consequences of each required some kind of commentary.

The subsequent fates of the poems vary. The Marian triplum dissolves into a formulaic descriptive/attributive poem. The motetus makes an allusion that is both apposite and topical. The subject calls upon the Tartars not to hesitate in the vengeance they will wreak on his behalf. This is a very rare use of this particular national group in French lyric poetry. There are no other examples in the motet repertory.

Richard Southern has pointed to a growing disenchantment with the crusading ideal towards the end of the twelfth century and to the hope of political change from beyond the Muslim world: from the Tartars.[57] This was fuelled by the conflicting reports of the conversion of the King of the Tartars, and the myth of Prester John. But by the middle of the thirteenth century, the Tartars, or Mongols as they have been known since the eighteenth century, had not only conquered the Muslim world, but were also threatening Western Europe. From the moment they destroyed Kiev and began their offensive against the West in 1241 until their final defeat by the Egyptian Mamelukes at Goliath's Well near Gaza in 1260, they were the source of concern, and occasional panic.[58] In the case of Matthew Paris, they elicited near hysteria. He wrote:

> They are inhuman and beastly, rather monsters than men, thirsting for and drinking blood, tearing and devouring the flesh of dogs and men, dressed in ox-hides, armed with plates of iron, short and stout, thickset, strong, invincible, indefatigable. . . . They have one-edged swords and daggers, are wonderful archers, and spare neither age, nor sex, nor condition.[59]

Exactly how much the author of the triplum text of our motet really knew about the Tartars is an open question. It is possible that he knew nothing more than their name. Nevertheless, it does suggest that, since the Tartars did not appear in the West until the 1240s, it would be unlikely that a poem would make reference to them in these terms at least until then. A text would probably not make such a reference until either 1245, when Innocent IV decided to treat with the Tartars, or 1248 when St Louis sent an emissary to their leader.

Although devotional poetry plays an important role in the vernacular motet, one cannot speak of the devotional motet as a 'genre'. The use of devotional texts may be set alongside other techniques found in motets that were discussed in Chapters 4 to 7. Those techniques are certainly important elements in defining the French motet of the thirteenth century, but they cannot be promoted to the status of subgenre. In the final chapter, the entire range of technical impulses may be reviewed within the context of a critical practice that gives meaning to the genre of the motet.

---

[57] R. W. Southern, *The Making of the Middle Ages* (London: Hutchinson, 1953) 59.

[58] Jacques Le Goff, *La Civilisation de l'occident médiéval* (Paris: Arthaud, 1964), trans. Julia Barrow as *Medieval Civilisation, 400–1500* (Oxford: Blackwell, 1988) 149–50.

[59] Henry Richard Luard, ed., *Mathaei Parisiensis, monachi Sancti Albani, Chronica majora*, 7 vols, Rerum britannicarum medii aevi scriptores 57 (London: Longman etc., 1874–83) 4: 76–7; translation from William Woodville Rockhill, *The Journey of William Rubruck to the Eastern Part of the World, 1253–1255 as Narrated by Himself*, Hakluyt Society, New Series 4 (London: Hakluyt Society, 1900) xv–xvi, cited in R. H. C. Davis, *A History of Medieval Europe from Constantine to St Louis* (London: Longman, 1970) 404.

8

The motet and genre

Genre

The motet is a genre. It invites us to ask how that genre is constituted, and to explain how its subgenres – if they exist – function as parts of the whole. The previous chapters have looked at suggestions of how genre functions in the thirteenth-century motet. It has been possible to isolate, admittedly with serious revision of conventional views, two subgenres: the *motet enté* (those works bearing the title in français 845 only, however) and the rondeau-motets of the Noailles chansonnier. By contrast, in the critique of these putative subgenres, we have uncovered a variety of techniques. They include, for example, the use of rondeau structures, devotional texts and repeating melodic patterns, as well as the construction of chains of refrains. These are general characteristics that are found in a wide variety of pieces. Motets exploit more than one technique at the same time, and their overall form is determined by the ways in which such technical devices interact. These techniques are in fact *modes*. They play a fundamental role in developing an interpretation of the motet. Understanding how *modes* interact with the genre or *Kind* (the motet) is an important first step in evolving a satisfactory interpretation of these dazzling pieces.

Contemporary genre criticism has moved away from questions of taxonomy and towards questions of interpretation.[1] In such interpretations, it is important to distinguish modes from other categories of genre. It is certainly true that any criticism will 'sink into incoherent confusion' unless it distinguishes between four categories of genre: *Kind* or historical genre, *subgenre*, *mode* and *constructional type*.[2]

Kind is the most general category that we are likely to encounter in the study of medieval music. Motet, conductus and chanson are examples. Subgenres include rondeau-motets (the types included in the Noailles chansonnier), *motets entés* (but only those works so titled in français 845), *conducti cum caudae* and *jeux partis*. These are all groups that genuinely mark themselves off systematically by *differentiae*

---

[1] David Hult, *Self-Fulfilling Prophecies: Readership and Authority in the First Roman de la Rose* (Cambridge: Cambridge University Press, 1986) 187.

[2] Alastair Fowler, *Kinds of Literature: An Introduction to the Theory of Genres and Modes* (Oxford: Oxford University Press, 1982) 55.

specificae.[3] Such relationships are straightforwardly taxonomic. In the case of the motet, however, they are either so general, or identify so small a portion of the repertory, that they leave a large part of the repertory undifferentiated.

The use of the term 'genre' however includes, in addition to simple taxonomies based on Kind and subgenre, the use of 'more or less unstructured modes' and 'purely formal constructional types'.[4] Constructional types concern ways of structuring works according to conventional formal plans, and are of marginal interest here. If, however, the focus of attention were to shift towards the monophonic chanson, and especially dance-songs, an evaluation of constructional types would play a greater role. One type however, the use of rondeau/rondet de carole structures, played a significant role in the discussion of the rondeau-motet in Chapter 5.

Modes assume a central position in this investigation. This is exactly where Alastair Fowler sees them: 'By being less historically circumscribed . . . modes seem to hold the key to a coherent ordering of literature'. Although it is clear from his general comments that he believes that modes should apply both to literary history as well as the specific criticism of cultural products, it is in the latter, more precise, sense that it is used here.[5] Modes are less easy to identify than constructional types because, as interpretative tools, they have to be explained in terms of the individual Kind. Modes in the conductus, then, will be different to those in the motet. For the motet, modes might include the ways in which tenors are appropriated from plainsong, the use of refrains, or the writing of Latin texts to polyphonic music. This last example shows how one mode can function within at least two Kinds simultaneously since Latin texts appear in conjunction with polyphonic music of two Kinds: motet and conductus.

This view of mode recalls some important comments made by Jurij Tynjanov in 1927. In an article directed towards the study of literary evolution, Tynjanov proposed a view of both literature and literary works as systems.[6] One could extract elements from these systems and examine them out of context. Literature, or the literary work, is then the result of the interrelationship between such elements. To borrow Tynjanov's own formulation: 'The interrelationship of each element with every other as well may be called the constructional *function* of the given element'.[7] The elements to which Tynjanov points are 'composition, style, rhythm, and syntax in prose, and the rhythm and semantics in poetry'.[8] These are technical matters which accord well with the similarly technical issues that stand at the forefront of our discussion of thirteenth-century music and poetry.

---

[3]   The term is borrowed from Porphyry. See *Isogoge, translatio Boethii*, ed. Lorenzo Minio-Paluello, Aristoteles Latinus 1, 6–7 (Rome: Union Académique Internationale, 1966) 5.

[4]   Fowler, *Kinds of Literature*, 56.

[5]   *Ibid.*, 111.

[6]   Jurij Tynjanov, 'O literaturnoj èvoljucii', *Na literaturnom postu* 4 (1927) 19–36; R *Arxaisty i novatory* (Leningrad: n.p., 1929; R [as Slavische Propyläen 31] Munich: Fink, 1967) 30–47; trans. C. A. Luplow as 'On Literary Evolution', *Readings in Russian Poetics: Formalist and Structuralist Views*, ed. Ladislav Matejka and Krystyna Pomorska (Cambridge, Mass., and London: Harvard University Press, 1971; R Ann Arbor, Mich.: University of Michigan, 1978) 67 (page numbers refer to 1978 reprint).

[7]   *Ibid.*, 68.

[8]   *Ibid.*, 67.

Tynjanov's view of literature and the literary work is inherently dynamic. The point of interaction between literature and the literary work is described as follows:

Since a system is not an equal interaction of all elements but places a group of elements in the foreground – the 'dominant' – and thus involves the deformation of the remaining elements, a work enters into literature and takes on its own literary function through this dominant.[9]

In other words, elements may be more important in some works than in others. This imbalance between components characterises the individual literary work.

In Tynjanov's concept of genre, 'the free or controlled association of elements' controls the form of a given work. 'Elements' encompass both Fowler's 'more or less unstructured modes' and his 'constructional types'.[10] Since the latter play such a minimal role in the motet, the terms 'element' and 'mode' may be used interchangeably here. Tynjanov argues that some elements emerge as 'dominants' in the dynamic interplay that informs musical or literary works. An individual work may be characterised by the concentration on one or more modes at the expense of others.

There is a wide range of musical and literary impulse in the thirteenth-century motet. It suggests that a view of genre in the musico-literary work that starts from the premiss of interrelating modes could be a plausible way of understanding the motet. Criticism of the work therefore depends on the identification of a distinction between 'dominants' and those components that are pushed into the background. To take an example, one motet might play off a dominant complex arrangement of refrains in its upper voices against one of the more popular tenors that is deployed in a neutral, or modally less valuable, fashion. Conversely, a motet might highlight its dominant tenor by allusion to its incipit in its upper voices, and by reflecting the tenor's phrase-structure in the construction of triplum or motetus. A successful interpretation of a motet that begins with descriptions, classifications and differentiations of components, continues with the exploration of how these distinguish the individual work from others.

The motet consists of a series of co-existing 'modes', and their exploration is a highly desirable basis for interpretation. This is still some way removed, however, from an adequate model for the treatment of the mid-century French motet. It takes no account of the sophisticated use of borrowed material, nor of the complexities of the identification and function of refrains that occupied parts of previous chapters. Some of the comments made by Chrétien de Troyes in the prologue to *Le Chevalier de la Charette* help to tune more finely an understanding of the differences between borrowed and original material.[11]

---

[9] *Ibid.*, 72.

[10] Indeed, as Fowler himself admits, the influence of Tynjanov's ideas is evident throughout the former's exhaustive study (*Kinds of Literature*, 250–1). But in his gloss on Tynjanov, Fowler criticises an 'overemphasis on conflict', that arises out of his characterisation of components in the literary system that 'do not co-exist, but struggle for preeminence'. Some may see this as something of a misrepresentation of Tynjanov's less than straightforward comments on this subject (*ibid.*, 250). Fowler's objections to Tynjanov however reside entirely within the domain of literary history. He points quite fairly to an inconsistency of reception as a serious obstacle to viewing literary history as an orderly system (*ibid.*, 251). Since we are here concerned with literary works and not literary history, such a disagreement is of marginal significance.

[11] Mario Roques, ed., *Les Romans de Chrétien de Troyes édités d'après la copie de Guiot (Bibl. nat. fr.794)*, 4 vols., Les Classiques français de moyen âge 80, 84, 86 and 89 (Paris: Champion, 1952–60) 3: 1–2.

Chrétien distinguishes between *matière*, *entencion*, *sens* and *conjointure* in the composition of his romance.[12] *Matière* is source material, and encompasses both verbal and literary matter. *Conjointure* represents the form of the work, and is therefore associated with questions of structure. *Matière* and *conjointure* correspond to Geoffrey of Vinsauf's terms *materia* and *ordo*.[13] *Matière* (subject matter) could have been selected by the patron, as could its mode of treatment (*sens*). Both were manipulated by the *entencion* of the poet, and resulted in the *conjointure* of the work.[14]

When these terms are transferred to the composition of motets, identification of *matière* is unproblematic. The 'source material' consists of borrowed material from the realms of plainsong, clausula, Latin motet, chanson and romance. The previous seven chapters have shown how intertextual relationships between plainsong, liturgy, narrative and chanson, and the motet are central to the composition of the motet. They are also central to its interpretation. This places the critic of the motet at an advantage since such well-preserved *matière* is a rarity in the study of romance. In *Le Chevalier de la Charette*, for example, it is impossible to isolate the *matière* because none survives.[15]

Conjointure and *entencion* emerge as the object of the critical process. *Conjointure* may be described as the combination of source materials (*matière*) governed by the *entencion* of the composer. *Conjointure*, in the shape of the completed motet, is simple to observe once the barriers of paleography and notation have been broken down. An understanding of *entencion* can emerge only from an identification of *matière* and the observation of *conjointure*. Although we may detect the traces left by *entencion*, it cannot be identified because it is not a body of material (as is *matière*) but an activity.

Manner of treatment (*sens*), so important in the romance, is elusive in the motet. Documentary sources that relate to the motet and that are analogous to those outlining *sens* in the romance are unknown. The prologue to *Le Chevalier de la Charette* tells us how Chrétien's patron, Marie de France, suggested a manner of treatment (*sens*) and how Chrétien responded (*entencion*). No descriptions of such a commission of a motet survive, and it is unlikely that the works were the result of such a process. We may conclude that *sens*, despite its central role in the romance, has little part to play either in the compositional history of a single work, or in the interpretative strategy developed here.

There are two types of freedom that the composer of the motet enjoys: the manipulation of *matière* (in much the same way as Chrétien handles his historical material) and the construction of new music and poetry. *Entencion*, and its Latin cognate, *intentio*, describes both the manipulation of *matière* and its union with newly composed material.

12   These terms have attracted significant comment. See, among others, Faith Lyons, '*Entencion* in Chrétien's *Lancelot*', *Studies in Philology* 51 (1954) 425–30; William Albert Nitze, '"Sans et matière" dans les œuvres de Chrétien de Troyes', *Romania* 44 (1915–17) 14–36; Douglas Kelly, *Sens et conjointure in the Chevalier de la Charette* (Paris and The Hague: Mouton, 1966); Kelly, 'The Source and Meaning of *Conjointure* in Chrétien's *Erec* 14', *Viator* 1 (1970) 179–200; Kelly, 'Chrétien de Troyes: The Narrator and His Art', *The Romances of Chrétien de Troyes: A Symposium*, ed. Douglas Kelly, The Edward C. Armstrong Monographs on Medieval Literature 3 (Lexington: French Forum, 1985) 13–47.
13   Kelly, *Sens et conjointure*, 91.
14   *Ibid.*, 32.
15   *Ibid.*, 35.

Distinctions between *matière* and *entencion* are important in drawing up Tynjanov's 'structured inventory of components'. We may confidently identify certain elements – plainsong tenors, clausulae or refrains, for example – as deriving from *matière*. As a consequence, the term is used in the following descriptions. *Entencion* is not an appropriate term to use in conjunction with such a structured inventory as Tynjanov proposes. It goes without saying, however, that the description of both newly composed material and the manipulation of *matière* are necessarily analyses of the traces of *entencion*.

This enquiry seeks to establish, on the basis of an identification of *matière* and the observation of *conjointure*, an interpretation of both the generic structure of the Kind and the internal processes of composition. The investigation is based on the hundred or so motets in the fifth fascicle of the Montpellier Codex. All are in three parts with two upper voices texted in French. There are two objectives. First, the different elements of the Kind – in other words the modes – are identified. Second, *conjointure* is described by reference to the co-existence of modes. The description and analysis of the elements follows the plan: music (*matière*), newly composed poetry, refrains (*matière*) and newly composed music.

Musical tradition (*matière*)

The Latin background is often critical in the growth of the French motet. Plainsong, tenor patterning, clausula and Latin motet may all play a part in the composition of a French work. The French motets in three parts in Montpellier are not in general subject to modes related to plainsong and clausula as are the Latin motets. Nevertheless, tenor patterning is important in our understanding of the range of modes functioning in French-texted compositions.

The most well-known musical traditions underpinning the Latin motet are those of building a motet on a borrowed plainsong tenor or on a borrowed polyphonic clausula. The elements of this tradition were explained in Chapter 2, and represent an obvious point of departure for an investigation of musical *matière*.

A variety of initial choices faced the composer of the motet – with French or Latin texts – and an enumeration of these is a contribution to an inventory of modes associated with *matière*.

1. A composer could text a pre-existent clausula, simply writing the text(s) of the motet himself.
2. At the other extreme, the composer could draw on nothing more than the melody of a plainsong. He would then structure the entire motet by assigning a rhythm to the tenor melody, and then supply both words and notes for the upper part(s).
3. A further possibility is that the composer could return to a clausula, but take only its rhythmicised plainsong tenor, and not its upper parts, and build the rest of the motet on this tenor.

The third alternative is interesting because the structure of the completed motet – its durations and proportions – is determined by its *matière*, exactly as if the composer had borrowed an entire clausula. The composer is still able to exercise his *entencion* in the construction of the upper voices. Some aspects of this procedure may be seen by examining a cluster of motets based on tenors and clausulae associated with the melisma *Omnes* (M1). Example 8.1 consists of the first eight perfections of a clausula: *Omnes* embedded in a two–part organum *Viderunt omnes* (M1) preserved in the Florence manuscript.

OMNES

Example 8.1 Clausula *Omnes* (M1), first eight perfections; *I-Fl* Plut. 29. 1, fol. 110r

This is the first of six rhythmically identical tenor *ordines*. There are three motets in the fifth fascicle of Montpellier (and one four-part composition in the second fascicle) that not only use the melody of the *Omnes* tenor but also borrow exactly the rhythmic patterning from the clausula in Example 8.1. (19) *Ci mi tient li maus d'amer* – (20) *Haro! Je n'i puis durer* – *Omnes* (M1) uses exactly the same tenor pattern as this clausula, but neither upper part of the motet bears any relation to the duplum of the clausula.[16] In *Ci mi tient*, the tenor pattern is used exactly four times. The disposition of the tenor of (11) *Je m'en vois* – (12) *Tiex a mout le cuer hardi* – *Omnes* (M1) again harks back to that of the clausula. Here, the pattern is stated seven and a quarter times. The last statement uses the first two perfections of the pattern only, and is presumably a result of attempts to match the tenor with the refrain in the motetus. The four-part motet (27) *A Diu commant cele* – (28) *Por moi deduire* – (29) *En non Dieu que que nus die* – *Omnes* (M1) behaves very much like the previous work: the tenor pattern is stated six and a half times with the result that the tenor ends on the pitch *d* rather than *f*. Again, this is because of the presence of refrains at this point in the upper parts.

Two extracts from the tenor of (17) *Tant me fait a vos penser* – (18) *Tout li cuers me rit* – *Omnes* (M1) are given as Example 8.2.

Example 8.2.1

Example 8.2.2

Example 8.2 (17) *Tant me fait a vos penser* – (18) *Tout li cuers me rit* – *Omnes* (M1), tenor, perfections 1–9 and 26–33; *F-MO* H 196, fols. 157v–8r

16 In all the cases where this tenor is used in a motet it is transposed down a fifth to begin on *f*.

The presence of the tenor pattern from the clausula given in Example 8.1 is clear, but it is prefaced by a single pitch, *f*, and the repetitions only extend to perfection 25, by which point – the exact centre of the piece – the pattern has been stated three times (Example 8.2.1). The second half of the piece uses a different rhythmic pattern (Example 8.2.2) that reverses elements found in the first. More interestingly, it may not have been composed for this work, since this pattern is shared with the first half of another motet: (9) *Amoureusement me tient* – (10) *Hé, Amours* – *Omnes* (M1).

The rhythmic pattern in the second half of the tenor of *Tant me fait a vos penser* is not found in any clausula. It is possible that the composer may have fashioned the rhythmic pattern for the first time in this motet, and that it was later copied by the composer of the other. At the end of *Tant me fait*, the tenor pattern is slightly distorted. It takes the last three notes that should be in the pattern L B L, and extends them as L L L. The *ordo* is lengthened by one perfection, and balances the addition of the single note at the beginning of the first half of the piece. This complex balance was borrowed by the composer of *Amoureusement me tient* who used the basic pattern of the *ordo* only in the first half of this motet.

These two motets demonstrate the function of a mode associated with the borrowing not simply of a tenor, but of its associated rhythmic pattern. *Tant me fait a vos penser* is a piece in which that mode may be viewed as one of Tynjanov's 'dominants'. Especially striking are the use of two palindromically related *ordines*, and the composer's interference with the tenor patterns at the beginning and end of the work. The focus of the piece is on manipulations of the tenor, rather than on the otherwise fairly routine refrain citations at the beginning of the motetus and end of the triplum.

Textual innovation

Two principal generic modes characterise the thirteenth-century motet: language of text and number of voice-parts. The exploitation of these modes has resulted in such apparent subgenres as the Latin two-part motet, French triple motet or bilingual double motet. Derived from the explicit classifications found in thirteenth-century sources, most particularly the *corpus ancien* of Montpellier, the use of these subgenres is present, unchallenged, throughout this study, and defines its subject. Although such traditional subgenres have a degree of value in terms of classification, especially for bibliographical purposes, they are limited as critical tools.

Identifying the literary mode of the poetry is important in coming to terms with the mass of French lyrics associated with the thirteenth-century motet. Two principal modes readily spring to the eye: the *pastourelle* and the *chanson-requette*. It is sometimes claimed that the lyric poetry of the French motet is derived from that of the trouvères. The observation fails, however, to define 'trouvère' song, and to ask if it includes, as well as the *grand chant courtois*, the *pastourelle* and rondet de carole. Many would want to dissociate the aristocratic trouvères from much motet poetry, and it is precisely these *popularisant* types of poem that play such an important role in the motet. There are various modes at work in vernacular lyric poetry, and to isolate them goes a long way towards a meaningful interpretation of motets. One group of these lyric modes is important for the rondeau-motet: the *type-cadre C'est la jus*. In conjunction with the *Bele Aeliz type-cadre*, these two represent a lyric mode that evokes the rondet de carole when present in the motet.[17]

Two types of poem are found in the motets of the fifth fascicle of Montpellier, and may be characterised as '*pastourelle*'-type and '*chanson-requette*'-type.[18] Outlining their differences is critical to an understanding of the motet. The texts of a single motet, (496) *Encontre le tans de Pascour* – (497) *Quant fuellent aubespin* – *In odorem* (M45), are good examples of the two modes. The motet from which they are taken is based on a clausula found in the Florence manuscript, and does not employ refrains. Musical innovation does not seem to be one of the dominants in this piece, and the poems are contrafacta of pre-existing Latin motets.

(Triplum)	(Motetus)
Encontre le tans	Quant fuellent aubespin,
De Pascour,	Qu'oisellon au matin
Que toz amans	Chantent cler en leur latin,
Mainent joie	Je, qui de penser ne fin
Et baudor,	Et qui por adrecier ting
Plus n'i demeur,	Seur mon cheval a droiture
Que ne soie	Sentier lés un chemin,
Renvoisiés et plains de joie	Trovai par desoz un pin
Et d'amour;	Pastorele au cors fin,
Sans sejor	Ou ele chantoit
Voeil fere un noviau chant.	Et si notoit;
Ne por quant	En son frestel menot joie
Ma joie est tornee en plor,	Ne quide, que nus hom l'oie.
Se ne puis avoir l'amor	Je la vi simplete et coie,
De cele, qui mon cuer a	Seule san Robin.
Et qui toz jours mes l'avra,	Vers li m'eslais,
Si li plaist; ele m'ocirra,	De moi li fis lais,
Tantost qu'on voudra.	Esbahie
Mon cuer a en sa baillie,	Fu, si se deslie.
Face en quanque li plaira.	Quant de li me vit pres,
Sa grant biauté m'a si pris	Si torne a la fuie
Et sorpris,	Et je apres.
De s'amor m'otroie;	Par la main l'ai prise;
Diex doinst, qu'ele soit moie!	Ce que li dis,
Si m'avroit trestout gari,	Mout petit prise,
An Diex, et resbaudi.	Ce m'est vis.
Ele a fresche la coulor,	S'amor qui m'atise
Blanche comme flor	Veut, que je soie a sa devise
Est, ce m'est avis:	Ses amis.

17   The distribution of these modes is restricted mostly to the motets found in Noailles, although one piece in the fifth fascicle of Montpellier, (678) *Bele Aelis par matin* – (679) *Haro, haro!* – *Flos filius eius* (O16), does depend in part on this mode.

18   The valuable, but non-medieval, phrase *chanson-requette* was coined by Paul Zumthor (*Essai de poétique médi-évale*, Collection poétique (Paris: Editions de Seuil, 1972) 262) and adopted by Bec (*Lyrique française*, 1: 218).

Cheveus blons, front vien assis,	Au col li mis
Les ieuz vairs, rians,	Mes bras et puis li dis:
Les sorcis haus et voutiz,	'Bele flour de lis,
Bouche vermelle et plesant.	Je sui vostre amis,
Diex, ne me puis	A vous me rent pris'.
Tenir, que s'amor	Tant fis et tant dis,
Ne demant!	Qu'audesus me mis,
Bele, que ferai,	Ma volenté fis
Se vostre amor n'ai?	Tout a mon devis;
Las, autrement	Dous ris ot et cler vis.
Sui a la mort	
Sans resort.	
Se m'ociés,	
Quant tot a vous m'acort,	
Diex, c'est a tort.	

(Triplum) At Eastertime all lovers live in joy and happiness, but I am no longer with them because I am not lighthearted and full of love and joy; I want to compose a new song without delay. But my joy has turned to tears, for I cannot have the love of her who possesses my heart and who always will, if that please her; she will kill me as soon as anyone asks her to. She has my heart in her power, let her do with it as she pleases. Her great beauty has so captured and taken me, I am so inflamed with love of her that I will live in complete joy, if she grants me her love; may God grant that she be mine! Then will she have completely cured me, by God, and cheered me. She has such fresh colour, as white as a flower, it seems to me; blonde hair, a pleasingly shaped brow, laughing, grey-blue eyes, high arched eyebrows, pleasing scarlet lips. God, I cannot keep from asking for her love. Fair one, what shall I do if I have not your love? Alas, otherwise death is my lot without recourse. You kill me when I give myself entirely to you. God, that is not right.

(Motetus) With the hawthorn bush turning leafy green, with the clear warbling of birdsong filling the morning, I, lost in thought, and keeping my horse to a path alongside a road, found a true-hearted shepherd girl beneath a pine tree where she was singing and accompanying herself; she was playing joyfully on her pipe, thinking that no one heard her. I saw that she was simple and calm and alone, without Robin. I approached her, drew her near to me and pledged my love to her. She was frightened and pulled away. When she saw me close to her, she turned and ran, with me in pursuit. I took hold of her by the hand. It seems to me that she did not think much of what I said to her – that the love of her which was exciting me wanted me to be her sweetheart as she would. I put my arms around her neck and said to her: 'Fair lily flower, I am your sweetheart and hand myself over, prisoner, to you'. With enough sweet talk and sweet gestures I was able to get cn top of her and take my pleasure as I desired. She had a sweet laugh and a bright face.

The triplum text on the left is a *chanson-requette*, and the motetus text on the right is a *pastourelle*. Their stylistic origins in lyrics associated with monophonic song are clear. This is particularly so in the case of the *pastourelle*. There are marked differences between the two poems. The *dramatis personae* are radically different: the *pastourelle*-type invariably uses a knight and a shepherdess with a shepherd as an optional character; the *chanson-requette*-type explores the world of the lyric *je*.

The *chanson-requette*-type is almost devoid of narrative action, and is cast in the form of a plea to the Lady accompanied by the appeals for divine mediation that are much in evidence here. By contrast, the *pastourelle*-type, like its *chanson* counterpart, depends on a colourful scenario and, occasionally, an even more colourful narrative. It always begins with a springtime *exordium*: flowers are in bud, shrubs turn green and birds sing. It is invariably morning. The knight-narrator, usually on horseback, encounters a shepherdess (in the example, the absence of her lover Robin is noted) and her attributes are briefly described. Attempted seduction follows, and responses range from enthusiastic acquiescence to outright and indignant rejection. This is another point at which the shepherdess's consort may be mentioned or occasionally even appear. In the example here, the shepherdess puts up a spirited resistance but eventually succumbs as the result of the knight's fine words: 'Bele flour de lis, / Je sui vostre amis, / A vous me rent pris'; there is a triumph of *aristocratisant* eloquence over low-born naïvety. The attributes given as an initial description, 'simplete et coie', are further amplified in an offhand manner at the very end of the poem: 'Dous ris ot et cler vis'.

The sententious *chanson-requette* contrasts with the narrative *pastourelle*. Sentience, sometimes derived from the text of a refrain, determines the content and tone of the *chanson-requette* poem. Here, the common conceit 'Se m'ociés / Quant tot a vous m'acort' determines the tone of the entire lyric. The tone of the characters is likewise highly contrasted. The lyric *je* and the Lady of the *chanson-requette* are serious contributors to the ideal of *amour courtois*. We have already seen how easily this mode merges into a devotional one by means of the assimilation of the Lady with the Virgin Mary. Of the characters in the *pastourelle*, the knight is a seducer, a flatterer and sometimes weak, and the shepherdess is ambitious and lubricious.[19]

Both types of lyric make frequent but differing allusions to music. In the *pastourelle*, pipe and tabor are often used as attributive elements in the knight's brief description of the shepherdess. The purpose of music in the *chanson-requette* is more abstract, and consists most frequently of the *Chanter m'estuet* topos. The texts that exemplify this discussion well illustrate this feature. In *Quant fuellent aubespin*, the shepherdess '. . . chantoit / Et si notoit; / En son frestel . . .', whereas in *Encontre le tans de Pascour*, the poet 'Sans sejor / Voeil fere un noviau chant'.

The differing tones of the two modes are reflected in the literary register of the poetry. *Pastourelles* tend towards consistency. Their narrator is an aristocrat and his use of feudal and military image is particularly evident in dialogue. 'I hand myself over to you as a prisoner' he says to the shepherdess, as his final and successful gesture of seduction. By contrast, the register of the shepherdess's conversation is strictly functional. She is silent in our illustration but in (122) *Hui main au doz mois de mai*, for example, she declares to the knight that 'A moi n'a touchés voz ja, / Quar j'ai mignot ami!'

Consistency of register in the *pastourelle* is matched by variety in the *chanson-requette*. This often depends on influences from other lyric types. In our example there is a fractional shading from the *pastourelle* in the opening gesture, 'Encontre le tans / De Pascour'. The appropriation of these *exordia* is common in the *chanson-requette* mode. The translation obscures the rhetorical use of feudal imagery – such an *aristocratisant* characteristic – in 'Mon cuer a en sa baillie / Face en quanque li

19 Bec, *Lyrique française*, 1: 121.

plaira', although it is plain elsewhere. In this poem, the register tends towards the lofty, and this is not untypical of the mode.

The use of names is a clear means of distinguishing between the *pastourelle* and *chanson-requette* modes. Proper names are hardly ever present in the latter, whereas they are essential in certain phases of the former. They are only ever used for the low-born characters. Robin and Marot and their diminutives are the two most common and best known. Attributive description is an important element in the *chanson-requette*. The portrayal of the Lady runs to seven lines in our example, and is typical. This is in marked contrast to the cursory depictions in the *pastourelle* which often only include a couple of adjectives.

There may occur a degree of interference between the two modes. Most noticeable is the influence of the *pastourelle* on the variable register of the *chanson-requette*. The combination of two poems, as in the motets in the fifth fascicle of Montpellier, raises the possibility of further registral interference. This sort of potential cross-relation has attracted most comment on the motet from literary scholars.[20] The foregoing discussion of *chanson-requette* and *pastourelle* modes suggests that identification of such registral interference is but one approach among the many that these texts invite. Two futher observations shade the discussion of these two modes. One is the statistical superiority of *chanson-requette* over *pastourelle*. Another is the fact that most of the *pastourelles* are paired with other poems in the same mode. Such examples as (496) *Encontre le tans de Pascour* – (497) *Quant fuellent aubespin* – *In odorem* (M45) present different modes in triplum and motetus. Although they serve well as examples to point up the differences between the modes, they are relatively rare among the motets in the fifth fascicle of Montpellier.

Refrains (*matière*)

Motets may be considered in two classes: those with, and those without, refrains. In principle, French motets based on clausulae or Latin motets are subject to a mode that eschews refrains completely, because they are based on music that ultimately derives from a Latin, sacred, environment. Composers of such French motets as those found in the fifth fascicle of Montpellier are able to select a mode either with or without refrains. The composition of a work is not dependent on the presence of a refrain in the same way that it is dependent on the presence of a borrowed tenor. In motets with refrains, either both text and music of the refrain or the refrain's text alone is used. This is a difference in terms of the relationship between *entencion* and *matière*, and is often difficult to determine. In many cases, where for example a refrain text is found with two or more different melodies, it is very difficult to demonstrate that a composer takes a refrain, both text and music, from a pre-existent source and then uses the text only.

An edition of the last sixteen perfections of (83) *L'autrier m'esbatoie* – (84) *Demenant grant joie* – *Manere* (M5), followed by both texts complete, is given as Example 8.3.

---

[20]   The relevant literature is cited above, p. 7 and note 14.

It allows us to probe some of the ways in which we may identify the presence of borrowed words and notes in the refrain.

Example 8.3 (83) *L'autrier m'esbatoie* – (84) *Demenant grant joie – Manere* (M5), last sixteen perfections; *F-MO* H 196, fols 112v-14r

(Triplum)	(Motetus)
L'autrier m'esbatoie	Demenant grant joie,
Et touz seus pensoie	L'autrier m'en aloie
A mon gré;	Lés un pré
S'en ai mieuz trové:	Au douz tens d'esté.
Fesant mout grant joie,	N'encore n'avoie
Encontrai	Nul home encontré,
Robin lés un pré,	S'iert il ajorné,
Ou Marot avoit chanté:	Et je chevauchoie,
'J'ai une amourete	Palefroi sejorné.
A mon gré,	S'ai trové
Qui me tient joliete'.	Un bergerot
Regrete	Cointe et mignot,
Son bergerot,	S'a chanté:
Qui mout li agree	'Hé Emmelot,
Et cointe et mignot.	Je t'ai tant amee,
Ainsi Robin sovent regretot:	Qu'om m'en tient por sot!'
'Grant folie est,	Bergerie
Je t'en tieng pour sot	Mout bele menot,

A ce mot,   Mes s'amie
Quant t'amie   Souvent regretot,
As deguerpie,   Tant qu'il ot
Marot'.   Entroïé
Quant oie   La chevrie
Ot la chevrie,   Marot.
Si chantoit: Par la pree
'G'irai toute la valee   Encontre li renotoit:
Avec Marot'.   *'G'irai toute la valee*
                                 Avec Marot'.

(Triplum) The other day I was amusing myself all alone and letting my thoughts wander as they would, but I found something better to do: I met Robin beside a meadow where Marot had been singing: 'I have love to my liking and it keeps me lighthearted'. She was lamenting because of the handsome, charming shepherd lad who suited her so well. And so she often mourned Robin in this way: 'It's great folly, and I proclaim you a fool for having abandoned your sweetheart Marot'. When Robin had heard the piping he sang: 'I will travel the whole valley with Marot'.

(Motetus) The other day in sweet summertime I went out beside a meadow with a heart full of joy. I hadn't met a soul, and day was dawning as I was riding along on my fresh palfrey. I found a charming, handsome shepherd lad who sang: 'Hey, Emmelot, I loved you so much that I'm taken for a fool!' He was playing on a lovely, fine pipe, but he often lamented his sweetheart until he heard Marot's flute. From across the meadow he answered back in song: 'I will travel the whole valley with Marot'.

The two texts both belong to the *pastourelle* mode. At the end of both the triplum and motetus is a refrain: *'G'irai toute la valee avec Marot'* (vdB 1157). It is possible to unravel the refrain's musical tradition and to show that it is borrowed from a pre-existing source. Although the refrain in the motetus represents a borrowing of both text and music, the music in the triplum is newly composed to the text of the refrain. The refrain, both text and music, is also found in another motet, (515a) *Quant l'alouete saut* – *Qui conservaret* (M50). This is in turn based on a clausula in Florence. The refrain most probably arose out of the process of texting the clausula, and then was borrowed in the motet currently under discussion. Example 8.4 gives the last eight perfections of the clausula, *Qui conservaret*, and its derivative motet: *Quant l'alouete saut*. They may be compared with the last eight perfections of Example 8.3. Even though they are based on different tenors, the refrains are more or less identical. The very first sonority is changed to an *e–b* fifth in *L'autrier m'esbatoie* because of the *e* in its tenor. The original clausula/motet had a *d–a* fifth in the same place. Apart from this alteration, and a few changes of rhythm, the melody of the refrain of *Quant l'alouete saut* is the same as the one in the motetus of *L'autrier m'esbatoie*. Although both text and music of the refrain appear at the end of the motetus of *L'autrier*, it is clear that the text alone of the refrain is used in the triplum. There are, therefore, two different modes at work simultaneously in this composition: the music and text of the refrain are quoted at the same time as the text alone of the refrain is equipped with new music.

(83) *L'autrier m'esbatoie* – (84) *Demenant grant joie* – *Manere* (M5) also provides a good example of the ways in which a refrain interferes with the musical structure of

[QUI CONSERVARET]

[QUI CONSERVARET]

Example 8.4 Clausula *Qui conservaret* (M50), *I-Fl* Plut. 29. 1, fol. 169v, and (515a) *Quant l'alouete saut – Qui conservaret* (M50), last eight perfections; *B-Lu*

the piece. Throughout much of the motet, the upper voices are cast in the second rhythmic mode with extensive *fractio* and *extensio modi*, over a regular Mode V tenor. The refrain flatly contradicts this. The tenor continues as before, but the upper voices switch into Mode I. This may be seen in Example 8.3. The rhythmic mode of the refrain is here the same as it appears in *Quant l'alouete saut* and its clausula. The newly composed music to the text of the refrain in the triplum mimics the shift of rhythmic mode in the motetus. The refrain participates in the functioning of the *pastourelle* mode, and it marks a shift from indirect to direct speech in both poems. The corresponding shift in rhythmic mode enhances this purpose.

There is a second refrain in this motet. It is found in the middle of the triplum: '*J'ai une amourete a mon gré / Qui me tient joliete*'. It is also found in a *salut d'amours* which is preserved without music. Unlike the terminal refrain, it does not disrupt the musical foreground of the piece; its rhythms and melodies match those in the rest of the upper voices. It marks a shift however to direct speech in the same way as the terminal refrain. The poetic structure of the refrain, '*J'ai une amourete*', does however affect the structure of the piece. The first seven lines of both poems are mostly of identical length and use the same rhymes. The line-lengths result in identical phrase-lengths and simultaneous upper-voice cadences. Even in the sixth line of each poem, where line-lengths are different, the composer sets each to a four-perfection phrase. But just before the refrain everything changes. As the triplum poem introduces a cue line, 'Ou Marot avoit chanté', the motetus parts company with it. What follows is characterised by divergent line-lengths, rhymes and phrase-lengths. This dislocation of the phrase-structure and upper-voice cadence ends with the eleventh line of the triplum and the twelfth of the motetus poems. With the following text-lines, phrase-length, length of poetic line and rhyme are resynchronised. The same sort of process occurs at the end of the piece, just before the refrain. The relationship between text-line and phrase is again entirely regular up to the beginning of Example 8.3. The congruity of music and poetry collapses. The voices regroup for the final eight perfections that include the refrain.

The effect of such a process is to sectionalise the texture of the piece into an ABAC structure: a regular passage (perfections 1–28), an irregular passage created by the refrain (perfections 29–48), and a further regular passage (perfections 49–80). This is followed by the final refrain which, together with its introductory lines, generates a fourth section.

The local impact of a mode that entails the use of a refrain may be disruption to phrase patterning and to poetic structure, and to the musical surface itself. There are four positions for refrains in a motet: terminal, medial, initial and divided. (83) *L'autrier m'esbatoie* – (84) *Demenant grant joie* – *Manere* (M5) presents examples of the first two of these. We have already seen an example of a terminal refrain in our discussion of (17) *Tant me fait a vos penser* – (18) *Tout li cuers me rit* – *Omnes* (M1). This was van den Boogaard's normal refrain, where he felt that no comment was necessary: the terminal variety. He identified medial refrains as *int[érieur]*, initial refrains similarly: *déb[ut]*. He used the term *motet enté* with impunity to describe the more specific of the two nomenclatures described in Chapter 4.[21] He described those occurrences of the refrain, divided into two and placed at beginning and end of the voice-part, as a *motet enté*.

At the end of Chapter 4, it was suggested that the subgeneric term '*motet enté*' should be reserved for the small group of compositions found in the manuscript français 845. In the context of a typology of refrain usage, an alternative term needs to be offered. Replacing the term *motet enté* with 'divided refrain' relocates the phenomenon as a mode rather than as a subgenre, and more accurately reflects the practice found in the thirteenth-century motet. This correctly aligns the usage with the other three modes of deploying a borrowed refrain in a motet's voice-part.

Refrains can disrupt the patterning of otherwise regular musical and poetic structures. A much more common phenomenon is the use of the refrain's line-length and especially rhyme to control the rest of the poem. The text of the triplum of (787) *Grant solaz me fet amors* – (788) *Pleüst Diu* – *Neuma* (Neuma III. Toni) is given below:

Grant solaz me fet amors	α
Quant a chanter m'avoie,	ß
Qu'enseignie ma' la voie	ß
A celi, qui je queroie;	ß
Por qui je maig si grant joie	ß
Car quanque je desirroie, en ai	a
Et pour sa valour la servirai;	a
Car *de ma dame vient la grant joie que j'ai.*	a
Ele m'aprent, ce que je sai;	a
Trop bon gré mon cuer en sai,	a
Qui s'enhardi, qu'onques osai	a
Tel dame amer.	b

---

[21] Van den Boogaard, *Rondeaux et refrains*, 23.

Bien me doi reconforter,	b
Rire et jouer,	b
Mal oublier,	b
Ce qu'a ma dame ai mis mon cuer et mon penser;	*b*
Ja ne l'en quier oster,	b
Mes en sa baillie	d
Mest ma vie.	d
Je ne l'ai mie avec moi,	*c*
Mon cuer, ains l'a m'amie.	*d*
Plene fu de courtoisie,	d
Quant de s'amor l'ai	a
Proiee; adonc chantai	a
Et quant oïe ot ma chançon,	e
Et Dieus, por quoi la regardai,	*a*
Quant si vair oel traï m'ont?	*e*
Par sa franchise m'apela,	γ
De s'amor m'aseura.	γ

Love comforts me greatly when he counsels me to sing, for she has taught me the way to the one whom I seek and on whose account I am so joyful. For whatever I would desire, I have, and because of her great worth, I will serve her, for the joy which I have comes from my lady. She teaches me whatever I know; I am very grateful to my heart which became bold, that I ever dared to love a lady such as this. I should indeed be comforted, laugh, play, and forget all trouble, for I have entrusted my heart and my thoughts to my lady; I will never want to remove them; rather, I place my life in her keeping. I no longer have my heart with me: my sweetheart has it. She was full of courtesy when I beseeched her for her love; then I sang for her, and when she had heard my song, and God, why did I look at her when her grey-blue eyes betrayed me? She courteously called me over and assured me of her love.

There are four refrains in this poem, italicised here. Each has widespread concordances and, in the case of the text at least, a fairly straightforward process of borrowing is at work. Two of the refrains are of two lines and two are of one. In the edition of text, the rhymes derived from the refrain are labelled with Roman letters, those not derived from the refrain with Greek.

Only the rhymes of the lines at the beginning and end do not derive from the refrain. The rest of the rhymes cluster around the refrains in which they are also found. The 'a' rhymes of the first refrain are found in the two lines that precede it and the three that follow. The 'b' rhymes of the next refrain then come into play, and control the next four lines. The refrain with the 'b' rhyme then follows, and the next line is the last to use that rhyme. The 'c' rhyme in the third refrain is not used in the body of the poem. Since the last refrain shares one rhyme with the first ('a'), this is found towards the end as well. The refrains act as a focus for the lines that are newly composed, and take on a structural function in the poem. The structural concerns are subtle, and enable a gradual overlapping of the change in rhyme. This contrasts, for example, with the rigid structural articulations of tenor *cursus* that divide the tenor into three equal sections of thirty-eight perfections each.

Dictation of poetic rhyme by the rhymes of the refrain is one mode in which the refrain can function. It is equally possible that the rhymes of the refrain may be studiously ignored in the rest of the poem until the appearance of the refrain itself. This is particularly common in shorter texts with perhaps one refrain at the end of the voice-part. The two texts of the motet (83) *L'autrier m'esbatoie* – (84) *Demenant grant joie* – *Manere* (M5) share vocabulary between the triplum and motetus poems.[22] The words '*bergerot . . . cointe et mignot*', and the third singular perfect of 'regreter', 'regretot' are found in the central lines of both poems. The -*ot* ending is derived from the refrain line in the triplum which dictates a large proportion of the rhymes in the central part of this poem. But it also controls rhymes in the motetus. This procedure is a significant extension of the functioning of the mode.

The refrain-mode can be further described according to the degree to which the refrain is assimilated into the rest of the poem. The first three refrains of *Grant solaz me fet amors* offer examples of two levels of integration of the refrain. '*Je ne l'ai mie avec moi / Mon cuer, ains l'a m'amie*' accords fairly well with the alternation of first and third person statements that surround it, although its sense is discrete. However, the first two refrains of *Grant solaz* are not only integrated grammatically by conjunctions, but their registers precisely match their environment. Particularly striking is the use of the word 'dame' to describe the woman both in the refrains and in the surrounding lyric. Examples of the quotation of refrains that disrupt the prevailing register are very hard to find. They occur, for example, in the *pastourelle*-mode, in which registral discontinuity is an inherent characteristic.

A refrain may interact with a motet voice by taking a pair of lines that makes sense on its own, and placing the first line at the beginning of a poem and the second line at the end so that they make sense in their new context. The motetus of (678) *Bele Aelis par matin* – (679) *Haro, haro!* – *Flos filius eius* (O16) is a good example:

> *Haro, haro! Je la voi la,*
> La riens du mont qui plus m'a
> Mis en desconfort;
> N'onques n'en oi deport,
> Mes ades en grant dolor
> Sans sejor m'a mis a tort.
> Biau samblant sanz cuer amoreus,
> Meschief et corros
> Ai adés en la bele trové,
> Et s'ai bone volenté
> D'atendre le guerredon
> *Cele, qui m'a en sa prison*

Ho, ho! I see her there, the one who has hurt me more than any other. I never have any joy from her; but continually, without respite, she has wrongfully inflicted me with great pain. Fair seeming without a loving heart, sorrow and ire are what I have always found in the fair one, and yet I am quite willing to wait for recompense from her who has me in her prison.

The refrain makes perfect sense on its own: '*Ho, ho! I see her there, / The one who has me in her prison*'. The first line is dovetailed into the second: '*Ho, ho! I see her there, / The one who, more than any other in the world, has / Hurt me*'. Again at the end:

[22] See pp. 159–60.

'I am quite willing / To wait for the recompense / From *the one who has me in her prison*'. Rhymes work in pairs throughout this poem (*aabbccddeeff*), and those of the refrain are integrated entirely into this structure.

A refrain can work as an interpolated parenthesis. The last refrain in the triplum of *Grant solaz me fet amors* shows how the poetry of the surrounding context functions perfectly in its own right: 'She was full of courtesy / When, for her love, I / Beseeched her; then I sang, / And when she heard my song, / *O God, why did I look at her / When her grey-blue eyes turned towards me?* / She courteously called me over, / And assured me of her love'. The refrain is slipped in neatly before the second line from the end as a parenthetical aside that disrupts the flow of the sense of the poem. As we have seen, however, it plays a critical role in the poem's structure.

The inclusion of a refrain often betokens a change from indirect to direct speech, or a change in voice. This is particularly common in the *pastourelle*, and is very much the case, for example, in the triplum of (235) *Quant voi le douz tans venir* – (236) *En mai quant rose est florie – Immolatus* (M14):

> En mai quant rose est florie,
> Par matin s'est esveillie
> Marot, s'a Robin trové,
> A lui reprové
> La bone compaignie,
> Qu'adés li a portee;
> Q'or li a le doz torné.
> Il li a dit et juré,
> Par la foi
> Qu'il lui doit,
> Qu'einsi n'iert il mie:
> '*Se j'ai demoré*
> *A veoir m'amie,*
> *N'est pas a mon gré*'.

In May, when roses bloom, Marot woke up one morning and found Robin; she reminded him reproachfully of the fair companionship he had always provided her, for now he had turned his back to her. He told her and swore by the faith he owes her that it was not so: 'If I did not come to see my sweetheart, it is not because I did not want to'.

This highly abbreviated *pastourelle* completely omits the contrast between courtly, chivalric elements and those that concern the shepherd and shepherdess. The *exordium* is contracted into six words. The encounter here is between Marot, the shepherdess, and the shepherd, Robin. These are the two active characters in a larger *pastourelle* narrated by the knight. Nevertheless, the refrain projects a direct speech that contrasts strongly with the indirect speech of the rest of the poem.[23] Such a change from indirect to direct speech is found less frequently in the *chanson-requette*. This is clearly an aspect of the registral flexibility that characterises this mode. For example,

---

[23] Although this is a common feature, it must be stressed that not all direct speech is composed of refrains. The assumption that direct speech pointed to the presence of a refrain was one of the doubtful criteria Gennrich used in his identification of 'refrains'.

in the motetus of (286) *Nus ne set les biens d'amors* – (287) *Ja Dieus ne me doinst corage* – *Portare* (M22), much of the dialogue is presented in reported speech. At the end of the poem, the final retort of the cuckolding wife is a refrain in direct speech: 'Fie, villain with the mad face! / You will not know today / Whose sweetheart I am'.

An elaboration of such procedures as these is the use of the refrain as a song. This is an important and very common element of the *pastourelle* mode. The song is always cued, and the narrator named, as at the end of the triplum of (182) *L'autrier trouvai une plesant tousete* – (183) *L'autrier, les une espinete* – *In seculum* (M13):

> . . . Puis a forment en souspirant chanté;
> '*Sadera li duriau durete,*
> *Sadera li duré*'.

These are the last three lines of a ten-line poem whose rhymes are all taken from the two rhymes of the refrain.

More rarely, refrains function as songs in the *chanson-requette*. Here, as might be expected, the tone, both of the refrain and the poem as a whole, is rather different in those poems that adopt the *registre aristocratisant*. For example the motetus of (787) *Grant solaz me fet amors* – (788) *Pleüst Diu* – *Neuma* (Neuma III. Toni) ends as follows:

> . . . Ainz chanterai:
> '*Pris m'a une amourete*
> *Dont ja ne partirai*'.

Refrains are a powerful force in the mid–century vernacular motet. The ways in which they are deployed may be classified according to their structural function, and level of interference or integration with both textual and musical elements. They may also be classified by the degree to which their intrinsic form determines or even dictates the structure of the rest of the motet into which they are introduced.

Musical innovation

The last of the four general areas of modal activity within the motet is specifically musical. In addition to the manipulation of borrowed text (in the refrain) and music (both in the refrain and tenor), the composer contributes new musical material to the motet. When the composer turns his hand to fusing borrowed tenor and perhaps a borrowed refrain, he does so by the addition of music. Consistent melodic patterning, characterised by repetitions of phrases, is something of a rarity in the parts of motets that are newly composed. Many phrases begin the same way but invariably change course after the first few pitches. We need to be able to quantify how this particular melodic style behaves. In the motetus of (83) *L'autrier m'esbatoie* – (84) *Demenant grant joie* – *Manere* (M5), there are two pairs of identical phrases, starting at (a) perfections 75 and 81, and (b) perfections 13 and 25. So many of the other phrases seem to begin in a consistent way, and then diverge. Example 8.5 graphs the melodic structure of the motetus in a manner familiar from the analysis of the *motets entés* from français 845 in Chapter 4.

The analysis shows how far removed is the melodic construction of this voice-part from that of the motets in français 845. Only two of the paradigms describe simple melodic repetition: C and E. Even paradigm E needs qualification. The graph shows the ways in which the paradigms break down. In paradigm B, for example, five phrases begin with the same four pitches and then change. There is a clear difference between the multiple evolution of phrases in paradigm B and the single repeated phrase in paradigm C. Exactly how the last two members of paradigm A function is open to question. The inclusion of the third, and especially the fourth, member of paradigm C is similarly dubious. The third member is found also in the triplum which is not graphed here. The triplum behaves in a broadly similar way, although its paradigms are different. From an analytical perspective, the shared material between the voice-parts, and the *exactly* repeating elements in paradigms C and E in the motetus, emerge as the modal dominants that characterise this particular motet. To the ear, however, the phrases under paradigm B that use the same opening formula and then diverge are the most striking. They too have a claim as modal dominants. Although this tension is an interesting characteristic of the motet, the point to be stressed is that the dominant mode is one that is associated with newly composed music, not, for example, refrain or poetic mode.

Some melodic practices are tied to melodic patterning in the refrain. In the discussion of (9) *Amoureusement me tient* – (10) *Hé, Amours* – *Omnes* (M1) in Chapter 6, we saw how two refrains were each used twice, once in each voice-part. Their music was presumably borrowed. Between them, they occupied a large proportion of the melodic superstructure of the motet. A further example of melody as one of the dominant modes of a motet is (290) *Emi, emi Marotele* – (291) *Emi, emi Marotele* – *Portare* (M22). Extracts from the work (perfections 1–4, 13–16 and 45–8) are given as Example 8.6. The refrain consists of the pair of lines: '*Emi, emi Marotele / Voz trairés l'ame de mi*'. These occur in other sources, but are here divided into two, and placed at the beginning and end of the motetus. The text alone of the refrain is duplicated in the triplum, both at the beginning and the end.[24] The music is different. We may be certain that the melody of the original refrain occurs in the motetus because it is also preserved in other sources of the refrain.

The concept of free melodic repetition is however new. Counterpoints are composed to accompany an imported melody, and come to be repeated with the imported melody, and hence to influence the structure of the motet. The contrapuntal line in the triplum that accompanies the second line of the refrain (i.e. the last line of the motetus) is repeated in the middle of the triplum. As may be seen in Example 8.6, perfections 13–16 and 45–8 are musically identical. These repetitions are independent of the refrain. Although the triplum music of the last four perfections of the piece draws analytical attention to the passage in perfections 13–16, the text of the triplum draws attention to the beginning and end of the motetus.

Sequence and canon are two compositional resources used to great effect in the organa of Perotinus. (459) *Navrés sui au cuer* – (460) *Navrés sui pres du cuer* – *Veritatem* (M37) is a motet in which melodic repetitions are found. A motetus phrase near the

---

24 This has already been seen in *L'autrier m'esbatoie* (see above pp. 158–60).

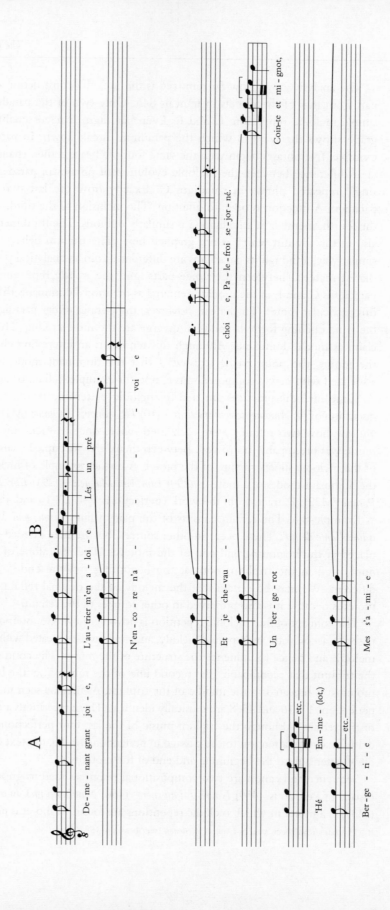

Example 8.5 (83) *L'autrier m'esbatoie* – (84) *Demenant grant joie* – *Manere* (M5), melodic structure of the motetus

Example 8.6 (290) *Emi, emi Marotele* – (291) *Emi, emi Marotele* – *Portare* (M22), perfections 1–4, 13–16 and 45–8; *F-MO* H 196, fols. 210v-12r

beginning of the piece is repeated towards the centre and clearly straddles the end of the first and the beginning of the second tenor *cursus*. This is a response to the organisation of the tenor. The repetitions in (661) *Quant define la verdour* – (662) *Quant repaire la dolçor* – *Flos filius eius* (O16) are slightly different. Example 8.7 gives an excerpt.

The repetitions in the motetus are clearly sequential. The participation of the triplum and tenor in the sequence is slight. The triplum follows the pattern only for the last two of the three limbs of the sequence. The last note of each of the three

[FLOS FILIUS EIUS]

Example 8.7 (661) *Quant define la verdour* – (662) *Quant repaire la dolçor* – *Flos filius eius* (O16), perfections 29–34; *F-MO* H 196, fols. 173v-4r

tenor phrases doubles the cadence note of the motetus. In (561) *Riens ne puet ma grant folie* – (560) *Riens ne puet plus doumagier* – *Aperis* (M69), three passages in canon are found. In the first, the second phrase begins only in the last couple of perfections of the first. But in the other two passages, the *comes* follows the *dux* at a distance of only one perfection. Particularly striking, however, are the verbal correspondences between the texts of triplum and motetus. The text in both *dux* and *comes* is the same. Textual processes in this motet lead musical ones.

There is a similar pattern in (124) *Vilene gent* – (125) *Honte et dolor* – *Hec dies* (M13), an edition of which is given as Example 8.8. Two phrases marked with brackets crossed once (motetus, perfections 17–20 and triplum, 21–4) behave similarly to those in *Riens ne puet ma grant folie*. The phrases share the same text and music. As the texts diverge, so do the musical phrases. These two phrases begin very similarly to the opening of the motetus voice. The other two phrases (motetus, perfections 9–16 and 25–32) are musically identical, but apart from rhyme, they share no poetic content. The first element ends with the words 'Vileine gent' that are found at the beginning of the triplum. The words are derived in turn from the first words of the refrain in the motetus, and prompt the refrain in the triplum. This is paralleled by the musical prompting of the refrain in perfections 43–5 of the triplum. The descending fifth *g* to *c*, that prompts the refrain in the triplum and begins it in the motetus, is also present in perfections 15–16. Here, it seems to highlight the end of the first phrase of melodic significance in the motetus, and the beginning of the simple canon that occupies perfections 17–24. It is also found in perfection 31, exactly at the end of the second statement of the second repeating phrase.

The use of a melodic repetition that is unrelated to textual duplication is one of several modes in this motet. We may add it to repetitions that include textual repeats, and the use of a terminal refrain in the motetus, as modal elements characterise the generic status of this work. There is, however, a structural importance to these apparently competing modalities. They are deployed in a linear and complementary fashion. There are very few points in the piece where one or other of these elements is not at work.

Example 8.8 (124) *Vilene gent* – (125) *Honte et dolor* – *Hec dies* (M13); *F-MO* H 196, fols 138v–40r

Musical repetition may occur in two voices simultaneously. Example 8.9 is an extract from (678) *Bele Aelis par matin* – (679) *Haro, haro!* – *Flos filius eius* (O16) where there is a melodic repetition of a piece of two-part counterpoint. The repeating triplum phrase cadences at the same time as the repeating motetus phrase begins. The passages are boxed in the example. Although the contrapuntal pairing of the first of the two phrases might be the result of the presence of the word 'deport' in both triplum and motetus texts, this is not the case with the second of the two phrases. A strictly musical impulse generated this patterning.

Much melodic repetition in the upper voices of motets is tied to the structure of the tenor. Such a procedure has the effect of enhancing the structural force of a multiple tenor *cursus*. In such cases a generic mode associated with melody creates a motet with a strong structural profile. The music in previous examples concentrated on outlining cross-references between portions of the melodic line or between two voice-parts. Two cases where the tenor is also included may serve as examples. The tenor of (13) *Qui bien aime, il ne doit mie* – (14) *Cuer qui dort* – *Omnes* (M1) consists of two *cursus* of sixteen perfections each. For the first five perfections of each *cursus*, the triplum is almost exactly the same. Similarly, (21) *Il n'a en toi* – (22) *Robin, li mauvés ovrier* – *Omnes* (M1) also has a tenor consisting of two *cursus* of sixteen perfections each (the pattern is different to the previous piece however). The motetus phrases in the second half of each *cursus* are, apart from fractional changes to the end of the second one, identical to their counterparts in the first *cursus*. The

Example 8.9 (678) *Bele Aelis par matin* – (679) *Haro, haro!* – *Flos filius eius* (O16), perfections
10–22; *F-MO* H 196, fols. 132v-3r

positioning of the repetitious part of the motetus is a precursor of the interaction of
upper voices and tenor in the fourteenth-century isorhythmic motet.[25]

When principles of melodic repetition take over the functioning of all three
voice-parts, the relationship between texture and structure that is one of the
consistent characteristics of the thirteenth-century motet is under severe threat. This
principle, carried to its logical conclusion, produces motets later in the century, the
structure of whose French-song tenors is reflected exactly in both upper parts. These
are critical to the evolution of polyphonic song *c*. 1300. We can see this principle in
embryo in (716) *Hé, Marotele* – (717) *En la praerie* – *Aptatur* (O45). There are three
identical statements of the tenor; each is of thirty-two perfections duration. In
perfections 17–23 of each *cursus*, not only does the motetus present exactly the same
melodic profile in each case, but the triplum also participates in the process.
Examples 8.10.1–3 show the three corresponding passages one above another. The
three motetus phrases are exactly the same with the exception of the last two notes
in the third statement. The role played by the triplum is rather more subtle. It
balances all three phrases. The first two phrases, (1) and (2), leave a perfection's rest
above the beginning of the motetus phrase. The triplum starts at the beginning of
the next perfection. In the third phrase, (3), this space is filled. However, the

25   Denis Harbinson, 'Isorhythmic Technique in the Early Motet', *Music and Letters* 47 (1966) 100–9.

Example 8.10 (716) *Hé, Marotele* – (717) *En la praerie* – *Aptatur* (O45); *F-MO* H 196, fols. 112v–14r.
Three corresponding passages

contrapuntal line in the triplum in perfections 3–4 of each phrase is identical in
phrases (1) and (3) and differs from phrase (2).

The recurrence of motetus phrases in a double *cursus* tenor permeates the entire
substance of (781) *Encontre le mois d'Avril* – (782) *Amours, tant voz ai servi* – *Neuma*
(*Neuma I. Toni*). In this three-part motet, two identical tenor *cursus* divide the piece
into equal halves. An edition is given as Example 8.11. The motetus consists of ten
phrases of four perfections each: five in the first half of the piece, five in the second.
The beginnings of both first phrases, both second phrases and so on are identical in
four out of the five instances. The pairs are marked A–D. The two A phrases begin

Example 8.11 Edition of (781) *Encontre le mois d'Avril* – (782) *Amours, tant voz ai servi* – *Neuma*
(Neuma I. Toni); *F-MO* H 196, fols. 189v-91r

in the same way, as do the two B phrases. Phrases C and D behave similarly. No
matter how far each phrase subsequently deviates, the next phrase always begins
again in exactly the same way in each half of the piece. The final phrase is different,
and imparts a degree of cadential function to a composition whose structure was
likely to be problematic with regard to closure. The triplum behaves in a rather
similar fashion, although the parallelisms are rather looser. Structural pitches and
contours remain the same, but ornamental figurations change.

A fundamental characteristic of the style of the mid-century motet is the disparity
between the poetic line-lengths and musical phrase-lengths of the two upper parts.
We have already seen one example, however, where the upper voices behaved

homorhythmically and were interrupted by a borrowed refrain. There is quite clearly an important generic mode to be uncovered here in which poetic line-length, musical phrase-length and rhyme play a role in the combination of the upper voices themselves and that of the upper voices with the tenor. (326) *De jolif cuer* – (327) *Je me quidai* – *Et gaudebit* (M24) is an excellent example of the ways in which these elements can interact. Both upper voices move systematically in phrases of exactly the same length throughout the piece because the poems share an identical structure. The end-rhymes are identical. The tenor consists of two complete *cursus* and one incomplete one. The first is constructed so that rests consistently coincide with the upper voices; the resulting texture is rather like that of the conductus. In the second and partial third *cursus* of the piece, the upper voices still move in similar phrase-lengths but they are now out of step with the tenor. Such a diversity of compositional viewpoint is in itself a modal attribute of the genre. The ability to choose whether or not to match articulations of the tenor with those of the upper parts is important. Deciding to do both in the same motet points to the relationship between tenor and upper-voice phrase as one of the work's dominants.

Conclusion

This outline of the various modes at work in the French motet has been given the form of examples, grouped according to, on the one hand, literary and musical divisions, and on the other, divisions between borrowed material (*matière*) and elements related to *entencion* or compositional purpose. Tynjanov's preference was for a structured inventory that laid out the modal possibilities of generic elements. An attempt at such a structured inventory follows. The divisions between music and text, *matière* and newly composed material, that have been used to organise this chapter are retained. Positive statements in the inventory include the possibility of the negative; 'refrain interrupts prevailing rhythmic mode' implies its opposite: 'refrain shares prevailing rhythmic mode'.

    MODE
      Music (*matière*)
        Clausula model
        Unrhythmicised tenor model
        Rhythmicised tenor model
        Tenor controls repetition patterns of upper voice(s)
      Textual innovation
        Language of text (subgenre)
          Latin motet
          French motet
          Bilingual motet
        Registral modes
          Aristocratisant
          Popularisant
        Pastourelle
        Chanson-requette

> Devotional motet
> Texting of clausula reflects original structure
> Upper-voice allusion
>> To tenor incipit
>> To text of plainsong
>> To elsewhere in liturgy
>
> Refrains (*matière*)
> Presence (absence) of refrain
> Text and music of refrain
> Text only of refrain
> Refrain interrupts prevailing rhythmic mode
> Refrain interrupts poetic pattern
>> Line-length
>> Rhyme
>
> Position of refrain
>> Initial
>> Internal
>> Terminal
>> Divided
>
> Upper voice(s) constructed exclusively from refrains
> Refrains control overall structure of work
> Refrains control rhyme-scheme of poem
> Poetic integration of refrain
>> Grammatically
>> Lexically
>> Choice of person
>> Tense
>> Mood
>> Register
>
> Musical innovation
> Autonomous repetition of melodic patterns
>> Sequence
>> Canon
>
> Repetition of melodic patterns related to refrain
> Repetition related to patterning of tenor
> Melodic repetition governed by textual repetition independent of refrains
> Parallel construction of series of melodic phrases
> Melodic repetition of two-part counterpoint
> Melodic repetition of entire texture (constructional type)

CONSTRUCTIONAL TYPE
> Rondeau-motet
> Cyclic structures

A generic definition of the motet may be derived from the way in which modes combine. Tynjanov stressed that the abstraction of elements is only a working hypothesis, and the function of such elements is the way in which they interact one with another in a given work.[26] This is the basis of Tynjanov's characterisation of a genre

---

[26] Tynjanov, 'On Literary Evolution', 67.

as a dynamic [musico-]literary system in which elements constantly interrelate by playing different roles. He draws a further distinction, that may be of value to our enquiry, between what he terms 'syn-function' and 'auto-function'. The syn-function of an element is the way in which it interacts with different elements in a single work. Most of the examples discussed in this chapter have stressed the ways in which competing modes interact. Auto-function is the effect of an element being 'interrelated with similar elements in other works in other systems'.[27] Tynjanov's example is the lexicon of a given work shared both with a literary and a linguistic vocabulary. There is no shortage of auto-functions in the modes that constitute the motet. We may identify plainsong tenors, for example, and point to their use in other *works* (other motets). Refrains are used not only in other works, but also in other systems (chansons and romances, for example).

We already use Tynjanov's concept of dominants to define a genre. So did medieval theorists. They defined the motet as a work based on a plainsong with more than one text. We might add some observations on format and notation. But this serves to distinguish between, for example, motet, conductus and chanson, not between subgenres or different works. Dominants of a work define that work's unique quality. In the light of the inventory of elements discussed in this chapter, we can point to at least two ways of stressing dominants. Some motets value one general element more highly than another (a concentration on melodic considerations or refrains for example). Others create a combination of modal emphases only found in that individual work (for example, a blend of a registrally ambiguous *chanson-requette* poem or a divided refrain, or some sort of melodic patterning). Dominants may be either newly composed or borrowed.

Such a flexible view of the genre of the motet prompts questions about the position of the composer and the nature of *entencion*. We speak habitually of the composer's 'choice' of tenor or of rhythmic mode. *Entencion* is however closely bound up with the question of the interaction of highly variable elements within the single work. Chrétien de Troyes mediated between the *matière* and *sens* given him by Marie de France, and the *conjointure* of the finished romance. Similarly, the composer of the motet reads his *matière* in the light of his own intention to create a work that explores a combination of modes. Some of these may involve the reworking of pre-existent materials, and others may involve more innovative construction.

From an exploration of various modes at work in the thirteenth-century motet, and from a contemplation of two contrasting but complementary theoretical positions, we can arrive at a view of the genre itself. Such a view is based in the first instance on a clearly defined and structured inventory of components. It is composed of modes and constructional types, but in practice concentrates on the former. It takes account of the distinction between *matière* and *entencion*. This inventory forms the basis for an interpretation of the musico-literary work based on the interaction of these modes. It is an interpretation in which the status of a given work is determined by the ways in which elements interact, and in which they are projected as dominants. This establishes the work's position within the environment of the Kind, and, ultimately, within the context of musico-literary history.

[27]   *Ibid.*, 68.

Bibliography

Gordon A. Anderson, 'Notre Dame Bilingual Motets: A Study in the History of Music, 1215–1245', *Miscellanea musicologica* 3 (1968) 50–144

'Notre Dame Latin Double Motets ca.1215–1250', *Musica disciplina* 25 (1971) 35–92

ed., *The Latin Compositions in Fascicules VII and VIII of the Notre Dame Manuscript Wolfenbüttel Helmstadt 1099 (1206)*, 2 vols, Musicological Studies 24 (Brooklyn, N.Y.: Institute of Mediaeval Music, 1971–6)

'A Unique Notre-Dame Motet Tenor Relationship', *Music and Letters* 55 (1974) 398–409

'Notre-Dame and Related Conductus: A Catalogue Raisonné', *Miscellanea musicologica* 6 (1972) 153–229; 7 (1975) 1–81

ed., *Motets of the Manuscript La Clayette: Paris Bibliothèque Nationale, nouv. acq. f. fr. 13521*, Corpus mensurabilis musicae 68 (n.p.: American Institute of Musicology, 1975)

ed., *Compositions of the Bamberg Manuscript: Bamberg, Staatsbibliothek, Lit.115 (olim Ed.IV.6)*, Corpus mensurabilis musicae 75 (Neuhausen-Stuttgart: Hänssler-Verlag; American Institute of Musicology, 1977)

Willi Apel, 'Refrain', *Harvard Dictionary of Music*, ed. Willi Apel (Cambridge, Mass.: Harvard University Press, 1944) 632–3

'Rondeaux, Virelais, and Ballades in French 13th-Century Song', *Journal of the American Musicological Society* 7 (1954) 121–30

P. Assion, 'Katharina (AIKATERINE) von Alexandrien', *Ikonographie der Heiligen*, 4 vols. ed. Karl Georg Kastner, Lexikon der christlichen Ikonographie 5–8 (Rome etc.: Herder, 1973–6) 3: 289–97

Pierre Aubry, ed., *Cent motets du xiiie siècle*, 3 vols (Paris: A. Rouart, Lerolle; Paul Geuthner, 1908; R New York: Broude Brothers, 1964)

Antoine Auda, ed., *Les 'motets wallons' du manuscrit de Turin: vari 42*, 2 vols (Brussels: chez l'auteur, [1953])

Rebecca Baltzer, 'Thirteenth-Century Illuminated Miniatures and the Date of the Florence Manuscript', *Journal of the American Musicological Society* 25 (1972) 1–18

'Performance Practice, the Notre-Dame Calendar, and the Earliest Latin Liturgical Motets'. Paper read at symposium *Das Ereignis Notre-Dame*, Herzog-August-Bibliothek, Wolfenbüttel, 15–20 April 1985

'Aspects of Trope in the Earliest Motets for the Assumption of the Virgin', *Festschrift for Ernest Sanders*, ed. Brian Seirup and Peter M. Lefferts (New York: Trustees of Columbia University, 1991) 7–42

James H. Baxter, *An Old St Andrews Music Book (Cod. Helmst. 628) Published in Facsimile with an Introduction*, St Andrews University Publications 30 (Oxford: Humphrey Milford; Oxford University Press; Paris: Librairie Ancienne Honoré Champion, 1931)

Pierre Bec, *La lyrique française au moyen âge (xiie-xiiie siècles): contribution à une typologie des genres poétiques médiévaux, études et textes*, 2 vols, Publications du Centre d'Etudes Supérieures de Civilisation Médiévale de l'Université de Poitiers 6–7 (Paris: Editions A. and J. Picard, 1977–8)

'L'accès au lieu érotique: motifs et éxorde dans la lyrique popularisante du moyen âge à nos jours', *Love and Marriage in the Twelfth Century*, ed. Willy van Hoecke and Andries Welkenhuysen, Medievalia Lovanensia 1: 8 (Louvain: Louvain University Press, 1981) 250–97

Jean and Louise Beck, eds, *Le manuscrit du Roi, fonds français no 844 de la Bibliothèque Nationale: reproduction phototypique publié avec une introduction*, 2 vols, Corpus cantilenarum medii aevi l; les chansonniers des troubadours et des trouvères 2 (London: Humphrey Milford; Oxford University Press; Philadelphia: University of Pennsylvania Press, 1938)

Jean Beck, ed., *Reproduction phototypique du chansonnier Cangé: Paris, Bibliothèque Nationale Ms. Français No 846*, 2 vols, Corpus cantilenarum medii aevi l; les chansonniers des troubadours et des trouvères 1 (Paris: Librairie Ancienne Honoré Champion; Philadelphia: University of Pennsylvania Press, 1927)

Samuel Berger, *La Bible française au moyen âge: étude sur les plus anciennes versions de la bible écrites en prose de langue d'oil* (Paris: H. Champion, 1884)

Stanley H. Birnbaum, trans., *Johannes de Garlandia: Concerning Measured Music (De mensurabili musica)*, Colorado College Music Press Translations 9 (Colorado Springs: Colorado College Music Press, 1978)

Maureen B. McC. Boulton, 'Lyric Insertion in French Narrative Fiction in the Thirteenth and Fourteenth Centuries' (M.Litt. diss., University of Oxford, 1979)

Willis H. Bowen, 'Present Status of Studies in Saints' Lives in Old French Verse', *Symposium* 1: 2 (1947) 82–6

Robert Branner, 'The Johannes Grusch Atelier and the Continental Origins of the William of Devon Painter', *Art Bulletin* 54 (1972) 24–30

Manuscript Painting in Paris During the Reign of St Louis: A Study of Styles, California Studies in the History of Art 18 (Berkeley, Los Angeles and London: University of California Press, 1977)

Julian Brown, Sonia Patterson and David Hiley, 'Further Observations on W_1', *Journal of the Plainsong and Mediaeval Music Society* 4 (1981) 53–80

Catalogue de la bibliothèque de F. J. Fétis acquise par l'état belge (Paris: Firmin Didot; Brussels: C. Muquardt, 1877)

Jacques Chailley, *Les chansons à la Vierge de Gautier de Coinci 1177 [78]–1236: édition musicale critique avec introduction et commentaires*, Publications de la Société Française de Musicologie 1: 15 (Paris: Heugel et Cie, 1959)

'Fragments d'un nouveau manuscrit d'Ars Antiqua à Châlons sur Marne', *In memoriam Jacques Handschin*, ed. Higinio Anglès *et al.* (Strasburg: P. H. Heitz, 1962) 140–50

Maria V. Coldwell, '*Guillaume de Dole* and Medieval Romances with Musical Interpolations', *Musica disciplina* 35 (1981) 55–86

Charles Edmond Henri de Coussemaker, ed., *Scriptorum de musica medii aevi nova series a Gerbertina altera*, 4 vols (Milan: Bolletino bibliografico musicale; Paris: A. Durand, 1864–76; R Hildesheim: Georg Olms, 1963)

Richard Crocker, 'French Polyphony of the Thirteenth Century', *The Early Middle Ages to 1300*, ed. Richard Crocker and David Hiley, New Oxford History of Music 2 (Oxford and New York: Oxford University Press, 1990) 636–78

R. H. C. Davis, *A History of Medieval Europe from Constantine to St Louis* (London: Longman, 1970)

Maurice Delbouille, ed., *Jacques Bretel: Le Tournoi de Chauvency*, Bibliothèque de la Faculté Philosophique et Lettres de l'Université de Liège 49 (Paris and Liège: Société de l'Edition 'Les Belles Lettres', 1932)

'Sur les traces de Bele Aëlis', *Mélanges de philologie romane dédiés à la mémoire de Jean Boutière (1899–1967)*, 2 vols, ed. Irénée Cluzel and François Pirot (Liège: Editions Soledi, 1971) 1: 200–18

Alexander J. Denomy, 'An Inquiry into the Origins of Courtly Love', *Mediaeval Studies* 6 (1944) 175–260

Luther Dittmer, ed., *Paris 13521 and 11411: Facsimile, Introduction, Index and Transcriptions from the Manuscripts Paris, Bibl. Nat. Acq. Fr.13521 (La Clayette) and Lat.11411*, Publications of Mediaeval Musical Manuscripts 4 (Brooklyn, N.Y.: Institute of Mediaeval Music, 1959)

ed., *Eine zentrale Quelle der Notre-Dame Musik: Faksimile, Wiederherstellung, Catalogue raisonné, Besprechung, und Transcriptionen*, Publications of Mediaeval Musical Manuscripts 3 (Brooklyn, N.Y.: Institute of Mediaeval Music, 1959)

ed., *Facsimile Reproduction of the Manuscript Wolfenbüttel 1099 (1206)*, Publications of Mediaeval Musical Manuscripts 2 (Brooklyn, N.Y.: Institute of Mediaeval Music, 1960)

ed., *Facsimile Reproduction of the Manuscript Firenze, Biblioteca Mediceo-Laurenziana Pluteo 29,1*, 2 vols, Publications of Mediaeval Musical Manuscripts 10–11 (Brooklyn, N.Y.: Institute of Mediaeval Music, [1966]–7)

'The Lost Fragments of a Notre Dame Manuscript in Johannes Wolf's Library', *Aspects of Medieval and Renaissance Music: A Birthday Offering to Gustave Reese*, ed. Jan LaRue (London, Melbourne and Cape Town: Oxford University Press, 1967) 122–33

Eglal Doss-Quinby, *Les Refrains chez les trouvères du xiie siècle au début du xive*, American University Studies 2: 17 (New York, Berne and Frankfurt am Main: Peter Lang, 1984)

Maurice and Wilfrid Drake, *Saints and their Emblems* (London: Werner Laurie, 1916)

Guido Maria Dreves, ed., *Lieder und Motetten des Mittelalters*, 2 vols, Analecta hymnica medii aevi 20–1 (Leipzig: O. R. Reisland, 1895)

Peter Dronke, 'The Lyrical Compositions of Philip the Chancellor', *Studi medievali*, Third Series 28 (1987) 563–92

Theodor Wilhelm Elwert, *Traité de versification française des origines à nos jours*, Bibliothèque française et romane, A: 8 (Paris: Editions Klincksieck, 1965)

John A. Emerson, 'Sources, MS, II, 5: Western Plainchant, 12th Century', *The New Grove Dictionary of Music and Musicians*, 20 vols, ed. Stanley Sadie (London: Macmillan, 1980) 17: 619–22

Beverly Jean Evans, 'The Unity of Text and Music in the Late Thirteenth-Century French Motet: A Study of Selected Works from the Montpellier Manuscript' (Ph.D. diss., University of Pennsylvania, 1983)

'The Textual Function of a Refrain Cento in a Thirteenth Century French Motet', *Music and Letters* 71 (1990) 187–97

Mark Everist, 'Music and Theory in Late Thirteenth-Century Paris: The Manuscript Paris, Bibliothèque Nationale, *fonds lat.* 11266', *Royal Musical Association Research Chronicle* 17 (1981) 52–64

French 13th-Century Polyphony in the British Library: A Facsimile Edition of the Manuscripts Additional 30091 and Egerton 2615 (folios 79–94v) (London: Plainsong and Mediaeval Music Society, 1988)

Polyphonic Music in Thirteenth-Century France: Aspects of Sources and Distribution (New York and London: Garland, 1989)

'From Paris to St. Andrews: The Origins of W₁', *Journal of the American Musicological Society* 43 (1990) 1–42

'The Sources of Trouvère Song' (Unpublished Paper)

Robert Falck, 'Richart de Fournival', *The New Grove Dictionary of Music and Musicians*, 20 vols, ed. Stanley Sadie (London: Macmillan, 1980) 15: 843

The Notre Dame Conductus: A Study of the Repertory, Musicological Studies 33 (Henryville, Ottawa and Binningen: Institute of Mediaeval Music, 1981)

Alastair Fowler, *Kinds of Literature: An Introduction to the Theory of Genres and Modes* (Oxford: Oxford University Press, 1982)

Maria V. Fowler, 'Musical Interpolations in Thirteenth- and Fourteenth-Century French Narratives', 2 vols (Ph.D. diss., Yale University, 1979)

Marcel Françon, *Leçons et notes sur la littérature française au xvie siècle*, 3rd edn with additional notes (Cambridge, Mass.: Harvard University Press, 1965)

'Sur la structure du rondeau', *Romance Notes* 10 (1968–9) 147–9

István Frank, '*Tuit cil qui sunt enamourat*: notes de philologie pour l'étude des origines lyriques 2', *Romania* 75 (1954) 98–108

Charles de Fresne [Ducange], ed., *Histoire de S. Louys IX. du nom Roy de France écrite par Iean Sire de Joinville, Sénechal de Champagne* (Paris: Mabre-Creamoisy, 1668)

Wolf Frobenius, 'Zum genetischen Verhältnis zwischen Notre-Dame-Klauseln und ihren Motetten', *Archiv für Musikwissenschaft* 44 (1987) 1–39

Friedrich Gennrich, *Musikwissenschaft und romanische Philologie* (Halle: Niemeyer, 1918)

'Die Musik als Hilfswissenschaft der romanischen Philologie', *Zeitschrift für romanische Philologie* 39 (1919) 330–61

ed., *Rondeaux, Virelais und Balladen aus dem Ende des xii., dem xiii., und dem ersten Drittel des xiv. Jahrhunderts mit den überlieferten Melodien*, 3 vols [1] Gesellschaft für romanische Literatur 43 (Dresden: Gesellschaft für romanische Literatur, 1921); [2] Gesellschaft für romanische Literatur 47 (Gottingen: Gesellschaft für romanische Literatur, 1927); [3 (titled *Das altfranzösische Rondeau und Virelai im 12. und 13. Jahrhundert*)] Summa musicae medii aevi 10 (Langen bei Frankfurt: n.p., 1963)

Die altfranzösische Rotrouenge, Literatur-historisch-musikwissenschaftliche Studien 2 (Halle: Niemeyer, 1925)

'Trouvèrelieder und Motettenrepertoire', *Zeitschrift für Musikwissenschaft* 9 (1926) 8–39 and 65–85

'Refrain-Tropen in der Musik des Mittelalters', *Studi medievali* 16 (1943–50) 242–54

'Refrain-Studien: sind die Refrains Fragmente von populären oder populär gewordenen Liedern oder vollständige Volkslieder', *Zeitschrift für romanische Philologie* 71 (1955) 365–90

Bibliographie der ältesten französischen und lateinischen Motetten, Summa musicae medii aevi 2 (Darmstadt: n.p., 1957)

ed., *Ein altfranzösischer Motettenkodex, Paris B.N. 13521*, Summa musicae medii aevi 6 (Darmstadt: n.p., 1958)

Bibliographisches Verzeichnis der französischen Refrains, Summa musicae medii aevi 14 (Langen bei Frankfurt: n.p., 1964)

Florilegium motetorum: ein Querschnitt durch das Motettenschaffen des 13. Jahrhunderts, Summa musicae medii aevi 17 (Langen bei Frankfurt: n.p., 1966)

Cantilenae piae: 31 altfranzösische geistliche Lieder der HS Paris, Bibl. Nat. Nouv. Acq. Fr. 1050, Musikwissenschaftliche Studienbibliothek 24 (Langen bei Frankfurt: n.p., 1966)

Graduale sacrosanctae romanae ecclesiae de tempore et de sanctis primum sancti Pii X iussu restitutum et editum Pauli VI pontificis maximi cura nunc recognitum ad exemplar 'Ordinis cantus missae' dispositum et rhythmicis signis a Solesmensibus monachis diligenter ornatum (Solesmes: Abbaye Saint-Pierre; Tournai: Desclée, 1979)

Hilda Graef, *Devotion to the Blessed Virgin*, Faith and Fact Books 45 (London: Burns and Oates, 1963)

Eduard Gröninger, *Repertoire-Untersuchungen zum mehrstimmigen Notre-Dame Conductus*, Kölner Beiträge zur Musikforschung 2 (Regensburg: Gustav Bosse Verlag, 1939)

Frederick F. Hammond, ed., *Walteri Odington Summa de speculatione musicae*, Corpus scriptorum de musica 14 (Rome: American Institute of Musicology, 1970)

Denis Harbinson, 'Imitation in the Early Motet', *Music and Letters* 45 (1964) 359–68

Henry Hawkins, *The History of S. Elizabeth* (n.p.: n.p., 1632; R [English Recusant Literature 1558–1640] London: Scolar, 1974)

Ernest Hoepffner, 'Virelais et Ballades dans le Chansonnier d'Oxford', *Archivum romanicum: nuova rivista di filologia romanza* 4 (1920) 20–40

Klaus Hofmann, 'Zur Entstehungs- und Fruhgeschichte des Terminus Motette', *Acta musicologica* 42 (1970) 138–50

　　Untersuchungen zur Kompositionstechnik der Motette im 13. Jahrhundert dargeführt an den Motetten mit dem Tenor IN SECULUM, Tübinger Beiträge zur Musikwissenschaft 2 (Neuhausen and Stuttgart: Hänssler-Verlag, 1972)

Richard H. Hoppin, *Medieval Music*, Norton Introduction to Music History (New York: W. W. Norton; Toronto: R. J. Mcloed, 1978)

Jacques Hourlier and Jacques Chailley, 'Cantionale Cathalaunense', *Mémoires de la Société d'Agriculture, Commerce, Sciences, et Arts du Département de la Marne* 71 [2e série 30] (1956) 141–59

Michel Huglo, 'De Francon de Cologne à Jacques de Liège', *Revue belge de musicologie* 34–5 (1980–1) 44–60

David Hult, *Self-Fulfilling Prophecies: Readership and Authority in the First Roman de la Rose* (Cambridge: Cambridge University Press, 1986)

Sylvia Huot, 'Transformations of Lyric Voice in the Songs, Motets and Plays of Adam de la Halle', *Romanic Review* 78 (1987) 148–64

　　'Polyphonic Poetry: The Old French Motet and Its Literary Context', *French Forum* 14 (1989) 261–78

Edward Järnström and Arthur Långfors, eds, *Recueil de chansons pieuses du xiiie siècle*, 2 vols, Annales academiae scientiarum fennicae B.III.1 and B.XX.4 (Helsinki: Imprimerie de la Société de Littérature Finnoise, 1910–27)

Alfred Jeanroy, 'Imitations pieuses de chansons profanes', *Romania* 18 (1889) 477–86

　　'Modèles profanes de chansons pieuses', *Romania* 40 (1911) 84–6

Alfred Jeanroy, Louis Brandin and Pierre Aubry, *Lais et descorts français du xiiie siècle: texte et musique*, Mélanges de musicologie critique (Paris: Welter, 1901)

Susan M. Johnson, 'The Role of the Refrain in Old French Lyric Poetry' (Ph.D. diss., Indiana University, 1983)

Douglas Kelly, *Sens et conjointure in the Chevalier de la Charette* (Paris and The Hague: Mouton, 1966)

'The Source and Meaning of *Conjointure* in Chrétien's *Erec* 14', *Viator* 1 (1970) 179–200

'Chrétien de Troyes: The Narrator and His Art', *The Romances of Chrétien de Troyes: A Symposium*, ed. Douglas Kelly, The Edward C. Armstrong Monographs on Medieval Literature 3 (Lexington: French Forum, 1985) 13–47

Janet Knapp, 'Polyphony at Notre Dame of Paris', *The Early Middle Ages to 1300*, ed. Richard Crocker and David Hiley, New Oxford History of Music 2 (Oxford and New York: Oxford University Press, 1990) 632–5

Vernon Frederick Koenig, ed., *Les Miracles de Nostre Dame par Gautier de Coinci*, 4 vols, Textes littéraires français 62 [vols 1 and 3], 92 [vol. 2] and 176 [vol. 4] (Geneva: Librairie Droz; Lille: Librairie Giard, 1955–70)

Karl Künstle, *Ikonographie der christlichen Kunst*, 2 vols (Freiburg im Breisgau: Herder, 1926–8)

Michael Kwatera, 'Book of Hours', *Dictionary of the Middle Ages*, 12 vols, ed. Joseph R. Strayer (New York: Charles Scribner's Sons, 1982–9) 2: 325–7

M. Francis Laughlin, 'Elizabeth of Hungary (Thuringia), St', *New Catholic Encyclopedia*, 17 vols (New York etc.: McGraw-Hill, 1967–79) 5: 282

Moshé Lazar, *Amour courtois et 'fin'amours' dans la littérature du xiie siècle*, Bibliothèque française et romane; série c: Etudes littéraires 8 (Paris: Klincksieck, 1964)

Peter Lefferts, ed., *Robertus de Handlo: Regule/Rules and Johannes Hanboys: Summa/The Summa: A New Critical Text and Translation on Facing Pages with an Introduction, Annotations and indices verborum and nominum et rerum*, Greek and Latin Music Theory (Lincoln and London: University of Nebraska Press, 1991)

Pierre Le Gentil, 'A propos de Guillaume de Dole', *Mélanges de linguistique romane et de philologie médiévale offerts à M. Maurice Delbouille*, 2 vols, ed. Madeleine Tyssens (Gembloux: Editions J. Duclout, 1964) 2: 381–97

Jacques Le Goff, *La Civilisation de l'occident médiéval* (Paris: Arthaud, 1964), trans. Julia Barrow as *Medieval Civilisation, 400–1500* (Oxford: Blackwell, 1988)

Victor Leroquais, *Les sacramentaires et les missels manuscrits des bibliothèques publiques de France*, 4 vols (Paris: n.p., 1924)

Les livres d'heures manuscrits de la Bibliothèque Nationale, 3 vols (Paris: n.p., 1927–43)

Robert White Linker, *A Bibliography of Old French Lyrics*, Romance Monographs 31 (University, Miss.: Romance Monographs, 1979)

Oliger Livier, 'Le plus ancien office liturgique de la B.se Isabelle de France (d.1270)', *Miscellanea Giovanni Mercati*, 6 vols, Studi e testi 121–6 (Vatican City: Biblioteca Apostolica Vaticana, 1946) 2: 484–508

Henry Richard Luard, ed., *Mathaei Parisiensis, monachi Sancti Albani, Chronica majora*, 7 vols, Rerum britannicarum medii aevi scriptores 57 (London: Longman etc., 1874–83)

Friedrich Ludwig, *Repertorium organorum recentioris et motetorum vetustissimi stili*, 2 vols (1/1 – Halle: Verlag von Max Niemaeyer, 1910; R [ed. Luther A. Dittmer, Musicological Studies 7] Brooklyn, N.Y.: Institute of Mediaeval Music; Hildesheim: Georg Olms Verlag, 1964); (1/2 – [345–456 ed. Friedrich Gennrich including R of 'Die Quellen der Motetten ältesten Stils', *Archiv für Musikwissenschaft* 5 (1923) 185–222 and 273–315, Summa musicae medii aevi 7] Langen bei Frankfürt: n.p., 1961; R [345–456], [457–783, ed. Luther A. Dittmer, Musicological Studies 26] [Binningen]: Institute of Mediaeval Music, 1978); (2 – [1–71 ed. Friedrich Gennrich, Summa musicae medii aevi 8 – 65–71 in page proof only] Langen bei Frankfürt: n.p., 1962; R [1–64, 65–71 corrected], [72–155 ed. Luther A. Dittmer (Musicological Studies 17)] Brooklyn, N.Y.: Institute of Mediaeval Music, n.d.; Hildesheim: Georg Olms Verlag, 1972)

'Die geistliche nichtliturgische und weltliche einstimmige und die mehrstimmige Musik des Mittelalters bis zum Anfang des 15. Jahrhunderts', *Handbuch der Musikgeschichte*, ed. Guido Adler (Frankfurt am Main: Anstalt, 1924) 157–295

Faith Lyons, '*Entencion* in Chrétien's *Lancelot*', *Studies in Philology* 51 (1954) 425–30

Finn Mathiassen, *The Style of the Early Motet (c.1200–1250): An Investigation of the Old Corpus of the Montpellier Manuscript*, trans. Johanne M. Stochholm, Studier og publikationer fra Musikvidenskabeligt Institut Aarhus Universitet 1 (Copenhagen: Dan Fog Musikforlag, 1966)

Paul Meyer, 'Légendes hagiographiques en français', *Histoire littéraire de la France*, 411 vols (Paris: Imprimerie Royale etc., 1733–1981) 33: 328–458

'Le Salut d'amour dans les littératures provençale et française', *Bibliothèque de l'Ecole des Chartes* 28 (1867) 124–70

'Mélanges de littérature provençale 2: motets à trois parties', *Romania* 1 (1872) 404–6

'Notice du MS. 535 de la Bibliothèque Municipale de Metz renfermant diverses compositions pieuses (prose et vers) en français', *Bulletin de la Société des Anciens Textes Français* 12 (1886) 41–76

Rudolf Adelbert Meyer, 'Die in unseren Motetten enthaltenen Refrains', Albert Stimming, *Die altfranzösischen Motette der Bamberger Handschrift nebst einem Anhang, enthaltend altfranzösische Motette aus anderen deutschen Handschriften mit Anmerkungen und Glossar*, Gesellschaft für romanische Literatur 13 (Dresden: Gesellschaft für romanische Literatur, 1906) 141–84

Wilhelm Meyer, 'Der Ursprung des Motett's: vorläufige Bemerkungen', *Nachrichten von der königliche Gesellschaft der Wissenschaften zu Göttingen: Philologisch-historische Klasse, 1898*, 4 vols [paginated consecutively] (Göttingen: Luder Horstmann, 1898) 2: 113–45; R in *Gesammelte Abhandlungen zur mittellateinische Rhythmik*, 3 vols (Berlin: Weidmannsche Buchhandlung, 1905–36; R Hildesheim: Georg Olms, 1970) 2: 303–41

Eric George Millar, *The Parisian Miniaturist Honoré* (London: Faber, 1959)

William Albert Nitze, '"Sans et matière" dans les œuvres de Chrétien de Troyes', *Romania* 44 (1915–17) 14–36

Patricia L. P. Norwood, 'A Study of the Provenance and French Motets in Bamberg Staatsbibliothek Lit.115' (Ph.D. diss., University of Texas at Austin, 1979)

'Performance Manuscripts from the Thirteenth-Century?' *College Music Symposium* 26 (1986) 92–6

Christopher Page, *The Owl and the Nightingale: Musical Life and Ideas in France 1100–1300* (London: Dent, 1989)

'Johannes de Grocheio on Secular Music: A Corrected Text and a New Translation', *Plainsong and Medieval Music* 2 (1993) 17–41

Thomas B. Payne, '*Associa tecum in patria*: A Newly Identified Organum Trope by Philip the Chancellor', *Journal of the American Musicological Society* 39 (1986) 233–54

'Poetry, Politics, and Polyphony: Philip the Chancellor's Contribution to the Music of the Notre Dame School', 2 vols (Ph.D. diss., University of Chicago, 1991)

Dolores Pesce, 'The Significance of Text in Thirteenth-Century Latin Motets', *Acta musicologica* 58 (1986) 91–117

'A Revised View of the Thirteenth-Century Latin Double Motet', *Journal of the American Musicological Society* 40 (1987) 405–42

Guy de Poerck and Rike van Deyck, 'La Bible et l'activité traductrice dans les pays romans avant 1300', *La Littérature didactique, allegorique et satirique*, 2 vols, ed. Jürgen Beyer and Franz Koppe, Grundriss der romanischen Literaturen des Mittelalters 6 (Heidelberg: Winter; Universitätsverlag, 1968–70) 1: 21–39 and 2: 54–69

Porphyry, *Isogoge, translatio Boethii*, ed. Lorenzo Minio-Paluello, Aristoteles Latinus 1, 6–7 (Rome: Union Académique Internationale, 1966)

Gaston Raynaud, ed., *Recueil de motets français des xiie et xiiie siècles publiés d'après les manuscrits, avec introduction, notes, variantes, et glossaires*, 2 vols, Bibliothèque française du moyen âge (Paris: F. Vieweg, 1881–3; *R* Hildesheim and New York: Georg Olms Verlag, 1972)

    Bibliographie des chansonniers français des xiiie et xive siècles comprenant la description de tous les manuscrits, la table des chansons classées par ordre alphabétique de rimes, et la liste des trouvères, 2 vols (Paris: F. Vieweg Libraire Editeur, 1884)

Gilbert Reaney, *Manuscripts of Polyphonic Music (11th – Early 14th Century)*, Répertoire International des Sources Musicales BIV₁ (Munich and Duisberg: G. Henle Verlag, 1966)

Fritz Reckow, ed., *Der Musiktraktat des Anonymus 4*, 2 vols, Beihefte zum Archiv für Musikwissenschaft 4–5 (Wiesbaden: Franz Steiner Verlag, 1967)

Gustave Reese, *Music in the Middle Ages with an Introduction on the Music of Ancient Times* (London: J. M. Dent, 1941)

Georg Reichert, 'Wechselbeziehungen zwischen musikalischer und textlicher Struktur in der Motette des 13. Jahrhunderts', *In Memoriam Jacques Handschin*, ed. Higinio Anglès *et al.* (Strasburg: P. H. Heitz, 1962) 151–69

Erich Reimer, ed., *Johannes de Garlandia: De mensurabili musica: kritische Edition mit Kommentar und Interpretation der Notationslehre*, 2 vols, Beihefte zum Archiv für Musikwissenschaft 10–11 (Wiesbaden: Franz Steiner Verlag, 1972)

Revised Medieval Latin Word-List from British and Irish Sources, ed. R. E. Latham (London: Oxford University Press, 1965; *R* 1983)

Colin A. Robson, 'Vernacular Scriptures in France', *The West from the Fathers to the Reformation*, ed. Geoffrey William Lampe, The Cambridge History of the Bible 2 (Cambridge: Cambridge University Press, 1979) 436–52

William Woodville Rockhill, *The Journey of William Rubruck to the Eastern Part of the World, 1253–1255 as Narrated by Himself*, Hakluyt Society, New Series 4 (London: Hakluyt Society, 1900)

Edward H. Roesner, 'The Origins of W₁', *Journal of the American Musicological Society* 29 (1976) 337–80

Ernst Rohloff, ed., *Der Musiktraktat des Johannes de Grocheo nach dem Quellen neu herausgegeben mit Übersetzung ins Deutsche und Revisionsbericht*, Media latinitas musica 2 (Leipzig: Komissionsverlag Gebruder Reinecke, 1943)

    ed., *Die Quellenhandschriften zum Musiktraktat des Johannes de Grocheio im Faksimile herausgegeben nebst Übertragung des Textes und Übersetzung ins Deutsche, dazu Bericht, Literaturschau, Tabellen und Indices* (Leipzig: VEB Deutscher Verlag für Musik, [1972])

Yvonne Rokseth, *Polyphonies du treizième siècle*, 4 vols (Paris: Editions de l'Oiseau Lyre, 1935–9)

Mario Roques, ed., *Les Romans de Chrétien de Troyes édités d'après la copie de Guiot (Bibl. nat. fr.794)*, 4 vols, Les Classiques français de moyen âge 80, 84, 86 and 89 (Paris: Champion, 1952–60)

Samuel Rosenberg, Review of Eglal Doss-Quinby, *Les refrains chez les trouvères du xiie siècle au début du xive*, American University Studies 2: 17 (New York, Berne and Frankfurt am Main: Peter Lang, 1984), *Speculum* 62 (1987) 410–12

Rotulus (1 conductus & 9 motets), early 14th c. ([Brussels]: Alamire, 1990)

Henri Roussel, ed., *Renart le nouvel par Jacquemart Gielee publié d'après le manuscrit La Vallière*. Société des anciens textes français (Paris: Editions A. and J. Picard, 1961)

Nicolas Ruwet, 'Methodes d'analyse en musicologie', *Revue belge de musicologie* 20 (1966) 65–90, translated with introduction by Mark Everist as 'Methods of Analysis in Musicology', *Music Analysis* 6 (1987) 3–36

Raymond C. St-Jacques, 'Bible, French', *Dictionary of the Middle Ages*, 12 vols, ed. Joseph R. Strayer (New York: Charles Scribner's Sons, 1982–9) 2: 218–19

Ernest Sanders, 'Peripheral Polyphony of the Thirteenth Century', *Journal of the American Musicological Society* 17 (1964) 261–87

'The Question of Perotin's Œuvre and Dates', *Festschrift für Walter Wiora zum 30. Dezember 1966*, ed. Ludwig Finscher and Christoph-Hellmut Mahling (Kassel etc.: Bärenreiter, 1967) 241–9

'The Medieval Motet', *Gattungen der Musik in Einzeldarstellungen: Gedenkschrift Leo Schrade*, ed. Wulf Arlt *et al.* (Berne: Francke Verlag, 1973) 497–573

'Motet, Medieval, Ars Antiqua', *The New Grove Dictionary of Music and Musicians*, 20 vols, ed. Stanley Sadie (London: Macmillan, 1980) 12: 617–24

Karlheinz Schlager, ed., *Alleluya-Melodien I bis 1100*, Monumenta monodica medii aevi 7 (Kassel etc.: Bärenreiter, 1968)

Oscar Schultz-Gora, 'Ein ungedruckter *Salu d'amors* nebst Antwort', *Zeitschrift für romanische Philologie* 24 (1900) 358–69

Darwin F. Scott, 'The Three- and Four-Voice Monotextual Motets of the Notre-Dame School' (Ph.D. diss., University of California at Los Angeles, 1988)

Norman Smith, 'The Earliest Motets: Music and Words', *Journal of the Royal Musical Association* 114 (1989) 141–63

Robyn Smith, 'Gennrich's "Bibliographisches Verzeichnis der französischen Refrains": Paper Tiger or Fat Cat?' *Parergon* 8 (1990) 73–101

Clive R. Sneddon, 'A Critical Edition of the Four Gospels in the Thirteenth-Century Old-French Translation of the Bible', 2 vols (D.Phil. diss., University of Oxford, 1978)

'The *Bible du xiiie siècle*: Its Medieval Public in the Light of its Manuscript Transmission', *The Bible and Medieval Culture*, ed. W. Lourdaux and D. Verhelst, Mediaevalia Lovaniensia Series 1: Studia 7 (Louvain: Louvain University Press, 1979) 127–40

R. W. Southern, *The Making of the Middle Ages* (London: Hutchinson, 1953)

Hans Spanke, ed., *Eine altfranzösische Liedersammlung: der anonyme Teil der Liederhandschriften KNPX*, Romanische Bibliothek 20 (Halle: Verlag von Max Niemeyer, 1925)

G. Raynauds Bibliographie des altfranzösischen Liedes, Musicologica 1 (Leiden: E. J. Brill, 1955)

Georg Steffens, 'Der kritische Text der Gedichte von Richart de Semilli', *Festgabe für Wendelin Foerster* (Halle: Niemeyer, 1902) 331–62

Edmund Stengel, 'Die altfranzösische Liederzitate aus Girardin d'Amiens *Conte du cheval de fust*', *Zeitschrift für romanische Philologie* 10 (1886) 460–76

John Stevens, *Words and Music in the Middle Ages: Song, Narrative, Dance and Drama, 1050–1350*, Cambridge Studies in Music (Cambridge: Cambridge University Press, 1986)

Albert Stimming, *Die altfranzösischen Motette der Bamberger Handschrift nebst einem Anhang, enthaltend altfranzösische Motette aus anderen deutschen Handschriften mit Anmerkungen und Glossar*, Gesellschaft für romanische Literatur 13 (Dresden: Gesellschaft für romanische Literatur, 1906); a modified version of x–xxxvii is *idem*, 'Altfranzösische Motette in Handschriften deutscher Bibliotheken', *Mélanges Chabaneau: volume offert à Camille Chabaneau à l'occasion du 75e anniversaire de sa naissance (4 Mars 1906) par ses elèves, ses amis et ses admirateurs*, no ed. (Erlangen: Fr. Junge, Libraire-Editeur, 1907) 89–103

Hermann Suchier, ed., *Œuvres poétiques de Philippe de Rémi, Sire de Beaumanoir*, 2 vols, Société des anciens textes français (Paris: Firmin Didot, 1884–5)

Herbert Thurston and Donald Attwater, eds, *Butler's Lives of the Saints*, 4 vols (London: Burns and Oates, 1956)

Hans Tischler, 'Classicism and Romanticism in Thirteenth-Century Music', *Revue belge de musicologie* 16 (1962) 3–12

'Perotinus Revisited', *Aspects of Medieval and Renaissance Music: A Birthday Offering to Gustave Reese*, ed. Jan LaRue (London, Melbourne, and Cape Town: Oxford University Press, 1967) 803–17

ed., *The Montpellier Codex*, 4 vols [vol. 4 ed. and trans. Susan Stakel and Joel C. Relihan], Recent Researches in the Music of the Middle Ages and Early Renaissance 2–8 (Madison, Wis.: A. R. Editions, 1978–85)

ed., *The Earliest Motets (to circa 1270): A Complete Comparative Edition*, 3 vols (New Haven and London: Yale University Press, 1982)

'Pérotin and the Creation of the Motet', *Music Review* 44 (1983) 1–7

The Style and Evolution of the Earliest Motets (to circa 1270), 4 vols, Musicological Studies 40 (Henryville, Ottawa and Binningen: Institute of Mediaeval Music, 1985)

'New Data on the Evolution of the Parisian Organa', *Journal of Musicological Research* 5 (1984) 85–91; R in *La musique et le rite sacré et profane: actes du xiiie congrès de la Société Internationale de Musicologie, Strasbourg 29 août – 3 septembre 1982*, 2 vols. ed. Marc Honegger and Paul Prevost (Strasburg: Association des Publications près les Universités de Strasbourg, 1986) 2: 75–84

Leo Treitler, '"Centonate Chant": *Übles Flickwerk* or *E pluribus unus?*' *Journal of the American Musicological Society* 28 (1975) 1–23

Jurij Tynjanov, 'O literaturnoj èvoljucii', *Na literaturnom postu* 4 (1927) 19–36; R *Arxaisty i novatory* (Leningrad: n.p., 1929; R [as Slavische Propyläen 31] Munich: Fink, 1967) 30–47; trans. C. A. Luplow as 'On Literary Evolution', *Readings in Russian Poetics: Formalist and Structuralist Views*, ed. Ladislav Matejka and Krystyna Pomorska (Cambridge, Mass., and London: Harvard University Press, 1971; R Ann Arbor, Mich.: University of Michigan, 1978) 66–78

Karl D. Uitti, 'French Literature: Before 1200', *Dictionary of the Middle Ages*, 12 vols, ed. Joseph R. Strayer (New York: Charles Scribner's Sons, 1982–9) 5: 232–54

Nico H. J. van den Boogaard, *Rondeaux et refrains du xiie siècle au début du xive: collationnement, introduction, et notes*, Bibliothèque française et romane, D: 3 (Paris: Editions Klincksieck, 1969)

Hendrik van der Werf, *Integrated Directory of Organa, Clausulae and Motets of the Thirteenth Century* (Rochester, N.Y.: Author, 1989)

Mary Josephine Ward, *The Splendour of the Rosary* (London: Sheed and Ward, 1946)

Eithne Wilkins, *The Rose-Garden Game: The Symbolic Background to the European Prayer-Beads* (London: Victor Gollancz, 1969)

Nigel Wilkins, ed., *The Works of Jehan de Lescurel*, Corpus mensurabilis musicae 30 (n.p.: American Institute of Musicology, 1966)

Mary Wolinski, 'The Montpellier Codex: Its Compilation, Notation and Implications for the Chronology of the Thirteenth-Century Motet' (Ph.D. diss., Brandeis University, 1988)

Jeremy Yudkin, ed., *The Music Treatise of Anonymous IV: A New Translation*, Musicological Studies and Documents 41 (Neuhausen-Stuttgart: American Institute of Musicology, 1985)

Music in Medieval Europe, Prentice Hall History of Music (Englewood Cliffs, N.J.: Prentice Hall, 1989)

Paul Zarifopol, *Der kritische Text der Lieder Richarts de Fournival* (Halle: Niemeyer, 1904)

Paul Zumthor, *Essai de poétique médiévale*, Collection poétique (Paris: Editions de Seuil, 1972)

Index of compositions

Index

A